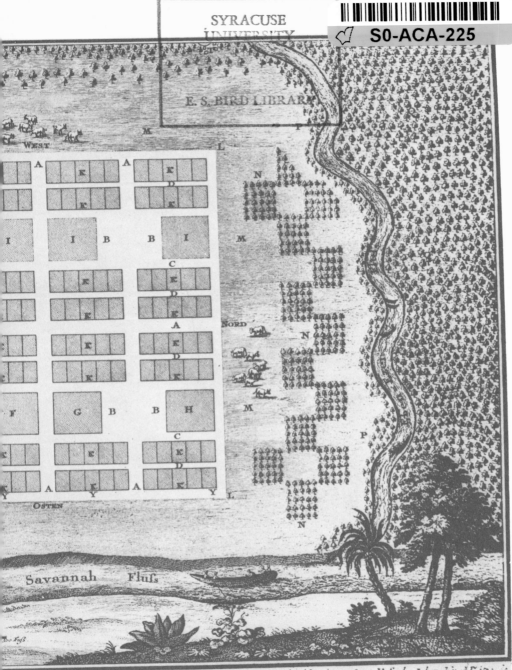

Detailed Reports on the

Salzburger Emigrants

Who Settled in America . . .

Edited by Samuel Urlsperger

JOHN WESLEY

Detailed Reports on the Salzburger Emigrants Who Settled in America . . .

Edited by Samuel. Urlsperger

VOLUME FOUR, 1737

Translated and Edited by
GEORGE FENWICK JONES
and
RENATE WILSON

WORMSLOE FOUNDATION PUBLICATIONS
NUMBER TWELVE

UNIVERSITY OF GEORGIA PRESS
ATHENS

Contents

Dritte
CONTINVATION
der ausführlichen Nachricht
von den
Saltzburgischen
Emigranten,
die sich in America niedergelassen haben.
Worin enthalten sind
I. Das Tage-Register der beyden Prediger zu EbenEzer
in Georgien vom 1. Ian. 1737. bis auf den 30. Iun.
1737.
II. Der Prediger in EbenEzer, wie auch einiger Saltzburger
Briefe, vom Jahr 1737. 1738. und 1739.
III. Eine kurtze Aufmunterung zu einer Christlichen und frey-
willigen Liebes-Steuer vor EbenEzer, 2c.
Nebst
einer Vorrede
herausgegeben
von
Samuel Urlsperger,
Des Evangelischen Ministerii der Stadt Augspurg Seniore und Pastore
der Haupt-Kirchen zu St. Annen.

HALLE,
In Verlegung des Wäysen-Hauses, M DCC XXXX.

Third

CONTINUATION

of the Detailed Reports
of the

SALZBURG
EMIGRANTS

who have settled in America
in which are contained

I. The Diary of the two ministers at Ebenezer
in Georgia from 1 Jan., 1737, to 30 June,
1737.

II. Letters from the ministers in Ebenezer, and
also from several Salzburgers, from the years
1737, 1738, and 1739.

III. A short encouragement for a Christian and
voluntary charitable donation for Ebenezer, etc.

together with

A PREFACE

edited

by

SAMUEL URLSPERGER,

Senior of the Evangelical Lutheran Ministry of the
city of Augsburg and pastor of St. Anne's Church

HALLE

Published by the Orphanage Press, M DCC XXXX

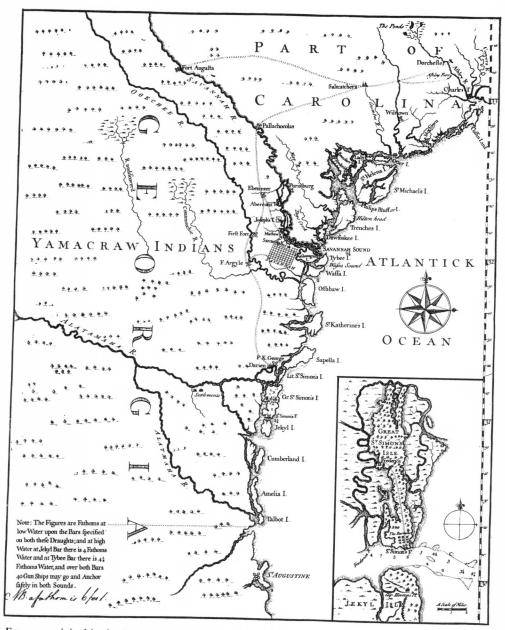

From an original in the De Renne Collection, University of Georgia Library. It is supposed to have been drawn during the period 1741–1743. It has been reproduced in several publications, including Urlsperger's *Ausführliche Nachrichten, 13te Continuation, Erster Theil* (Halle and Augsburg, 1747).

 *Foreword*

THE Wormsloe Foundation is a non-profit organization chartered on December 18, 1951, by the Superior Court of Chatham County, Georgia. In the words of its charter, "The objects and purposes of this Foundation are the promotion of historical research and the publication of the results thereof; the restoration, preservation, and maintenance of historical sites and documents and the conduct of an educational program in the study of history in the State of Georgia, and in states adjoining thereto."

As its first important activity, the Foundation has begun the publication of a series of historical works and documents under the title of "Wormsloe Foundation Publications." They consist of important manuscripts, reprints of rare publications, and historical narrative relative to Georgia and the South. The first volume appeared in 1955, written by E. Merton Coulter, the General Editor of the series, and entitled *Wormsloe: Two Centuries of a Georgia Family.* This volume gives the historical background of the Wormsloe Estate and a history of the family which has owned it for more than two and a quarter centuries.

The second publication of the Foundation was *The Journal of William Stephens, 1741–1743,* and the third volume was *The Journal of William Stephens, 1743–1745,* which is a continuation of the journal as far as any known copy is extant. However, there is evidence that Stephens kept his journal for some years after 1745. These volumes were edited by the General Editor of the Wormsloe Foundation series and were published in 1958 and 1959, respectively.

The fourth volume of the series was the re-publication of the unique copy of Pat. Tailfer et al., *A True and Historical Narrative of the Colony of Georgia . . . With Comments by the Earl of Egmont.* This volume is in the John Carter Brown Library of Brown University. In this publication there appears for the first time in print the comments of Egmont. With the permission of Brown University, this volume was edited by Clarence L. Ver Steeg of Northwestern University, Evanston, Illinois.

The fifth volume in the series was the long-missing first part of Egmont's three manuscript volumes of his journal. It was edited by Robert G. McPherson of the University of Georgia.

This volume contains the journal from 1732 to 1738, inclusive, and is owned by the Gilcrease Institute of American History and Art, Tulsa, Oklahoma, which gave permission for its publication.

In 1963 the Foundation published its sixth volume, *The Journal of Peter Gordon, 1732–1735*, which was edited by the General Editor of the series. Gordon came to Georgia with Oglethorpe on the first voyage; he began his journal on leaving England. The original manuscript was acquired in 1957 by the Wormsloe Foundation, which presented it to the General Library of the University of Georgia.

The seventh volume in the series was *Joseph Vallence Bevan, Georgia's First Official Historian*. It is a departure from the nature of the five volumes directly preceding, which are documentary. It was written by the General Editor, who brings to light a historiographer who was appointed Georgia's first official historian by the state legislature.

The eighth volume, *Henry Newman's Salzburger Letterbooks*, begins a series within the general series, for it is to be followed by several volumes of translations of the Urlsperger Reports (*Ausführliche Nachrichten* . . . , edited by Samuel Urlsperger, Halle, 1735ff, and dealing with the Georgia Salzburgers). This volume was edited by George Fenwick Jones of the University of Maryland, who has also edited later volumes of the Salzburger translations.

The ninth volume of the Wormsloe Foundation Publications is the first of several volumes of the Urlsperger Reports in translation to be published in this series. It appeared in 1968. The second volume of the Urlsperger Reports (being the tenth volume in the general series) was published in 1969, edited by George Fenwick Jones of the University of Maryland, as was the first, and extends over the years, 1734–1735. The third volume in the Urlsperger series (the eleventh in the general series) covers the year 1736, and was published in 1972. It was translated and edited by Professor Jones with the assistance of Marie Hahn of Hood College. The present volume, fourth in the Urlsperger series and twelfth in the whole number of the Wormsloe Foundation Publications, was edited by Professor Jones and translated by him together with Renate Wilson of The Johns Hopkins University.

E. MERTON COULTER
General Editor

 *Introduction*

THIS fourth volume contains the diary, written during the year 1737 by two Lutheran ministers assigned to a group of Protestant exiles from Salzburg who had settled at Ebenezer, near Savannah, Georgia, in the year 1734. Readers unfamiliar with the expulsion of these persecuted Protestants from their alpine homeland and their journey to the New World will find sufficient information in the introductions to the previous three volumes of this series and, in greater detail, in that to *Henry Newman's Salzburger Letterbooks.*[1] Most entries in the diaries were written by the older of these two divines, Johann Martin Boltzius, whose assistant, Christian Israel Gronau, wrote only on the days that Boltzius was absent in Savannah or else sick in bed.

After the tumult and turmoil of the year 1736, in which the Salzburger settlement had been moved, despite Oglethorpe's objections, from Old Ebenezer to the more fertile and accessible Red Bluff on the Savannah River, the year 1737 was a period of calm after the storm. Unfortunately for most readers of the diary, Boltzius could now give even more attention to the spiritual condition of his flock; yet, behind his predominantly religious concerns, we can still see his efforts to cope with the depressing problems of food and health, particularly with the suffering of the Third Transport, or third group of immigrants, whose supplies had been sent to Frederica on St. Simon's Island instead of to Ebenezer.

Boltzius' accounts of his dealings with Thomas Causton, the harried "mayor" or chief magistrate of Savannah and keeper of the storehouse, give us an insight into the chaotic conditions prevailing in that confused paradise, in which the grandiose schemes of the Lord Trustees and other benefactors were being so poorly realized. They also give us a glimpse of the religious life there, of the spiritual apathy of the English and the contrasting fervor of the Moravians. The latter, a cenobitic sect from Saxony in eastern Germany, left soon afterwards for Pennsylvania, partly because of the discouraging economic and health conditions in Georgia and partly because, as pacifists, they were unwilling to bear arms against the Spaniards in the War of Jenkins' Ear.

Boltzius calls these sectarians Herrnhuters, a name derived from Herrnhut, a religious community on one of Count Nicolas Ludwig von Zinzendorf's estates, in which they had sojourned after escaping religious persecution in Moravia. Boltzius' virulent prejudice against the Herrnhuters, which so amazed John Wesley and other Englishmen in Savannah, resulted in part from their literal acceptance of the priesthood of all believers, which made ordained ministers like Boltzius superfluous. It will be noted that Samuel Urlsperger, the contemporary editor of Boltzius' journals, removed all references to the delicate matter of the heretical Herrnhuters, who had previously caused embarrassment for the orthodox clergy at Halle. [Incidentally, all bracketed passages in the following text were deleted by Urlsperger from his edition[2] and are now being restored from the letterbooks of the Francke Foundation in Halle,[3] into which Boltzius' reports were regularly transcribed in their unexpurgated form.]

Boltzius' abhorrence of the Herrnhuters was so intense that his long entry for Wednesday, July 27, even suppresses the fact that Wesley had visited Ebenezer on that day in the company of August Spangenberg, the leader of the Georgia Herrnhuters. This journey must have taken place, for Wesley wrote in his journal under that date:

In the evening we came to New-Ebenezer, where the poor Saltzburghers are settled. The industry of this people is quite surprising. Their sixty huts are neatly and regularly built, and all the little spots of ground between them, improved to the best advantage. On one side of the town is a field of Indian corn; on the other are the plantations of several private persons; all which together one would scarce think possible for a handful of people to have done in one year.[4]

It will be noted that Boltzius did mention in his entry for 13 October that Wesley had visited Ebenezer on the previous Tuesday. This could hardly have been the same visit, in view of the great discrepancy in dates, since both of them used the old, or Julian, calendar. In any case, Boltzius failed to mention Spangenberg's visit.

Boltzius' relations with John Wesley were generally cordial, despite the latter's great admiration for the Herrnhuters and his inability to make the proper distinction between these dangerous innovators and the orthodox Lutheran clergymen in Ebenezer. Wesley, for his part, admired Boltzius and envied his control over his docile and obedient little flock. Despite Boltzius' disparaging remark in his entry for 13 January about Wesley's insistence upon total immersion, he seems to have respected his British counterpart. Wesley's sudden flight from Georgia, briefly related by Boltzius in his entry of 15 December, was caused by a conflict with Causton, whose niece Wesley had repelled from Holy Communion.[5]

In his entry for 23 August, Boltzius writes that he is imploring Causton, or in his absence Wesley, to come up to Ebenezer to inspect the damage wrought by the corn worms; and his next entry records that Causton is unable to come because of a "complicated matter." This was surely an understatement, for Boltzius must have heard of the furor in Savannah after 22 August, when Causton convoked a grand jury of fifty men to try Wesley for the crime of repelling his niece, Sophie Williamson, from Holy Communion. Since we do not have Boltzius' unexpurgated report, but only Urlsperger's bowdlerized edition, it is probable that Boltzius had given far more details about this sordid affair, which quickly divided Savannah into two hostile factions, motivated, no doubt, by political considerations more than by Wesley's rejection of his former fiancée from Holy Communion. Boltzius surely felt malicious satisfaction in Wesley's discomfiture, since Wesley had once repelled him too from Holy Communion for not having been confirmed in the proper (i.e. Anglican) church, which alone enjoyed the Apostolic Succession through the laying on of hands. (It will be noted that in his unfavorable entry for 13 January Boltzius had revealed Wesley's name, which Urlsperger later deleted.)

In addition to a steadily growing number of Lutherans in Savannah, mostly "Palatines" or indentured servants from the upper Rhineland, Boltzius and Gronau also tried to serve the few Lutherans and other Protestant Germans in Purysburg, South Carolina, across and down the Savannah River from Ebenezer. Boltzius' journal describes the misery not only of the Swiss in Purysburg but also of other Swiss settlers who passed by Ebenezer on their way up the Savannah River to Savannah-Town near Augusta. The leader of the Swiss settlers at Savannah-Town was Johannes Tobler, a former governor (*Landeshauptmann*) of the canton of Appelzell, who had the following words to say about Ebenezer a few years later: "They are all Germans there, yet they are in a flourishing state. They have two ministers. One of them, who is my esteemed friend, is named Martin Boltzius. He spares no pains to make the people there happy both in this world and in the next. There are, to be sure, people who claim that he meddles too much in secular matters, but who can please everybody?"[6]

The reader of these reports will probably agree with those who claimed that Boltzius meddled too much in secular matters, for example in discouraging the Salzburgers from seeking employment elsewhere or chastising them for accepting outrageous and unChristian wages for their labor, as he did in his entry for 5 July. However, Ebenezer soon became the most prosperous settlement in Georgia, and this was due in no small part to its pastor's shrewd understanding of economics and human nature.

Although primarily concerned with saving his parishioners' souls, Boltzius soon found himself responsible for their bodies as well, especially after he had successfully ejected the two commissioners, von Reck and Vat, and had lost the apothecary Zwifler. In a short time Boltzius assumed the functions of magistrate, quartermaster, business manager, town planner, deputy, doctor, and pharmacist. Health was, of course, the most serious single problem; for, as Boltzius confides in his entry of 30 July, his congregation had lost a quarter of its adults and more than a third of its children in slightly more than three years in Georgia. Malaria, which had afflicted the entire community the previous summer, had never entirely disappeared even in the cold winter months; and it raged again as soon as warm weather returned. It is safe to say that most of his people were sick most of the time; and it is a wonder that they were able to build their new settlement despite their constant chills and fever and racking pains. No doubt they would have been better off without the medications they received, to say nothing of blood-letting. It is sad to see Boltzius blaming the weather for diseases like dysentery, which we now know to result from lack of sanitation.

Boltzius' almost daily weather reports should help throw light on the activities reported in other chronicles of colonial Georgia. Also of interest are his references to cattle raising, an enterprise in which the Salzburgers and the Swiss surpassed all other colonists. Whereas agriculture was impeded by poor soil, bad weather, worms, and wild animals, enough progress was made in 1737 to prove Boltzius' contention that free enterprise was more productive than the communal work urged by Oglethorpe.

It seems incredible that the Salzburgers were nearly starving in a land teeming with game and along rivers abounding in sturgeon, eels, and catfish, all of which were rich men's fare in the old country. Perhaps centuries of harsh game laws in their homeland had discouraged the German settlers from learning to feed themselves from the bounty of the forest; for a single good coon-dog should have kept the community supplied not only with raccoons but also with opossums, which are as succulent as suckling pigs. And, with a hundred beaters at their command, they should have been able to surround and kill the deer and bear that so greatly damaged their crops, as well as quantities of marsh rabbits. Wild turkeys were then less wild than now, and wood ducks could have been trapped and netted. When Boltzius was finally offered an indentured professional hunter, he refused him because his heavy drinking might set a bad example. It is possible, of course, that Boltzius failed to report the taking of fish and game because his reports aimed to persuade the Trustees to continue provisions for another year.

As the dutiful pupil of his Pietist professors back at the University of Halle, Boltzius went to great pains to show in his diary, which he knew they would read, that he was teaching their doctrines in undiluted form. Over and over we see him contrasting the "true path of full conversion" with the "wrong, independent way of self-sufficient justice and piety" (5 June). The Pietists were afraid of "natural honesty" and "bourgeois respectability," through which some misguided sinners expected to achieve salvation without being reborn in the wounds of Jesus. To be reborn, one must acknowledge his absolute depravity and throw himself entirely on the mercy of Jesus. Consequently, Boltzius was often skeptical when his parishioners believed themselves saved.[7]

Like other Pietists, Boltzius was optimistic through all his hardships. Since God is all-knowing, all-powerful, and all-loving, He can only do what is best for us. Therefore, what seems a curse can only be a blessing in disguise; for a loving father chastises his child for its own good. "How beneficial it is for our soul, if matters do not go the way our flesh would want them to go, but we are instead led through many dark and perilous paths" (8 January). Boltzius repeated this thought in so many variations that even his congregation endorsed it, at least while talking to him. For example, a woman who had had only a mild attack of malaria explained that "she felt the need of being chastised with illness by the Lord; for days of health, while pleasing her flesh, might not be so wholesome for her soul as some suffering in her physical body" (23 June).

All entries in this diary are taken from Boltzius' unexpurgated reports as copied into the Halle letterbooks except for those from 1 August through 14 November, which were taken from Urlsperger's bowdlerized edition, since the original reports were lost in the mail. To be sure, Boltzius subsequently sent another copy that arrived in time to appear in Urlsperger's edition but, as far as the present editors know, was never copied into the letterbooks and was presumably lost. Facts revealed in the earlier unexpurgated parts make it easy to identify most of the names that Urlsperger so discreetly deleted. The number of notes in these volumes has been greatly diminished by identifying all proper names in the index. Biblical quotations in the diary, which were, of course, from Luther's translation, have been rendered in the language of the King James version. Because Boltzius was so steeped in the Bible, we can assume that he always quoted from memory; and it is not always certain that he was aware he was quoting.

This fourth volume, together with its three predecessors, represent only a fraction of the voluminous reports sent from Ebenezer by Boltzius before his death in 1765 and by his successors for a generation thereafter, to say nothing of a vast amount of correspondence likewise preserved in the archives of the Francke Foundation in Halle, in the DDR. The present editor, who will not live long enough to complete the task of translating and editing this material, will gratefully accept the aid of collaborators who might care to help in this interesting task. All that is required is a knowledge of the German language and enough perseverance to become familiar with the rambling literary style affected by the eighteenth-century Pietists.

As in the case of the previous volumes, the editors wish to thank the authorities of the University and State Library of Sachsen-Anhalt in Halle, DDR, for graciously supplying microfilms of Boltzius' diary, from which Urlsperger's deletions have been recovered. We also wish to thank both the American Philosophical Society for supporting the original research and the General Research Board of the University of Maryland for defraying typing costs; and we are especially indebted to the Wormsloe Foundation for publishing this volume.

George Fenwick Jones   Renate Wilson
University of Maryland   The Johns Hopkins University

Daily Register

Of the two pastors, Mr. Boltzius and Mr. Gronau
From January 1st to the end of the year 1737

JANUARY

Saturday, the 1st of January 1737 I.N.I. The weather has changed, and now it is pleasantly warm both day and night. Therefore, tonight we held our evening services, which many people attended full of joy in both body and soul. We are still omitting the repetition during the holidays; and in the meantime our pupils come into the hut of my dear colleague, who seeks to stimulate their devotion with singing, praying, and repetition of the Scripture they have heard and tries to lift up their hearts to our Lord Jesus.

Sunday, the 2nd of January. This has been a day full of fears and sighs, but also a day of much comfort and full of praise to the Lord, of which I can give no details at this point. God puts many a burden on us, but He also helps us. We have a God who helps and a Lord who saves from death. If this be felt with the fullness of our hearts, God will be large in our minds and strengthen our courage to bear all our further sufferings in Christian patience. For our part, we again have much evidence that God hears a faithful prayer, provided that we do not tire of waiting and hoping. His glorious name should be held high in praise for His kindness from here to all eternity.

Monday, the 3rd of January. The matter of provisions for the Salzburgers and our own circumstances would have required one of us to travel to Savannah today. Some obstacles came up, however; and for this reason the journey has been postponed for another week. We prefer to stay together over Sundays and holy days; and, since the Feast of the Epiphany falls on this coming Thursday, we had already made up our minds yesterday to spend this day in solemn celebration with divine help and with praise of the Lord for the cherished gospel which was given to

1

our heathen ancestors, and with urgent prayers for our flock and the poor heathen.

Tuesday, the 4th of January. As a result of the recent rains, the roads, and among them a certain path leading to the cattle pasture, have become so bad that our congregation will have to work together to build a new bridge if their cattle are not to suffer harm. This proposal was made tonight after the evening prayers were finished. Their cattle are now no safer from the wolves than in Old Ebenezer, inasmuch as the wolves not only howl terribly from quite close during the cold nights, but have also either eaten or injured calves, hogs, and poultry.

Wednesday, the 5th of January. Among her children Mrs. Helffenstein has a boy, fifteen years of age, whom she would like to have instructed in a trade; that is, she would like to have him become a tailor; and there would be an occasion for that with our friend H. [Herrnberger], who is a kind and devout man and very skillful at his work. The complete arrangements for this were made in my house today; and, according to the agreement, the mother will provide the boy with food and clothing, and on his part the tailor will teach him the trade in three years without any consideration being paid therefor. He will also give the boy time to attend my classes preparing the children for Holy Communion and permit him freedom to avail himself of other opportunities for his edification and the benefit of his soul. This H. [Herrnberger] has also accepted the tailor Christ as a companion in his work, since the latter (Christ) does not at this point feel that he can or wants to work in farming. Since, however, H. [Herrnberger] adjusts the payment for his work according to the poverty of our people and takes little, said Christ would not be able to subsist once our provisions run out. But in the meantime it will be of help to him, and God will provide for him afterwards.

Thursday, the 6th of January. On this Feast of the Epiphany, our Gracious Lord has much edified my heart through the large number of our Salzburgers who assembled tonight in the kitchen and hut of our herdsmen. Our conversations, songs, and prayers have again awakened our dear flock to a sincere Christian faith and a true gratitude for the precious gift of our gospel. Among other things, I told them how difficult it was, and how many obstacles had to be overcome, before our ancestors could be converted from their heathenish ways and made to recognize and accept the Christian religion. I tried to explain this to them by the many obstacles our heathens here have to overcome.

And, if God were only now making a start with us as with them and if we still had to be brought into the state into which God long ago placed our forebears, we would also find it hard going. For this reason we should arouse ourselves to praise the Lord God from the bottom of our hearts for not letting us stumble on our own way, as other blind peoples had to, but instead so brightly lighting the candles of His gospel amongst us.

I further illustrated this by showing our flock what advantages God's paternal care and our esteemed benefactors had given them over other Christian communities, in that, for example, we not only enjoyed full freedom in setting up and holding our services, and were not burdened by anyone with extraneous matters, ceremonies, and other such customs, but provision has also been made so that they do not have to furnish their ministers (of which two had prudently been provided for them) with either salary or fees. In addition to this they could send their children to school without any payment and in accordance with our own ways; and they and their children are provided with many kind of good books, such as Bibles, hymnals, etc. Also, our gracious and loving God has provided some monies so that, under His guidance, it may eventually be possible to build some institutions which will also serve the children of strangers, and even some of the heathen. I showed them how, in practice, they might apply that which they had learned; and I read them some passages concerning the obstacles which had been encountered in the conversion of the heathen in Surinam and which, in the main, are very similar to the ways which we have encountered in this country.

Friday, the 7th of January. Today I have been busy writing a couple of letters, i.e., to Mr. Vernon and Court Chaplain Ziegenhagen. Lack of time and the business of the day did not make it possible to write more letters. [The letter to Mr. Vernon was so written that it may be communicated to the Lord Trustees, since I have described, in humble terms, that which conscience and duty would make me write concerning the bad garden plots of the Salzburgers and of their future plantations, which might not be any better. I furthermore pointed out again that of the third transport not more than ten families had received cows but no other livestock, nor had they yet been given the necessary tools.] My diary has not progressed far at this point; and there remains a matter to be included, for which we would have to inquire with Mr. Causton. For this reason, we shall send it at the next occasion, together with several letters.

These letters will again be addressed to Mr. Eveleigh, a merchant in Charlestown, who thinks very well of us and is quite willing to be of service. God willing, we shall send to Savannah for provisions next Monday; and my dear colleague will likely go along on this journey on account of the aforementioned letters and other business.

Saturday, the 8th of January. In this first week of the new year, our glorious and merciful Lord has led me and my dear colleague into many internal and also external tribulations; but then He has also already fulfilled the merciful Word of His promise to us poor creatures and has given many signs of His help and comfort to us, whose trust is in Him. How beneficial it is for our soul, if matters do not go the way our flesh would want them to go, but we are instead led through many dark and perilous paths. Thus, our hearts can recognize many things that we failed to see before; and our Lord Jesus becomes ever so much closer and dearer to our hearts with His great merit and salvation, which is extended even to the greatest of sinners. Also, such circumstances teach us to have more pity and understanding for those who undergo the same or similar trials; and we can thus comfort them with the very comfort with which God has comforted us. The song: "O Lord Jesus, Your manger is, etc."[8] is thus a wonderful hymn; and the words of Sirach, Chapter 11: 10–13: "Look at the examples etc.," strengthen my heart much. The Lord will help us through all the misery which we have encountered in our pilgrimage; for He has said, "I will not forsake thee etc."[9] When the godly members of our flock notice our grief and suffering, they help us pray, without any reminder on our part, even more faithfully and fervently; and they praise God from a full heart for the help rendered us. This we know and feel full well. God be praised for all His blessings, and also for all the trials and tribulations He imposes on us, from now until eternity, Amen.

Sunday, the 9th of January. This year on Sunday afternoons Luther's small catechism is read and applied for the edification of all. During the period of Advent and in the following holy days, the catechization was based on some sayings proper to the holy days.

Monday, the 10th of January. Kiefer, the herdsman from Purysburg, was here yesterday with his two sons and brought a boy[10] whom his mother, a widow in Purysburg, wants to place in our school. She is willing to contribute to his food and clothing whatever is within her means to give, provided only that the boy may be instructed in the Christian faith and other necessary knowledge. For a number of days now we have had a heavier freeze by day and night than we have experienced all winter long. These repeated changes in the weather cause in many of us a quite marked change in physical condition. Many have a relapse of their fever unless they take great care to protect themselves from the cold and to avoid too much exertion at work.

Tuesday, the 11th of January. Veit Lemmenhoffer and his wife are both still quite ill. The woman in particular is in such a bad state because of daily attacks of the fever and also because of another ill that has befallen her, that we are gravely worried about her getting well again. They both acquiesce in the will of the Lord and in the cross that He has given them to bear, and I cannot find any sign of complaints or impatience in them. The two N. N. people [the Balthasar Rieser couple][11] are not yet rid of their fever either, and they have lost almost all strength. The man has become so mellowed and humbled as a result of this chastisement that he is seeking to have more true insight into himself and into this world, to which he was quite attached in his heart; and he is trying to understand more of the ways of our Lord Jesus, the Savior of Man. He now knows so well the teachings of the gospel and the ways of salvation; and he speaks of these matters so thoughtfully and edifyingly that I know hardly anyone of our flock who could equal him in this respect. He is a good example of how much man can achieve in the historical recognition of spiritual things by his own natural gifts and how much it cost our Lord in order to tear our hearts completely away from self-love and love of this world. The two oldest boys, one fifteen and the other thirteen years of age, help their sick parents much more and much better in their work than when they were well.

Wednesday, the 12th of January. Our people here need a smith more than anything else. Their tools are put to much use; and, since these are not made of iron and steel as good as it is found in Germany, the tools are easily damaged. Previously, the smith in Abercorn gave them good service; but he has been grievously ill with fever for a long time and is not quite well yet. Also, because he has much other work to catch up with, he will not be able to work for us for some time to come. The road to Abercorn is a long one; and, since the people have been forced to go there in vain many times, it is quite a burden on them. This man is still inexpensive, whereas the smiths and other artisans in Savannah are so expensive that poor people cannot afford to pay them; and, in addition, the work never gets done. At present, Mr. Causton no longer has things repaired for our people, and they have to pay for everything that they order to be made or repaired. I have asked him to repair the grist mills, especially since the third transport did not receive any and thus must grind their grain with those belonging to the first and second transports. He let me know, however, that he could not fulfill my request. It is to be hoped that, in one of the future transports which are expected, provision will be made for a smith and a cobbler; but they should bring along their tools.

Thursday, the 13th of January. In Savannah an old physician asked my dear colleague to baptize his child, which is already nine months old. My colleague refused this, however, because they have their own minister in Savannah. The people there are much displeased that Mr. N. [Wesley] does not wish to baptize children other than by immersing them in water unless he can be convinced that the infants could not stand such treatment due to their feeble health.[12]

The son of a poor widow from Purysburg has now arrived; and his mother has provided him with as much rice and beans as her means allowed. Our heavenly Father, who will not even let a bird die of hunger, will see to the rest. We have placed him with a couple who will give him shelter and supervision, and it is to be hoped that he will be well taken care of and instructed to apply himself to his prayers and other beneficial work. If our Salzburgers only had time, something should be built, in the name of God, for poor children and for the sick.

Friday, the 14th of January. In our evening prayer meeting, I have begun to repeat with questions and answers what we have also catechized daily in my house, basing it on the *Compendium theologicum* of the Reverend Freylinghausen. I had learned that many of our flock would have liked to participate in this if their time and work would but allow it. But this repetition is held only once a week, so that we will not be delayed in pursuing our study of the Bible stories, which are still blessed by the Lord. For some time now the cold has become so severe that I cannot see much difference between winter in Germany and here. One blessing is the abundance of firewood here; and this cannot be spared, since we are lacking in stoves and other convenient arrangements.

Saturday, the 15th of January. The English preacher who has been sent here for the conversion of the heathen[13] has requested the help of some of our people to prepare a piece of land which he has been given by the Indians. However, everybody is so busy with his own work that it seems impossible to take up work for others. As we have noticed, this preacher is most concerned with learning the language of the Indians; it may be said that he has ample time for this, since he has no children other than a single Indian boy whom he instructs in his school. This week we too had some Indians, together with many children, whom we would like to have in our school if their parents would but permit it. These children spent today watching how our children sang, prayed, and were instructed in school.

Sunday, the 16th of January. I have had occasion to notice that some of our listeners are much interested in learning about the tyranny and horrors of the Papist doctrine. For this reason, I have started with some of our people, who come to one of the huts for simple edification and common prayer, to read from the life of our blessed Luther, which offers me many suitable occasions to edify them with useful reminders and testimonies of the past and present corruption of the doctrine and life of the poor Papists. At the end of the meeting,[14] all those present attested their pleasure and thanks for the beginning we had made. The blessed work of the Reformation well deserves our remembering it with praise and thanks and giving others an opportunity to learn of it.

Monday, the 17th of January. More than a year ago two cows and a calf joined our herd, and it has been impossible to determine whose property they were. Recently we heard that they belong to a tailor and a clerk in Savannah, who would be quite willing to leave the cattle where they are now if only they could find someone willing to buy them, since it would cause much expense and difficulty to return them to Savannah. At the present time cattle are very expensive, and poor people could not think of paying for them. A good cow with a calf will go for 3 £ sterling or more. If our esteemed benefactors in London cannot see their way to provide the last group of Salzburgers and Austrians with cattle, as they have done before for the second and the first transport, these people will be very badly off as regards manure, milk, and meat; for it will be many years before they will be able to buy their own livestock. It remains to be seen how the Lord Trustees will resolve my most recent humble intercession on behalf of these poor people. They have bought as many hogs and as much poultry as their meager resources would permit, so that they might slowly be able to breed their own livestock.

Tuesday, the 18th of January. The bitter cold still persists by day and by night; and, furthermore, the wind has become so harsh and biting that hardly anybody ventures outside. The winds in this country are often of great violence. A few fences around our people's gardens have come down today because the crossbars to which the long slats are tied were only fastened with wooden nails.

Wednesday, the 19th of January. Some of our people, while working in their gardens in the strong wind, had lighted a few fires. Although they had good reason for it, this was most incautious; and the fires quickly spread and covered a large area. It has caused some damage in that a part of the common fence, and a pile of slats burned. If the people had not taken precautions in time, the fire could have spread much farther and have attacked a few of the huts and some fences around the gardens. The grass is now so dry and the ground so covered with dry leaves that a fire will start easily. The forest itself is not so easily affected except for a few dry trees, which burn down slowly. It is the custom here in these two and the following months to occasionally light a fire among the grass and the reeds, so that young grass can sprout more easily, and the cattle will benefit therefrom. But this is usually done with much care and not in such a high wind.[15]

Thursday, the 20th of January. The son of Mrs. Helffenstein has already grown weary of his master and of the profession of tailor, and after the first few weeks which were set as a trial period he is now back helping his mother. He claims that he would rather be a cobbler than a tailor. The mother has many children, and the two oldest can work the ground, but not cut trees, so that they will not be able to do much planting, although they do not lack good will and effort. We already have a few fenced-off plots of which we will give some to Mrs. Schweighoffer and some to this widow for planting until such time as arrangements can be made for the sustenance of these two widows. We again have a few Indian families with us who have brought us fresh meat; but they ask much for it. Among them can be found honorable, good, and kind men who are easy and pleasant to get along with. They stop often at our huts, and there is nothing we would like more than to render them spiritual help. They have many children with them; and these, as well as the grown men, wear nothing but a woolen cloth or a leather hide around their body.

Friday, the 21st of January. I was much impressed when a woman told me that her little child who is but three years old and until now has not wanted to speak, uttered as his first word, "Hallelujah," so clearly that it could be well understood. This happened when she and her family were singing the hymn, "Hallelujah, Praise, honor and glory, etc."[16] Some of our schoolchildren show much pleasure in singing holy songs formerly not known among them; and, since we all try hard to teach them such unknown and lovely melodies and have them sing these songs before the others, the adult members of our group find much pleasure and edification in them. The members of our congregation now all have the same hymnals, so that, when something unknown is sung, they can read it later until such time as they have learned these melodies.

Saturday, the 22nd of January. N. N. [The watchmaker, Müller] complained much of his oldest son, who, he said, is nearly nineteen years old and almost able to gain his own bread.[17] But he is very wilful, does not speak kindly to his parents, and claims many liberties because he can do the most work. Also, the father added, he encourages the other children to disobedience and disorderliness. The other day he wanted to join in Holy Communion, but for good reasons I told him to wait for the next occasion. Now I am much pleased that I made him wait, since I heard these stories about him, which urge me to work very seriously with him and those like him before the next communion takes place. The two oldest daughters of this N. [Müller] have proved to be very well behaved in school and understand the truths we try to teach them quite well.[18] At noon, I asked the men of our village to join me in a meeting, because I wanted to consider with them several matters which would serve for great safety and better management. God bless everything for His glory and our physical and spiritual benefit.

Sunday, the 23rd of January. Recently, under the date of 8th August 1736, we mentioned Schoemannsgruber,[19] an inhabitant of Purysburg who had tried to deliver himself of his poverty and his miserable circumstances by his own efforts and much endeavor, but this only led him to even greater ruin and much misery. Now he has died of a burning fever while travelling on a boat; and he has left a widow and two children in poverty. His wife has returned to Charleston, and she has asked me for a certificate attesting to the death of her husband. However, this service should be rendered by an English preacher in Charlestown, who will be in a better position to verify her husband's death.

Monday, the 24th of January. The weather being pleasant today, we visited a few Salzburgers who were working in their gardens. Several have already cleared their two acres of land of trees and brush. If the lengthy sickness of some had not prevented it, there is no doubt that all the gardens would by now be so well prepared. If those able to finish the work on their gardens in a few days (excepting the fences, for which they have to wait for their neighbors) had already been given their forty-eight acres, they could start work on that land, too. Such land would be of great benefit for those, in particular, whose gardens are entirely on sandy ground. If only they had those forty-eight acres, they could select the best lands and work them to greater benefit and with more pleasure than is now the case. [The food being as bad and entirely insufficient as it is, the people exhaust themselves in their work in order finally to gain their own bread; but, where the land is so terribly poor as are some of the lots, they are forced to work without reward and find little joy in it. We are impatiently waiting for news as to how the Lord Trustees will deem to resolve the matter for which we interceded with them on behalf of these poor people. There is no doubt in my mind that, if the Lord Trustees were themselves to see the miserable land and the unending industry of the Salzburgers as well as their continuing poor circumstances, which are due solely to the wrong provisions made for these poor people, their hearts would break in commiseration and they would soon be inclined to provide real help. As long as our conditions here are described to them by others, who may well have ulterior motives, little benefit can be expected to result for our poor people. May God in His mercy keep watch over us. Good land is available here, but no one is willing to give it to our people—this is hardly in accord with the promises extended to them and with Christian fairness.]

Tuesday, the 25th of January. Several parents have asked to excuse their older children from school for several hours of the day because they are needed to work in the fields. Mrs. Holtzer, an Austrian widow, and her daughter are quite eager to prepare part of the two acres in their possession so as to use the land for gardening. A single man, who does not have any good land and who will benefit from half of the produce, is helping her in this endeavor.

We now often have Indians in our village. Both grownups and children are sometimes present while we teach our children; and, during our evening prayer meeting today, a man and his child sat down quietly on the bench with the rest of the congregation, while outside the church the women and girls spent their time laughing and running around.

[Wednesday, the 26th of January. The smith in Abercorn has sent me a note through one of our Salzburgers and informed me that, by order of Mr. Oglethorpe, Mr. Causton will no longer pay for the repair of any tools that our people bring there; they will have to pay for such things themselves from now on. In addition to the repairs now under way, our congregation owes him the sum of 3£, etc. I can hardly believe that it should be the will of the Lord Trustees that impoverished and hardworking people such as ours, who work for the very bread they eat, should be forced to pay for the repair of such necessary tools as axes, hoes, etc. It would seem to me also that they have been deprived of this privilege since they moved from Old Ebenezer, perhaps from secret revenge, for otherwise I cannot see how they could owe as much as 3 £ sterling, particularly since the smith has been unable to work for quite a time due to his high fever.]

Thursday, the 27th of January. Last night Mrs. Ernst gave birth to a daughter, who was baptized this morning. This woman had been confined to her bed with fever for more than six months; but, as the husband told us, God helped her in that her delivery was easy and without much difficulty. [Yet these two ungrateful people will not recognize this or other things as a gift of God. Today, the schoolmaster's wife returned by land, accompanied by a suspicious-looking guide. She had been gone since the 5th of December, that is, almost 8 weeks. This is hardly becoming for a schoolmaster's wife.]

Friday, the 28th of January. A pious Salzburger came to me today and complained that he had much trouble with the work on his poor land. He could hardly believe that God could make it possible for him to find sustenance on such bad earth. He recounted that, as soon as one doubt and worry is laid to rest, some new trouble occurs, etc. He is now carrying manure on his back to the garden, which is, however, quite far away. He is one of those who have already cleared the trees from their garden plots and would like to start work on the rest of their land, if it had only been surveyed. [Those who have read our previous messages in this respect and who judge our situation with an impartial mind must agree with us in our belief that not much is thought of the Salzburgers in this country and that the provisions made for their sustenance are not as promised. If this were not the case, other means for their support would have been provided from the very outset, which would hardly have consumed a third of the expenses actually made. It is much to be regretted that those gentle benefactors whose purpose in sending the Salzburgers here was but to honor God and provide for their spiritual and physical welfare cannot be with us and see their numerous miseries. I am sure that, if they could but see us, different provisions would be made and the Salzburgers would be helped].

Saturday, the 29th of January. Those of our young people who receive instruction at lunchtime in the *Compendium theologiae* of the Reverend Pastor Freylinghausen now find it necessary to stay outside all day at their work in the gardens and even to cook their meal there. For this reason I would like to shift the hour for this instruction to another time, if it were but possible. Early in the morning it is too cold, and most of them are busy with their livestock and with their housework. In the evening we have our prayer meetings; and on Sunday, after the public services, we visit our flock or the children come to us for prayer and simple conversations and in the evening we have a meeting with some of our people. In any event, this noontime lesson will only be given for another fortnight or so, since half of the articles of faith have already been seen and studied in accordance with the aforementioned *Compendium*. Not much of it has been repeated in public, because in accordance with the wishes of some of the audience I had wanted to expound the story of Jacob in connection with a certain point I wished to make.

We much regret that our huts are so uncomfortable and unsuited to pray privately with the *preparandis ad S. Coenam*[20] and to talk to them about the condition of their souls. Perhaps God will direct the hearts of our benefactors to have a suitable house built for us. The houses built of boards are quite expensive and, at that, are too cold in the winter and too hot in the summer. In addition, every word, even if it is not spoken in a loud voice, can be heard in the street, which is quite inconvenient for a minister who wishes to speak privately and seriously with his parishioners, and which also makes his listeners feel ill at ease. Only recently something was said to me in my hut which was heard by one or several persons, and this had some ill effects. If only some sums were allocated for this purpose, it would be possible—and far less expensive than the English manner of building is—to have the Salzburgers erect a few good houses better suited for our purposes, health, and office. We do not know, of course, whether a suggestion to this effect made to the proper persons in London would be well received.

Sunday, the 30th of January. In the last few days the cold weather has diminished and a warm rain has fallen, which is still continuing today. We do not know whether the persistent fever of some of the Salzburger men is due to this inconstant weather or what the real reason of their malady is. There are hardly any means to buy flour and butter, which in normal times is their healthiest and best nourishment.

Monday, the 31st of January. On the occasion of the recent fire in the woods, during which two hundred long shingles were burned, a quarrel and some ill will developed among two of our young people. One of them in particular thought he was entitled to something which was not due to him; and my suggestions in this matter were not well received. Today I stopped at his home to inquire as to his present state of mind regarding this presumed insult. He now admits that his ill will on that occasion was sinful, and he recognizes that what he refused to accept formerly was but right and just. He said that yesterday God had prepared him for this change of heart through His Word, and he much appreciated my reminder of his rage and bad temper and my advice based on the Lord's Word.

Kieffer, the herdsman from Purysburg, is now taking serious steps to move his entire family into the vicinity of our settlement on the Carolinian side. He has exchanged his land in Purysburg for the land here, so that he and his family might be closer to the school and the place of worship. He is now hurriedly building a hut, for which some of our people have prepared clapboards, against a consideration. At this point almost everybody is leaving Purysburg, for people find neither physical nor spiritual sustenance there. [Many complain of the preacher at that place,[21] who is quite careless in the exercise of his functions and much too interested in the things of this world.]

FEBRUARY

[Tuesday, the 1st of February. Mr. Zwiffler is still getting ready for his departure, and for this purpose he is selling whatever he can sell. For some time he has been behaving very friendly and helpful toward us and our congregation and sets a good example through his regular attendance at divine services. After his departure the people at our place will be most concerned about blood-letting, because they are very accustomed to it. May God look with mercy upon us in this matter and send us a Christian and experienced man who is suitable for the congregation and its needs.]

Wednesday, the 2nd of February. This afternoon I had another conference with the men of our parish on some material matters and arrangements. In particular, the herding and care of the cattle had given rise to some misunderstandings and a degree of confusion, so that it is high time to bring about some changes if many head of cattle are not to be lost as a result. We have now arranged for guarding the herd by dividing it; and for this purpose two herdsmen have been appointed who will be sufficiently rewarded so that the parish may not have as much cause for complaint as previously. Some of the ten cows that were given to the third transport have been lost now for a month. Presumably, as is often the case here, they have wandered back to their old place in Carolina; this had also happened with some of the cattle of the first and the second transport. Some have died, and many calves have been either devoured by wolves and bears or by dogs belonging to the Indians. The former herdsman has not done his job here as well as was the case in old Ebenezer, and for this reason two men were chosen who will be more careful and responsible.

Thursday, the 3rd of February. I had sent our boat to Savannah to get meat, corn, and rice for the third transport. However, it returned empty; because at this time there are no provisions left in the store-house. And, although our people were told by Mr. Causton to go to Josephtown to Capt. Maccay to ask for corn, they could not get anything there, unless we were to consent to take 150 bushels of sweet potatoes.[22] However, in view of the shortened rations, this would constitute a considerable loss for our people, since each pound of potatoes is counted equal to a pound of corn or beans and it is said that most of the potatoes are rotten and we would not have a chance to pick them over and choose the good ones. Thus I will have to go to Savannah myself on Monday to look after provisions, of which the third transport in particular is suffering a great lack.

[Some time ago, Rheinlaender had sent his son to Savannah so that he might learn the cobbler's trade with the Herrnhuters. He has now brought him back and does not want to send him there anymore. He claims that the cobbler there does not know his trade; the Herrnhuters would have caused much disgust and repulsion in the boy with their slanderous remarks regarding the preachers at Ebenezer, whom, as I understand, they call any number of vile names.[23] The parents recount much of what their son has told them regarding the different and peculiar arrangement of their worship; but one cannot believe everything they say. Mrs. Helfenstein has now agreed with them (the Herrnhuters) to place her son as an apprentice with their cobbler for three years. It is the son who left the tailor Herrnberger after a short time. She has asked my advice on this matter; but I can advise her neither pro nor con, and must leave the decision to her own judgment and her information on the conditions obtaining there. She became very familiar with the Herrnhuters in London. Her boy is not worth much, and he has bad habits and manners. The mother is much too lenient with him, and I have had much occasion to remonstrate with her on this point.]

Friday, the 4th of February. Yesterday six men found a good cattle pasture only two hours from here, and today the whole parish has gone there in order to build a hut for the herdsmen and an enclosure for the cattle. There were too many cows and calves at our place because, due to the negligence of the former herdsman and to the illness of our people, all the cane had been grazed away around the village. In the winter the cattle could not be driven to pasture far away from the village because they were too weak; and we might have lost them had we not proceeded to separate them in two herds, in such a manner that the cows giving milk are now to be herded close to the village and led back every night, whereas cows that will bear calves shortly and the cows and calves that are not producing at this time will be entrusted to the second herdsman. The parish hopes to gain much from this new arrangement. Although we now have two herdsmen, the people in their present poor circumstances will not incur any more expense, since they will pay one shilling sixpence per year for a cow and sixpence for a calf that still must be raised.

Continuation of the Diary

Saturday, the 5th of February. N. N. [Mrs. Schweighofer] was much chagrined about her children, who do not wish to obey her properly. She does not wish to be at fault for their insufficient education and their corruption; and, therefore, she asked me to assist her and punish the disobedient children in her stead. In class we have not found these children, of which there are three, to be seriously disobedient, although their frivolity and lack of application require a sharp and watchful eye for their own good. [The mother has lost the use of her right hand because of a stroke, and she is low in spirit. She loves her children and treats them with much tenderness, and thus her admonitions and threats do not carry much weight.

[Sunday, the 6th of February. Ernst and his wife are very evil people who annoy their neighbors and others in many ways. As long as they receive kindnesses and favors from others, they know how to dissemble and play the hypocrites; but, once their unpleasantness, malice, and wickedness are uncovered, they not only offer much in the way of explanations and excuses but become quite coarse and impudent in their replies. It is said that as regards lying, cursing, fighting etc. the wife is even worse than her husband. It was announced today that we will have Holy Communion in two weeks or so, and we will have much effort and little gain with these people. They cannot be convinced of the error of their ways and of the horror of their unconverted hearts. He now misses the public services with many pretexts; for his wife is in confinement and he remains at home, pretending that he has to take care of her.

[Monday, the 7th of February. The privation of the poor people at our place is getting worse and worse, and particularly the third transport is lacking in the most necessary staples. Since we have not been able to learn whether the provisions for this transport will be continued for another year, and since, moreover, the period for which the first and second transports were to receive provisions will run out this coming March, we have felt it necessary to approach Court Chaplain Ziegenhagen again and describe to him the misery and suffering of our dear flock. We have taken the occasion to send along our diary up till this point. Also, I have sent with today's boat a letter to Mr. Causton raising a number of important and urgent points concerning the miserable circumstances of the Salzburgers and the poor regard in which they are held; I have stated these matters with much concern, most humbly yet frankly, and I fear that this may not be too well received.]

Tuesday, the 8th of February. During his last severe fever and illness, N. N. [Stephan Riedelsperger] had felt so much remorse and disquiet concerning his former life that words failed him when he expressed his grief to me. He offered God so many promises on this occasion that I felt very joyous and was quite confident of the seriousness of the Christian life he was going to lead. Shortly after his recovery, however, he relapsed into his former indolence and, although he was reminded of his resolutions and his promises, it did not have the desired effect. Now God has arranged it that the evil nature of his heart may become quite open for all to see, and it is to be hoped that this will lead both to his mortification and to his eventual improvement. He has entered into a bargain and barter with a simple Salzburger which is so obviously unfair that others have seen it and informed me of it. When I refused to approve of such an injustice and gave him good admonitions, he became so insolent and rude that I was much surprised. I would not have expected such evil manners in him. It has thus become necessary to make public his ill manners and shameful suspicion next Saturday, when the congregation will assemble for some necessary discussions; and pious, conscientious, and reasonable people will have an occasion to judge this unjust barter, as well as my attitude in this matter. It is my hope that he will recognize how shameful his rudeness was, and that others may be warned by this example. [Riedelsperger had a similar dispute in Old Ebenezer in Mr. Vat's time; and, while the bargain was unfair, Mr. Vat held it to be equitable and valid under English law, although the partner to the bargain, who had entered into it too hastily, obviously suffered a loss and regretted it afterwards and can still be heard to voice his discontentment concerning this matter.]

Wednesday, the 9th of February. Yesterday during evening worship we reflected on what is written in Genesis 34 on the godless behavior of the sons of Jacob and of his only daughter. I took this occasion to demonstrate the horror of both subtle and obvious sins against the sixth commandment,[24] addressing myself particularly to our young listeners, in view of the past and the future; and I gave them much instruction on which their salvation both here and in heaven will depend, if they but follow it. This morning I learned of two in whose hearts the teachings of last night had such an effect that each recognized his sins in the past with many tears. Many hidden sins are on the conscience of some people, and they comfort and reassure themselves until God in his wisdom so arranges it that such hiding places are laid bare and all their comfort and assurance is taken from them. In studying the Biblical stories, we have often noticed that the venerable patriarchs led themselves and their own into much more serious temptation whenever they went into or near the cities than when they stayed in solitude as pilgrims and strangers, far from the noise and cries of this world. Those among us who possess the proper understanding well realize the advantage which we, in our retirement in the desert, have over those who live in the cities.

Thursday, the 10th, till Saturday, the 12th, of February. The boat that arrived yesterday brought the news that the people in Savannah are much worried about the Spanish, who are making considerable preparations for war and seem to have their eye on this colony. Mr. Causton had been informed of this by a fast boat from Charleston, and he wished to be informed of some matters relating to our defense. Since such matters cannot be discussed by mail but should be arranged directly, I decided to go on this journey myself. Mr. Causton again showed me much consideration, and he agreed to a number of things which will be to the benefit of our community and which I would hardly have achieved had I only written to him. He intends, this once, to pay the smith in Abercorn the three pounds and some shillings which are still owed for repairs on our people's tools, although the orders given to him had not provided for such payment. He gave permission for the Salzburgers, after work on their gardens has been terminated, to look for plots of land on their own and choose those which they wish to prepare for planting. If such plots should be allocated to others once the land is surveyed, the new owners would have to recompense the Salzburgers for their labors. So far, there are no provisions yet in the store-house, but he has hopes of receiving some by next week, and we should send the boat back. He will also provide our village with muskets, powder, and lead, since we have been lacking these until now. In Savannah there is only levity and joking with regard to the Spanish and their impending campaign. It would be better if the people there repented of the sins which so flourish in that city and thus arrest God's judgment and retribution.

This afternoon the men of the parish again congregated with me to discuss some points which I wished to bring up, and also to prevent some offenses and misunderstandings. I availed myself of this occasion to recall N. N. [Stephan Riedelsperger] and his recent conduct in such a manner as I felt would be of the greatest benefit to him and to the congregation. We know from experience that such meetings serve a good purpose, and we will arrange for them in the future whenever the circumstances warrant it.

Sunday, the 13th of February. Despite all the sorrows I feel in my heart because of some members of the congregation and

other circumstances regarding our people, our dear Lord has
given me so much spiritual comfort today that even the frail
flesh has benefited from it. He has shown me by several examples that my last, as well as today's, sermon of His word have
been blessed by His love. Some consciences have been moved
because of the sins that they committed in their youth. We had
shown in the last sermon, by means of Genesis 34, the distasteful
and abhorrent sin against the sixth commandment;[25] and today,
when explaining the seventh commandment, we demonstrated
the sin of hidden and open injustice and dishonesty with regard
to one's own possessions and those of his neighbor.

One of those among our congregation whose conscience had
been moved said to me that he had often asked God to put in
his mouth only that which a simple man needed to know, in
particular how he should go about obtaining true peace in
Christ and the certainty of His merciful forgiveness for his sins,
and that God had indeed granted him his wish. But, although
he had asked our Lord's pardon for his sins in many a prayer,
had detested his former ways, and had often felt that he was sure
of God's mercy and relieved of His curse and wrath, he knew
full well that he could not find true relief and peace, because
he had shied away from making an open confession and restor-
ing what he had unjustly acquired. The fact that such transgressions had been committed in the years of his ignorance and that
many circumstances had led him to believe that he had justly
acquired the belongings of another could not now offer any
comfort to him.

Such repentants who let the word of God ripen in themselves
are not rare. They have sinned in their past but have not made
amends for their deeds; and, despite all serious admonitions and
advice, they persist in their frivolous ways and evil manners; and
thus it is that things seem to go worse with them. [Muggitzer
is such a one. He is not one of the Salzburgers but came to us
with the second transport. If he were not so desperately poor
and thus in need of the help of others, and also of a timid
disposition, he would cause us much sorrow. Back in Germany
he committed a serious transgression which may have been kept
quiet until he had left. The same is probably true of Michael
Rieser, for whose improvement there is little hope.]

Monday, the 14th of February. In my small hut it is impossible
for me to do justice to myself and the worried souls who wish
to seek my advice and counsel, and I cannot fulfill my office in
these circumstances. They admitted that they are reluctant to

open their hearts to me here, not only because any passerby can hear almost every word that is said here, but also because the noise of housekeeping and the presence of my family interrupt all talks in this poor and miserably kept dwelling. And, since my health urgently requires a change in this respect and the consent of the Lord Trustees is not required in this matter, I have decided, at my own expense, to have some of the Salzburgers build a well-constructed house from dressed lumber as soon as they have tilled their fields. It will be built in the middle of the town at the site intended for the minister's house and other public buildings, although this location has not yet been fully measured and fenced in by the surveyor. I lack funds for this plan, but shall trust that our heavenly Father will provide for me in this respect, since it is based on urgent necessity.

For several days we have had the most pleasant spring weather by night and by day, which seems well suited for sowing and planting, but our experience makes us fear that there will still be several harsh night freezes such as those which, last year and on other occasions, killed all garden plants which had been put out too early.

Tuesday, the 15th of February. A young Englishman who is employed at the store-house in Savannah as a clerk travelled here by land last Thursday and asked my dear colleague to come with him in order to perform his marriage with a woman from Savannah, since Mr. Wesley had been hesitant to perform this ceremony in view of some of the rites customary in their church. My dear colleague consented to this request and departed this last Saturday, after I had returned from Savannah. But he made the condition that he would discuss the matter first with the English minister there. While Mr. Wesley did not object and assured my colleague that he would not look with disfavor upon such a ceremony, the circumstances made it clear that not much could be gained and some ill will might be incurred by such an exercise of our ministerial functions. For this reason, my dear colleague returned yesterday without having accomplished the purpose of his journey; but he stopped at Purysburg on Sunday afternoon to preach the word of the Lord to the congregation there.

S. [Mrs. Schweighofer] sent for me and revealed the worry that filled her soul: the day before yesterday, after the service, she had started to pray so as to examine her soul in the light of His word as it had been read. And doing this in the face of the Lord, she had been attacked by such fear and trepidation that she could neither pray, nor eat, nor drink; and she was thus in great need of instruction, comfort, and help to assure her that her soul would not suffer any danger. This occasion reminded me of the words in Isaiah 66:2, "and trembleth at my word." She is most painstaking in her use of the means of grace, most circumspect in her Christian life, and always hungry for the mercy of the Lord.

Wednesday, the 16th of February. N. N. [A young Salzburger] was so depressed by the sin of impurity which he had committed in his 15th year that he appeared at my door, looking quite lifeless, almost incapable of speech, and barely able to utter his words with sighs. He is quite honest in all other ways and is much loved by everyone for his godfearing, quiet life and faithful application to his work. But as there was something left here and there in his heart which displeased the clear eye of the Lord, he could not find true peace. How common the sins against the sixth and seventh commandments[26] are among Christian people, yet how rarely are they recognized as most despicable and how little remorse is felt for them. This being so, all good intentions and resolutions must remain vain and cannot lead to true conversion.

On his recent stay in Purysburg, my dear colleague was asked to return as soon as possible to perform Holy Communion, as the women there who have children find it hard to travel to our village. Therefore he departed this morning with our boat, which was sent for provisions. May God bless him in the exercise of his duty.

Mr. Z. [Zwifler] also informed me that he wished to take Holy Communion this coming Sunday. It will be his last time in this country, since he has resolved to return to Europe within three weeks via Charleston.[27] He testified that during the last months God had again blessed the effects of His word in him, and I only pray that he will have the faith and fidelity [that is required if he not to fare like some of the others from the first transport who, while always professing to be much regaled by the preaching of the gospels, never let themselves be led to a complete denial of the world and of themselves. For this reason, God's holy judgment will make such people fare worse and worse. Rauner, Gschwandel, and Schweiger have sinned so much by intemperate drinking that nothing remains but to proceed with them under the power that the Lord has vested in his servants. This is doubly true since they should have learned from the example which had been set in other cases and by our actions in these matters. Stephan Riedelsperger is not much better than they, since it was he who gave them occasion for such abuse and excess, of which we learned only yesterday.]

Thursday, the 17th of February. Last Monday a young woman sent me word through her spouse that I should visit her as soon as my affairs would permit it, as she had to talk to me concerning the salvation of her soul. However, I was not able to go to her until yesterday afternoon because of the people who were registering for Holy Communion. She was waiting for me at at the garden gate all in tears; and her words, which were uttered with much weeping, bore witness to the realization of the serious sins which she had committed in N. Before confiding the facts about her transgressions to me, she begged me that, while she was willing for me to accuse her of her detestable deeds before the entire congregation, she did not wish to be rejected [by her husband and her small child.] If I should so tell her, she would reveal her sins to a certain person [her *facinora* to her honest husband,] and also the news thereof should be sent to Germany; for she would rather become an object of derision and scorn in this world than suffer on the day of judgment, etc.

She talked so loudly and cried so bitterly that I was hard pressed to quiet her for fear that she might be heard by her neighbors, whose well-being could hardly be furthered by learning of another's sins in such a way. She further told me that she had long prayed to God by day and night for forgiveness for this and her other sins and had believed that all had been forgiven her in the blood of Christ; but, since she had still harbored wilfulness in her heart and had failed to confess her sins, she had run deeper and deeper into misery. This lasted until God let someone [her pious husband] tell her what had been read at the service last Sunday from Genesis 34 [for her and her child's condition is so weak that she cannot leave the house at night]; and this had stricken her conscience so deeply that she could hardly bear the pain and had neither eaten nor drunk nor slept.

Before she would confess her sins, I asked her to kneel with me in prayer; but she started to pray on her own and, amidst a current of tears, revealed her entire heart to me so that I was much shocked by the sins which she had committed before her marriage in N. I added my prayer and begged our heavenly Father for wisdom so as to find the proper way to help this soul, which has been betrayed and seduced by the devil but which is now being sought by Christ. I freely confessed to her my shock at this plethora of sins, but I told her that there was still hope for redemption and mercy. It was not in vain that God had borne with her so long and with such untiring patience, had given her a most pious husband and now attacked her conscience so strongly. All these were signs of God's mercy, which pursued her and desired her salvation. If she continued as seriously as now to seek the heart of Christ in prayer and tears, she would learn that His blood suffices to wash even her sins away, although life would continue to bring her doubts, fear, and hard fights with her conscience on many occasions. However, if she remained faithful, these would be to her own best and eventual salvation.

She seemed to urge me to absolve her formally, but I hesitated to do so at this point. Instead, I referred her to our service of repentance, confession, and absolution, to be held next Saturday with the other communicants. In the meantime, and since she begged me for it, I promised her to pass by daily if my time would at all permit it so as to pray with her and instruct and comfort her with God's word. *Firstly:* as concerns her desire to confess her former sins to another intimate person [her most pious and devoted husband,] I would not object to such a course, in particular as in his case this might bring more benefit than harm. However, I counseled her not to act too rashly in this respect, but to wait until he himself could reveal his worries to me, as he had let me know he wished to do. Meanwhile she should constantly address herself to the Lord in this matter. *Secondly:* it would be quite fruitless to make known her sins and her remorse in this respect to our congregation (since they had not been vexed by it), and much less to announce it in letters to Germany. Regarding the sin against the seventh commandment[28] however, she should undertake to make restitution to those concerned until God would enable her to make actual amends for the damage. I told her that, if she considered it better and more helpful for her true peace of mind to see restitution of the stolen goods made as timely as possible, I would be prepared to inquire in this regard with N. N. [the Honorable Senior Urlsperger]; and she was much pleased to hear this.

Friday, the 18th of February. The tailor, N. N. [Herrnberger], could not find a good opportunity to talk to me in my house about his spiritual condition and therefore asked me to visit him in his dwelling. The uppermost complaint on his mind is his lack of faith in spiritual matters which, he fears, may have caused his doom as mentioned in Hebrews 6:4-6. I did not have the time to go into a full explanation of this passage and into the true intent behind it, which I shall make up for on another occasion. But I reminded him instead of another passage, which is better suited to his condition, that is, Revelations 2:4-5. He was quite shy and fearful to partake of Holy Communion now. But this morning he came back to tell me of his intended participation. He told me that during the night he had had a dream in which he had climbed a high mountain with much effort. At the peak he had seen no one; but he had heard clearly these words: "For the just, the light will always rise, and joy will be for the heart that is devout." I compared this with Psalm 112:4. He brought me a little sermon in duodecimo of the justification, which the blessed Luther had preached in Marburg and which, as he [Herrnberger] told me, had taught him much.

At present, there are many horrible stories making their way from town to town to the effect that it is not only the Spanish from St. Augustine who threaten this colony with an attack, but much animosity is feared from a nation of Indians who live up in the mountains. In Savannah they are short of money as well as food, which is expected to come with the next ships from England. [And relations with the neighboring province of Carolina are far from good, so that on reasonable assessment the prospects for this colony can hardly be said to be encouraging.] When this terrible news arrived, we had reached, in our prayer meeting, the strange circumstances recounted in Genesis 35:5, which gave us much strength and confidence in the powerful help of the Lord. May God grant us only that we be seriously committed to fulfilling our oft-repeated pledges, as Jacob did there, and we shall not lack in the help of the Lord, in whatever way His wisdom dictates.

Saturday, the 19th of February. N. N. N. [Gschwandel, Rauner, and Schweiger, all men of the first transport] have drunk themselves into a stupor with rum furnished to them by N. [Stephan Riedelsperger], whom they had helped with the building of his house. Since this has caused much provocation and anger in the congregation, and in particular Rauner has much transgressed in this respect, I felt it my duty to make mention of their repeated wickedness and heavy sins in the prayer meetings this week. Also, I have excluded them from Holy Communion until they show sincere remorse. N. [Gschwandel] and N. [Schweiger] have shown much contrition and humility, and their sin has caused them much fear. N. [Rauner], however, remains obstinate and refuses to see the light, for which the honest and godfearing men of our community are much annoyed with him. The other two have assured me that they remonstrated with him for his obstinacy and his wicked conduct and would keep after him in this respect.

Since I am not always aware of such happenings, be it that they took place in some remote corner of the village or because I was absent on a mission, and since there have been some occasions where such miscreants, to the vexation of the congregation, have taken Holy Communion despite their misdeeds, I have publicly declared that I shall henceforth announce, on the Sunday preceding the Communion, the names of the communicants who have told me of their desire to take communion. Thus, there will be an occasion to advise me of any wicked person among them. At the same time I counseled the congregation that in such cases it is their duty to save their poor neighbor from the morass of his sins and disorderly life, which could indeed be done by making public his misdeeds and reckless sins. For, were they not to help the sinner, they themselves would have to bear some measure of guilt.

Furthermore, I proposed to the congregation that they should choose four godfearing men from among them who should not only, as was the case in Mr. Vat's time, assist in guard duty and other external matters, but also watch over the conduct of the community and confer with me on the spiritual and physical welfare of its members; and whom, moreover, I could instruct on the management of this or similar matters that might arise, as they might see fit. These men will come to my house once a week at a pre-arranged time to discuss the conditions of the community and means for their improvement. And we shall pray with each other for ourselves and on their behalf if there should not be any specific matter to discuss.

Sunday, the 20th of February. Today, forty-two persons have partaken of Holy Communion, among them a few souls who, by true repentance, have shed the burden of their former deeds and injustices and whose atonement for their sins has borne beautiful fruits, much to our hearts' delight. Some of the older children whom I have been preparing for this step were not admitted; instead, they will come to me more often for prayer and admonition. Once we notice a true change of heart in them and a spiritual hunger for the precious treasures immanent in Holy Communion, they will be confirmed in the pact that was entered into on their behalf through their baptism, as we have done with others of their age previously, and admitted to Holy

Communion. May the Lord take pleasure in our work in Christ. My dear colleague has not yet returned, and I presume that he felt this day well suited to celebrate Holy Communion in Purysburg. Late in the evening our people returned from Savannah by boat and brought pork. Tomorrow I shall dispatch some other men to go back there and get more provisions, in particular corn, of which there is great need.

Monday, the 21st of February. As yesterday was the first Sunday of the Lenten season, the reading of the catechism was suspended; and, since the passion of Christ is to be the basis for our lectures during this season, I began by asking questions about the marvelous story of Joseph, which was due for reading in our prayer meetings, to point out those passages in which he appears as a clear prefiguration of our self-humiliating and subsequently exalted Savior.[29] In the application I read them a passage from the most edifying life of the late Provost Porst, which served in a most pleasant manner to underline and reinforce the preceding. In our small meeting at night, I discussed with those present the life of the late Princess of Anhalt-Coethen; and I attempted to impress on my listeners, for this application, every aspect of her last words and struggles. Today I have experienced what I already mentioned yesterday, that is that the good Lord greatly blesses our instruction and reading, which may He continue to do for the sake of His son until the last day.

This evening my dear colleague returned home from Purysburg and told me how he had had the occasion to preach the word of the Lord, once on weekdays and twice yesterday, during Holy Communion and that the people there had come eagerly to hear him and wished to hear him more often. [The preacher there[30] is most negligent with respect both to his sermons and the performance of his other duties and causes much vexation to everybody by his conduct, which is quite obviously directed toward the matters of this world only.]

Tuesday, the 22nd of February. Some of our people are still quite weak from the fever and cannot do much work in the field. Some of the pious Salzburgers have therefore resolved, without recompense, to work their gardens for them and ready them for planting, lest they lie fallow and not bring any harvest. [It may well be that the Honorable Trustees had the weak and disabled members of our group in mind when they made provisions for communal work; but their intention is much better realized in this manner, now that the people are free in their manner of

working, than would have been the case with the forced communal labor originally planned, as we all know from experience.
As most have now finished their work on the two acres of land
which had been surveyed and parcelled out to them for gardens,
and as the work on the other unsurveyed land is an uncertain
and disagreeable enterprise, some of the men wish to go to
Savannah and seek work there in order to earn some food and
clothing. In particular, Mr. Causton needs many laborers for the
fortifications there and only recently has employed four men,
who had gone to Savannah for provisions, for the day. I feel that
I can counsel them neither for nor against this work, but they
are in great need. Both money and food are lacking; corn and
beans cannot be had even for money, and Mr. Causton cannot
give any help or counsel in this respect. Some of the people have
taken the risk of starting to clear some of the unsurveyed lands.]

Wednesday, the 23rd of February. I have now had a small
room prepared in my hut as well as is possible in the circumstances so that I might be able, at least for the summer, to talk
in private with the members of the congregation, which has
heretofore been most difficult. It will hardly be possible now to
build the house that I had in my mind; for the carpenters, after
taking a closer look at the matter, informed me that it would
come to more than 60 £ sterling, which the Lord Trustees and
our other benefactors will hardly be willing to expend for this
purpose. The house was to have had only one story, with two
rooms and one chamber, and was to have been made of whole
timbers. A dwelling made of clapboards, such as we had in
Old-Ebenezer, also costs much and would not serve for the
purpose I have in mind. It matters little whether one lives in a
well-made hut or in one of these shingled houses. Those who
know the building trade have said that walls of clay cannot be
used here in this hot climate unless, as is done in Charleston,
such walls are covered on the outside with clapboards which
would make the expense even greater.

I am now learning from some examples how hard true conversion is for those who as servants years ago had become unfaith-
ful to their masters and appropriated their belongings without
their knowledge or consent [insciis et invitis Dominis]. They are
not able to restore the stolen goods; and even their confession
and their resolution to make restitution once they have acquired
the means therefor do not suffice to give them peace of heart.
This may serve as a serious warning to all servants not to burden
their conscience with such disloyal acts, which is one of the most

common sins among this class of people. Some among us have been driven or at least tempted to such acts by the harshness and injustice of their masters, but this will not give those peace and comfort whose hearts have been enlightened at a later date.

Thursday, the 24th of February. We have had a cold rain all day after it had been most pleasant and warm the previous nights and days. Some children and older people again complain of attacks of the fever, and it is hard to establish what may be the cause of such attacks. During the hot summer months everybody said that the fever would end with the coming winter and cold. But not only have some men and women been plagued by the fever all winter long, but even some of those who had been rid of it have had several relapses in the course of the winter. I, for one, suffer from feverish attacks when I eat smoked meat or pork; but whether this is the cause of fever in others, it is hard to tell with certainty. There are few supplies of fresh and wholesome foods in this country, and the food that is available is quite dear and we are forced to adjust our expenses to our income.

Friday, the 25th of February. Since Mr. Zwifler intends to return to London next Monday, we shall take the opportunity to send with him some letters to our friends and benefactors which we are now preparing to write.

[Saturday, the 26th of February. I am beginning to lose all hope for the Rheinlaenders' conversion to God. If they can only benefit therefrom, they do everybody's bidding and do not hesitate to join in sinful behavior as long as they can see some profit in it. Although they believe themselves much cleverer than anyone else, their whole household is going backwards and does not amount to much, which must be a sign of God's judgment. The same holds true for Michael Rieser, who is a dyer by trade. His impenitence and evil manners (though this is not yet so apparent) keep God's blessing from his fieldwork, and it would seem that nothing much will become of him if he does not make more room for the word of God in his heart than he has done so far. When I was at their house yesterday, both the man and his wife told me of some improper occurrence which somebody, whom they mentioned by name, had caused in a state of drunkenness; however, they deny the whole matter from their fear of men, for which they certainly deserve strong censure.]

Sunday, the 27th of February. This morning among our audience there were some men from Purysburg who had helped with the construction of the mill in Old Ebenezer. Together with

some Englishmen, they have been called away from their work
because they are needed for the fortification of Savannah. Toward evening the men who had been sent down for provisions
last Monday returned; but they brought nothing but two small
barrels of meat after having waited vainly for some days for
more provisions which had been expected in Savannah. They
also brought with them the boy from Purysburg who had been
placed in our school but has already run away twice to go back
home.[31] The mother cannot make him obey, and she asked that
he be dealt with strictly so that some good may come out of it.
The boy has been placed with a pious Salzburger who supervises
him and attempts to make him follow the path of righteousness
but finds much resistance in him. Also, the three orphaned girls
have been entrusted here and there to some good and pious
people who will care for them and supervise them and who are
paid some little money every year for their trouble. It does not
seem possible at this point to make arrangements for a separate
place for poor children or even to build a house for this purpose,
although God had in His grace provided some funds for that
previously. Since food is so scarce here, and since laborers are
expensive, the children will have to be cared for as best we can
for the time being. Moreover, the land intended for the preachers' houses, for the church, the school, and therefore also for
such an orphanage, has not yet been surveyed, as much as we
would like this done.

Monday, the 28th of February. [Several people are close to
starvation and will die of hunger unless some help is given them
promptly. I had some seed corn and peas left, as well as some
rotten corn to be fed to the hogs, which I have given to those
who are worse off than the others; but this cannot last for long.
The sorrow which I feel in this respect requires me to go to
Savannah tomorrow, although my feverish condition should
keep me home. Moreover, the boat which returned almost
empty yesterday brought the news that there are no provisions
in the store-house.] In order to get some supplies, I shall again
approach Mr. Causton and submit some suggestions to him. [It
remains to be seen whether anything will come of my efforts.
If it had been known that the supply of corn from the store-
house would be so meager and unreliable, the Salzburgers
would have kept the thirty-seven bushels of corn they had been
forced to sell to Mr. Causton for the workers in Old Ebenezer,
and for which they have yet to be paid.] These and similar trials
which are set down in this diary are as little meant to be read

as a criticism of our dear benefactors as Moses meant to criticize the Lord and his many blessings when he carefully set forth the want, hunger, and thirst of the Israelites in the desert. The reasons for which these passages have been set down have been stated elsewhere. Such matters will not harm us, but will partly reveal what lies hidden in the hearts of men and partly teach us to open our eyes so as to realize the blessings we have received and to cherish them; for, in the absence of want and hunger, little attention is given to what we have and far too little thanks are offered to the Lord for his blessings. Other people, particularly those in N. [Purysburg], suffer much more grievously, which is well understood by our Salzburgers.

MARCH

Tuesday, the 1st to Thursday, the 3rd of March. God has again blessed my travels; for a large shipment of corn has just arrived in Savannah, of which Mr. Causton let me have forty bushels immediately. And, although I had come only in our small boat accompanied by but three Salzburgers, it so happened that we managed to bring the corn to Purysburg with the help of three men, of whom only one had to be paid. From there we brought the corn to Ebenezer in a larger boat borrowed for this purpose. Also, I found a man who let us have sixty bushels of seed potatoes,[32] for which Mr. Causton has paid, and who will also provide us with seed corn and peas. As for the surveyor, Mr. Causton cannot offer any help at this stage, but I have managed to obtain a number of advantages for our community [and only hope that nothing will interfere with these arrangements].

The fortifications in Savannah, on which a hundred men are working every day, will be completed in a fortnight. The cost of this enterprise will run to 5000 £ sterling. In Purysburg, too, they are building such fortifications for fear of the Indians, while they do not fear the Spanish as much as previously. This work is most inconvenient for the people in Purysburg, as it is the time for planting and sowing.

Friday, the 4th of March. Our letters to England and Germany are all written, and Mr. Zwifler will take them along next Monday. In our letters to the Honorable Society and to Mr. Oglethorpe we have again mentioned our material conditions and have asked for good land as well as for a prolongation of the supply of provisions until the next harvest; we also asked for cattle and tools for the third transport. To the Society, we have

mentioned matters concerning the spiritual well-being of the
congregation and our pupils, also making reference to the inconvenience of our quarters in the little hut, although we passed
over this matter with a few words and without anger. May God
bless [messages and] everything [else], to His glory and our
happiness and salvation.

Saturday, the 5th of March. This afternoon I again met with
the men of the community and talked to them about some matters concerning the proper order of things and their material
well-being. The four men chosen by the congregation to watch
over order and propriety, and who come to my hut every Friday,
have proven to be of much service to me. Through them I learn
of many things that come to pass here and there in our village;
also, they are versed in matters of work and husbandry and thus
can give good advice which is made public later. Thus, much
damage can be prevented that might otherwise occur.

Continuation of the Diary

Monday, the 7th of March, 1737. Yesterday we had a thunderstorm accompanied by an extraordinarily heavy cloudburst
mixed with hail, which has caused the water of the river to rise
far above its usual level. Kieffer, the herdsman from Purysburg,
is badly off, since the land which he had cleared in Carolina
across from us is flooded a good five feet high. His hut is flooded
almost up to the roof, his tools and those of his belongings
which he had stored there before his departure are floating
about, and he will be much aggrieved upon his return from
Purysburg. I have given instructions to collect those of his belongings which are adrift and to store them in my lodgings so
that he may not lose them altogether.

This morning Mr. Zwifler took leave from us and left for
Charleston, whence he will travel to London on the earliest
occasion. He intends to stay in London for some time so as to
earn some money for his return to his home in Hungary.[33] He
had shown much willingness to be of service recently and has
taken much trouble with his patients, e.g., in bloodletting. Also,
upon my request, he has made a written list before his departure
of all the medicines he has left here, with instructions regarding
their use. [We have taken occasion to refer to his services here
in our letter to the Society. Maybe it will be possible to reimburse him for his services. He has taken our letters with him and
will deliver them in London].

Tuesday, the 8th of March. The mother of the boy sent here

from Purysburg to attend school has asked us urgently to take care of her child to the best of our ability.[34] She is extremely poor and unable to provide him with the necessary provisions and clothing for his sustenance. The boy is well endowed by nature and skillful in his tasks; and he speaks English well. However, he has been quite untidy and willful, as his mother has herself admitted. As long as he conducts himself well and follows our admonitions and instructions, we shall do for him whatever we can.

Wednesday, the 9th of March. The three poorest widows among us, Mrs. Schweighoffer, Mrs. Helfenstein, and Mrs. Holtzer, have been provided with so much fenced-in and cleared land this spring that, with God's blessing, they should be able to harvest as much as the others here. In addition to the plots allotted to them, the Salzburgers are willing to let them have some parcels of the fields which had been prepared last year for common use. Mrs. Resch and Mrs. Riedelsperger, although they too are widowed, are much better off and in quite different circumstances. The former takes care of Gschwandel's household and is well provided for; while the latter holds part of the common land in consideration of her husband and may well marry again in the near future. I recently inquired of Mr. Causton regarding the fate of the widows and orphans once the provisions are terminated; he promised me to take steps for their sustenance and asked me for a list of their names.

Thursday, the 10th of March. [Mrs. Ernst has not yet recovered and is still confined to her bed; and her small child, which is but six weeks old, suffers more than anybody from this state of affairs. She is quite malicious, temperamental, and cantankerous so that it is quite clear that she cannot get well, whatever remedies she may take. I talked quite seriously to her today, but to no avail, other than that she listened to me in her husband's presence, interrupting me, as is her want, with many extraneous matters. He works hard, but there is little hope for him, as is true for Michael Rieser and Rheinlaender. The child is not cared for at all and will hardly survive for long. Much care and thought have been spent in this respect, but to little avail.]

Both yesterday and today we have had a very strong wind, and the rain yesterday was as strong as last week. Our boat, which had been sent for provisions last Monday, may well have been delayed by this inclement weather. We miss those of the Salzburgers who are absent more now than ever before, as there is much apprehension of an attack by the Spanish and the Indians.

Friday, the 11th of March. Much shooting has been heard from Savannah; and our boat, which arrived today, brought news from Mr. Causton that he has learned of the safe arrival of Mr. Oglethorpe in London. It is said that this news has caused much pleasure in Savannah. This morning N. [Rauner] asked for an opportunity to see me privately, on which occasion he asked for my forgiveness for his recent rudeness which he had shown when I blamed him for his drunkenness and kept him from taking Holy Communion. He was in tears, and it seems that God moved his heart during last night's prayer meeting. He confessed to me and confided in me several matters which caused me some grief but which I recommend to the wisdom of the Lord. Since our duties here are not confined to the exercise of our spiritual functions but also include material affairs, we are forced to swallow many a bitter pill, all in the name and for the glory of the Lord. Even our Savior could please only a few, much less we, who are but frail humans and His unworthy servants. I firmly believe that we would find it much more rewarding to take care of the souls in our custody were it not for the fact that we are charged with all sorts of other matters extraneous to our calling. I have little time left to visit the people in our congregation; and the many unpleasant occurrences which, if God is to be well served, cannot be handled roughly as if with a sword, take much of my strength and prevent me from learning the Indian language and attending to a number of other matters.

Saturday, the 12th of March. It being again the anniversary of our arrival in this country, where God has brought us by such wonderful ways and we have seen so many marks of His love and providence both in spiritual and material matters, we have held a memorial and thanksgiving service today. The texts read in the morning and in the afternoon were Psalms 81:14–17 and Lamentations of Jeremiah 3:22–24. A few Englishmen attended, among them Mrs. Musgrove and her betrothed[35] who came to be married here; but we could not accede to this request since our spiritual powers do not extend to the English population, unless there is an emergency. I much regretted having been forced by this matter to offend a woman who is well regarded by Mr. Oglethorpe and by all the Honorable Trustees.[36] She finally seemed to get over her irritation, in particular as I promised her to take the matter up with Mr. Causton next Monday and request his opinion as to whether the Lord Trustees and the Honorable Society might consent to my performance of marriages if some people should come here for this purpose and should prove the legitimacy of their request in the proper manner, particularly since the preacher there is so scrupulous in incidental matters. She told me that the deacon in Savannah, Mr. Ingam, who had begun to take instruction in the Indian language from her, had traveled to London by way of Pennsylvania because of it [because he wanted to travel both to and from England in the company of Mr. Spangenberg, who is still in Philadelphia. Presumably, Mr. Spangenberg and this Mr. Ingam will go further up among the heathen nations, since he well sees that nothing much can be accomplished among the Indian vagabonds here]. Mrs. Musgrove showed great pleasure when she heard our schoolchildren pray and sing with my dear colleague after the noon service.

Sunday, the 13th of March. Contrary to my assumption, Mrs. Musgrove has stayed over until today, still hoping to be married here. She is expecting two other betrothed couples who will come down here in their boat and are expected to carry some words from Mr. Causton addressed to me. If they should not come, and as I do not wish to marry her in the absence of a clear statement by Mr. Causton concerning his views on this matter, I have promised her to accompany her to Savannah in order to make inquiries in this respect with Mr. Causton and the English minister there. We would rather be spared such affairs that do not fall within the province of our congregation proper, [particularly as such people are not so much concerned about the divine blessing which would accrue to them from such a marriage ceremony, but rather have other things in mind which are displeasing to the Lord]. Since there is an English minister available and thus no *casus necessitatis*,[37] I shall attempt to rid myself of such demands in Savannah.

Monday, the 14th, to Wednesday, the 16th of March. This morning after six o'clock I asked the members of our community to meet with me so that I might inquire into several matters concerning their welfare to be taken up with Mr. Causton. After the meeting, the aforementioned Mrs. Musgrove and I embarked on our journey by boat to Savannah; but, when she learned in Purysburg that three other couples from Savannah had been married by the French preacher in Purysburg and since she felt that this privilege was due also to her, she stayed in Purysburg while I and my Salzburgers proceeded to Savannah.

It was my intent to inform Mr. Causton that my dear colleague and I did not intend to get involved in matters such as these marriages in the absence of a *casus necessitatis,* since any other conduct might leave us open to just criticism. [Mr. Wesley was much amazed at the stand taken by the preacher in Purysburg and addressed a letter to him in which he expressed his surprise and suggested that he would do better to abstain from such functions which are not properly part of his duties. He also intends to write to the bishop in London in this respect. In particular, it is most improper and irresponsible that said preacher should have performed the ceremony in French whereas none of the couples understands the French language.]

Mr. Wesley is much discouraged by the recalcitrance of his congregation, although it is certain that he makes every effort to convert them by means of thorough and edifying exposition of the Divine word, as much as is within his power. I returned home after having discussed matters concerning our community with Mr. Causton. [The river was high and the currents stronger than any I have seen before, and our journey was delayed by these conditions. There is neither money nor provisions in Savannah, and we also are much affected because our stipend has been withheld].

Thursday, the 17th of March. Last Monday we sent our large boat to the plantation of Mr. Montaigut to fetch forty bushels of Indian beans, for which our people will pay. These beans did not yield a good harvest this year and are therefore expensive, and we consider it a benefit to have been able to purchase some. [Mr. Montaigut knows that our land has not been surveyed yet and therefore recently stated to my dear colleague as follows: "The Salzburgers will, if things continue in this manner, either remain beggars or starve."]

Friday, the 18th of March. [We are again having much trouble and sorrow with the Rheinlaenders. They have been dissembling for a while, in the hope of deceiving our eyes and of reaching their narrow and material goals. But, since it had again become necessary to reveal the woman's evil heart, and since we did not appoint the man, as we had recently done for four Salzburgers, to the post of a vestryman of the congregation, both have become quite spiteful and talk of moving away, as they fear that they will not obtain the material benefits here which they have been seeking so avidly. Much has been tried with this ungrateful family, and much good has been done unto them, but they remain adamant in their sinfulness and they will yet frustrate our dear Lord's hope for their repentance and conversion.

They are so struck with blindness that, notwithstanding all their spiteful and scandalous deeds, they deceive themselves that they have been redeemed and are enjoying God's mercy. When faced with remonstrations and reminders of their conduct, they will give a thousand and one excuses, in which attempt their clever minds and natural skillfulness serve them in good stead. We are praying for them and beg God for the wisdom to deal with them properly; they cause us much heartache. The final disposition of their case will have to be in the hands of the highest bishops of the congregation of Jesus Christ. If they should leave us now, as things stand, they will carry horrible tales of our ministry and our congregation, in which their clever tongues will help them to convince others, although they are well known hereabouts and have shown themselves as inconstant wanderers who cannot settle down anywhere].

This morning our boat has been sent off to Savannah for provisions. The dates have to be watched carefully in this respect, and we have to send for provisions when we know that they are available in the store-house. We also need seed grain and beans, which have not yet reached Savannah. If it were only possible, we would keep our people here during this time of planting, for there is much work for them at all times.

Saturday, the 19th of March. We have received definite news that the surveyor,[38] who was to survey and apportion our plantations, has joined the armed forces in Port Royal. While I have informed Mr. Causton of this (he had already heard the news), he let me know that he cannot assign another surveyor to us, and thus the surveying of our land will probably have to wait until the arrival of Mr. Oglethorpe. In accordance with the latter's instructions, I am now distributing the last provisions for the first and second transport; as of this time I have not yet received enough corn and meat for the third transport. [The Lord Trustees and Mr. Causton can well imagine the difficulties which our poor people will encounter after the provisions have been terminated and the obstacles which they will meet in trying to obtain food and sustenance, in view of their hard work and their complete lack of funds.] Tomorrow we will study the scriptures, John 6 ff.; and we shall try to strengthen each other's faith in the living God and His fatherly providence on our behalf.

Sunday, the 20th of March. Today the bans were published for the marriage of Kogler and the widow Riedelsperger. As the English Church seems to insist on the bans being published thrice, and as Mr. Wesley does not wish to yield on this point of church law even though it appears this requirement can be waived in London with the bishop's permission, the English couples who wished to be married here have asked me to publish the bans for them in our congregation. They made this demand in the hope that I should thus be able to perform the marriage without much responsibility in this respect. However, such publishing of bans here would be mere sham, so nothing came of it. [It is mere arrogance and conceit on their part that they do not wish to do it in Savannah.]

[The Rheinlaenders had intended to stay away from church rather than to listen with discontented hearts. But today they were more eager than previously in our meeting. Both they and others have been preached enough of the Lord's law and the gospels to have no excuse on that day unless they see the light and reform and repent.

Monday, the 21st of March. [Bishop, who had been sent from London as my servant, has acquired some strange notions from the Englishmen who sometimes come to our village; and as a result he has become much less satisfied with conditions and quite spiteful. He clearly longs for the English and their free manner of living.] Good and faithful servants are so rare in this country that those who manage to take into service a quiet, industrious, and faithful person are considered lucky. [My dear colleague has taken the Maurer woman, an unmarried female from Salzburg, into service as a maid; but he is not well taken care of in this respect. Not only is she simple by nature; but she is also spiteful, ill-natured, and insolent and thus is quite different from the nature and feelings of the honest Salzburgers. Initially, she had been in the service of Mr. von Reck, where she did not conduct herself as a faithful servant, as I learned after his departure, although she had not, contrary to what has been maintained, been dismissed by him without any payment for her services.]

Today the men of the village will get together to fence in the gardens and other plots of land which they have cleared of trees and shrubs. This joint work is being done so as to give those who have only poor and sandy soil a chance to plant their corn and beans as early as possible. I am often asked what dispositions will finally be taken concerning the plantations and the forty-eight acres destined therefor; also, whether they could still hope for good land. But I cannot give any definite answers in this respect and refer them to the expected answers to the letters written to the Lord Trustees and the Honorable Society.

Tuesday, the 22 of March. This morning I have distributed the few provisions which arrived yesterday by boat. Our boat was loaded to barely half its capacity, because there is not much left in the store-house in Savannah. It is hardly worth the trouble to send our people down to Savannah during the planting season for so little return. Brandner's fever will not abate but seems to get more virulent with the coming of the warm weather. He is a young, industrious, and quite devoted man. He has borne his cross for these many months with much patience and acquiesces entirely in the guidance and the will of the Lord; may the Lord continue to do unto him as He wishes.

Wednesday, the 23rd of March. There is much hard work in setting up sturdy fences around the cleared land. If everyone were to fence in his own garden this time, the men could not possibly be finished before the start of sowing and planting. This will be made easier for them by the fact that all those whose land lies together have joined for the fencing work. The alleys which are to be left on the sides and at the rear of the lots will also be fenced in now, except for the most important passageways. [Those with poor soil, who have had much work not only with the previous clearing but now with the fencing, are much discouraged, because they remember from their experience in Ebenezer that in the natural way of things they can only hope for a poor harvest. We take every opportunity in our sermons, in the prayer meetings and in our private conversations to draw their attention to the plan that God has in all these tribulations.]

The two oldest sons of N. N. [the watchmaker, Müller], had formerly been so disrespectful to their parents that both father and mother complained bitterly of them. We have gone to great pains with them; and now the parents have testified that they have made much and commendable progress after their last Holy Communion. The parents hold themselves and their offspring strictly to the Lord's word, and the children gain much profit from their schooling and give us much pleasure.

Thursday, the 24th of March. N. N. [Gschwandel] has resolved to return to Germany this coming fall. A devout Salzburger to whom he confided his intention asked him whether he was sure of God's will in this matter? To which he answered that he would pray for more guidance. This poor man's heart is still full of love for this world; and God cannot do much more to move him with His word than touch his soul many times and cause him to sigh, to wish for his betterment, and to profess his good intentions. [His selfishness governs all his actions in matters of this world, and this has caused his reputation with the congregation to be quite low. Rheinlaender is more determined than ever to move with his family to Charleston, because he feels that he cannot find his subsistence here. Because of their quick intelligence, their facile arguments, and their improper intentions, both he and his wife are more of a bad influence on the congregation than of any service; and, inasmuch as they do not wish to improve themselves, our village will be as well off without them.]

As the widowed Mrs. Riedelsperger will move into Kogler's house and thus give up the hut and the site held by her deceased husband, Pichler has agreed with him to move here instead. He will make a small payment for the garden fence, the hut, the stables, and kitchen. Until now he has had his lot in a deep valley where much water accumulates during the rainy season and which at all times is muddy and unhealthy. If we had not been able to effect this change, he and his wife and child might have suffered grievously as to their health. It is true that he had already invested much work in his former place, but health is of greater concern than work and other advantages. He may keep the lot there for planting until somebody else wishes to settle there.

Friday, the 25th of March. N. [Sanftleben] has asked for me in order to discuss the state of his soul. He has been ill for the last week, and on his sickbed God has again revealed his sins to him and he is much dejected. He told me that on the occasion of his last voyage, on which he went with the others to fetch beans, he had become involved in an argument with N. [Rauner] concerning material things. On this occasion, he had sinned by the use of harsh and irate words; and he believes that his present physical weakness may well have been imposed upon him by the Lord as a punishment and to bring him to penance. I gave him some instruction based on the Lord's word and prayed with him.

[We have heard that the schoolmaster's wife is much annoyed and has sinned by making malicious judgments, because we have not used the services of her husband in the teaching of English to the children but have preferred to do this ourselves. His pronunciation of English words is quite wrong, and what he does know he seems incapable of imparting to the children, so that we cannot use him. If he would apply himself, his work with the smaller children should keep him quite busy.]

Saturday, the 26th of March. Kieffer from Purysburg wishes

to place four girls in our school, two of whom are full-grown and should be prepared for Holy Communion. The other two are quite young. Ruprecht Steiner will give them shelter in his hut, and they will be in good hands with him. Against all expectations, cold weather returned last week; but it seems that it has not affected the vegetables sprouting in the gardens. Worms are doing much damage to the cabbage, radishes, beets, and other plants. Like the caterpillars, they are often buried in the ground and come out at night to feed on the green leaves and tops. If there is anything to be left for harvesting, these pests will have to be searched out and destroyed, which is hard work, and often we find several hundred of them in a small bed.

Sunday, the 27th of March. For a number of days now I have been incommodated by the three-day fever;[39] and today, immediately after the morning service, it got much worse so I have had to postpone the repetition. I hope only that the Lord will make it bearable for me, as in previous times, so that I will not be too much impeded in the performance of my work. The chastisement is quite salutary for the soul and therefore I am grateful for it.

Monday, the 28th of March. There are again many Indians in our village who come either by land or by boat. We live in an area also inhabited by a small Indian nation called the Uitzschy Indians,[40] whose language is quite different from that spoken by the so-called Creek Indians of this locale. We sent our boat down to Savannah again for provisions; and my dear colleague went in my stead, since the accounts have to be submitted to Mr. Causton. Also, an early answer is expected to my letter in which I explained the lack of provisions for the first and second transports. According to Mr. Oglethorpe's orders, the already shortened rations and provisions for the first and second transport will be terminated. And, since our people will have nothing to live on until the next harvest, Mr. Causton has promised me to have the accounts inspected to determine whether they have received, in the form of provisions, the entire monies stipulated by the Lord Trustees at 3 Pounds 3 Sh. 6 P. Sterling, or whether they still stand to receive provisions in this respect. In my letter I reminded Mr. Causton of this, as well as of the still unrewarded public labor about which I had recently given him a specified statement at his request.

Tuesday, the 29th of March. Last night I again convened the men of the village to discuss and consider with them some matters relating to the difficult work of building fences, the

planting, their cattle, etc., so as to forestall loss and misunderstanding. N. N. [The tailor, Hernberger,] has recently worked
in my hut for several days, and on this occasion I have realized
even better than before the rich treasure of mercy and desire
for grace which lives in his heart. It pleases our dear Savior to
lead him along many dark paths of temptations and spiritual
trials, which will teach him not only to understand the corruption of our hearts and the fall into sin, but also to recognize the
importance and the value of the dear redemption owed to Jesus
Christ; and he pines after the state of grace without cessation,
sighing, praying, and weeping.

The present severe melancholy which envelops his spirit is
due to an act of faithlessness committed many years ago in
Hungary, where, in order to please his brother and his other
Catholic friends, he let himself be involved in *Asotion*[41] and thus
forfeited the state of grace which he certainly enjoyed at that
time. For a while, he comforted himself in his state of sin with
God's mercy, Christ's merit, and human frailty, etc.; but finally
he had been awakened by God's eternal mercy and compassion
in such a way that he could no longer stay in Hungary but had
hastily departed, his conscience wounded and stirred by the law,
to seek a renewed chance to save his soul through a true conversion, which he hoped to find in Protestant communities. While
God had subsequently shown him many signs of compassion
and mercy for his conversion, he had not, since the time of this
relapse, been able to reach a state of joy and certain awareness
of God's merciful forgiveness of his sins.

He again revealed his grief concerning the passage in Hebrews 6:4-6, whose true import, however, was shown to him in
the light of the mercy and recognition of the truth which God
had bestowed, in addition to a few other passages from the
gospel on the general love and mercifulness of God in Christ.
His sin rested even more heavily on him because his Catholic
brother, to whom he had previously been able to teach much
of Christ's word, had been injured by his godless collaboration
and had been confirmed in his errors and godlessness by his bad
example.

Wednesday, the 30th of March. S. [Mrs. Schweighofer] is
much in need of frequent visits and help, by advice and deed,
in her spiritual and material needs. She is a faithful disciple of
Our Lord Jesus, and it causes her much suffering and sighs and
tears that she should be so feeble and full of sin and defects in
her love for Him. Her former sins cause her much unrest, yet

drive her even more strongly to seek the innocent Lamb of God which has carried away the sins of all of us and of the entire world. The three of her children who are still with her cause her much sorrow, because she cannot, despite all her admonitions and punishments, bring them to the state which she would desire for them; and she is much afraid that they will succumb and be lost. As she feels she is incapable of the proper education of her children, she has asked me to take charge of two of them, that is, the boy and the smallest girl, and to see to their spiritual well-being, which I have promised her to do.

Thursday, the 31st of March. With today's boat we received a letter from the Honorable Senior Urlsperger and a beautiful gift of linen, bonnets, shirts, etc. for the adults and the children in the community. Among the lot was a length of cotton and two fine kerchiefs for our helpmates. This is another proof of the fatherly concern of our heavenly Father. He knows the poverty and want of our people, and He finds ways and means to relieve it. In our want, such benefactions and others are much welcome, and with God's blessing cause much good. His name be praised, and may He bless our benefactors. The Honorable Senior Urlsperger has also enclosed a kind and impressive letter to Mr. Oglethorpe, which we were supposed to forward. Since the latter departed for London last November, and since this is well known in Germany, I assume that the representations made therein have already been made in London and we will not have to send the letter there. Nonetheless, we consider it useful to let Mr. Causton have a copy of the letter in translation.

APRIL

Friday, the 1st of April. Last night I was told that I speak too harshly to some in the congregation and have not been preaching enough of the gospel as previously. This comment was caused by my last sermon, *Dominica Judica*,[42] in which I spoke of the wretched nature of the children of darkness as exemplified by the Jewish people. My grief at such talk and reflections on my thinking was dispelled this morning upon awakening, for a pious woman of our congregation appeared at my door, crying bitterly and demanding to speak to me privately. She told me that she and her family had spent a terrible night full of lamentations and abject prayer to which they (father and mother) had been driven by their oldest daughter. The child had been dreaming, and in her dreams the faithless and ungrateful nature of their conduct and criticism of the preaching of the gospels had been so strongly impressed upon her that she and her kin would have to make haste if their souls were to be saved. This statement of penance on the part of their child so moved the parents and caused them such grief at the many sins adhering to them and rendering them indolent that I could hardly calm the woman's mind by arguments taken from the gospel. The girl insists that we should advise the congregation of this happening, and should impress upon them that the time for conversion and penance is running out, although some might yet be saved. The mother added that she felt she should thank us on her knees for having attempted to reveal to her and to others their corruption, lack of faith, and spitefulness so seriously while relying on the Lord's words.

Saturday, the 2nd of April. Last night I read to the congregation the Reverend Riesch's[43] letter, as well as a portion of the recent letter of the Honorable Senior Urlsperger. This gave me renewed opportunity to speak of the paternal providence of the Lord for our congregation, in that He has bestirred many of his faithful servants to think of us in prayer and love and with good deeds. And, as we know of some who are inclined to a change of place [animum mutandi locum], it was shown to them how they would deprive themselves of many spiritual and material benefits by their spiteful and ungrateful conduct. We take every occasion to demonstrate to such erring people the damage and evil consequences of thoughtless behavior [mutatio]. Our counterarguments [argumenta dissuadentia] can be summed up as follows: 1. If they seek to escape from our dear Father and from the school of trials and the cross which He has prepared for them, they will run into their spiritual perdition. Until now, they claimed that they had left their motherland not for food and drink but out of their desire for the gospel and the Holy Sacraments, and now God was testing, by the imposition of want, whether their professed goals were true, etc. 2. It is the way of pious Christians to make all changes in the light of God's will as revealed to them, for otherwise we commit sin and court disaster. 3. Such people will commit blasphemy against the name of the Lord and will cause the good odor of the congregation of Ebenezer to stink, which can only bring the curse of the Lord down upon us. 4. Also, this is gross ingratitude for the many benefits which they have received and will much displease our benefactors in Germany and England. Finally, 5., those who decide to move away will not be welcomed anywhere, for what is the reputation of those who are unsteady in their manner of life? It will be said: "if you were worth anything, you would have stayed." [In many places, it is said of the Salzburgers that they cannot settle anywhere permanently but prefer to move about, and such views and imputations would only be confirmed by such as those who leave Ebenezer.] 6. What would be the final good to come from such departure? Those who would leave would again have to enter service and eat another's bread, whereas here they would eventually have their own land and enjoy freedom and independence. If some could not reach their goal here and thus laid themselves open to God's judgment, many a one might even fall back into [the Papist] darkness and error, of which sad examples are known. We have the grievous news concerning the brother of the late Adam Riedelsperger, God rest his soul, that for the love of his wife and material things he has relapsed [into Papism]. At the very least, such defectors will expose themselves to much spiritual danger and temptation.

If it should not prove possible to apportion good fertile land to the community, and if they should not be able to find sustenance on the land given to them, we place sufficient trust in the Lord and the love of our benefactors to believe that different arrangements will be made for their well-being, for in that case teacher and flock would remain together of their free will. [In the meantime, it is true, materially the poor Salzburgers are badly off, and it should not cause surprise if they seek strange ways to relieve themselves of their misery and want. It would almost appear that there is purpose behind the failure to enable these poor people to regain their strength and their own means of sustenance. What misery will arise if the 4th transport, which according to the letters we received is in the process of being assembled, should arrive here, when even the present settlers must fight to keep alive and do not even have their own land, as much as they would want to work for it.] Many of our honest flock are of good spirits despite all their want, consider themselves unworthy of even the smallest benefits, and both by word and letter praise with grateful and obliging words every good deed from which they benefit, [but this should not lead anyone to believe that the congregation is provided for even as concerns the bare necessities, and that the promises made to us have been kept.]

Sunday, the 3rd of April. After the morning service those stayed behind who wished to enter their names for next Friday to partake in the Lord's supper. At the end, we knelt down and prayed to God for His blessing for this important task. This public announcement has the advantage not only of giving us previous knowledge of those who wish to take Holy Communion and thus an opportunity to prepare for private communication with those whose circumstances warrant it, but also of letting the intended communicants know early in the week with whom they will share this feast. Thus they can remind each other as necessary of their trespasses in a brotherly manner or else inform me as required. Their names are also read publicly to the congregation.

One of the Salzburgers talked to me today concerning his spiritual condition; and his words, based as they were on his inward experiences, gave me much pleasure. After God had led him through many temptations and dark paths and finally shed the light of His mercy on him so that he knows where his true belief lies, he feels little burdened by material things which might be hard to bear in other circumstances. His present coarse and simple food tastes better to his tongue, now that his conscience is light and relieved, than fine foods ever tasted to him in Salzburg.[44] Since God saved him from the pain and sorrow in his soul, material worries are as nothing to him. He has placed his fate in the hands of the Lord and believes firmly that everything will turn out for the best, in which belief he was much confirmed by our recent reading of Psalms 81:14–17, "Oh that my people had harkened unto me."[45] He diligently prays to the Lord and wishes that more of us would follow his example more often, that is, that God would convert all members of our congregation and bring them to obedience to His word, for then we will not be wanting. He could not keep from me any longer that my sermons in Dover had seemed much too harsh to him; but, when he made closer acquaintance with the late Moshammer, and learned to know him better, God rest his soul, the latter had convinced him of the contrary and assured him from his own experience that there is no other way to God's mercy and forgiveness for our sins than the path of repentance and discipleship in Christ, with which the Old Adam cannot live. He keeps a fond memory of Moshammer and honors him as his spiritual father.

Monday, the 4th of April. This morning our boat was again dispatched to Savannah, for Mr. Causton had sent for it to fetch seed grain. I availed myself of this opportunity of forwarding the translation of the letter which the Honorable Senior Urlsperger had written to Mr. Oglethorpe, [adding that I felt much grief in my heart at the prospect of having a new transport of Salzburgers sent over when so little provision had been made for the support of the Salzburgers now here, in particular the third transport. I also tried to warn him of the impression which any newcomers would gain of my dear colleague and myself, and how the reputation of our office would suffer, if they were to find nothing but need, deprivation, and misery in our material conditions, whereas they had gained a quite different impression from the published news concerning the satisfactory state of our people, which news they would doubtless attribute to us.[46] My spirits are so depressed on this account that I often feel that I lack the joyful inclination to speak to our congregation for their edification. We know from experience what happened in this respect upon the arrival of the second and third transports.

[I also implored Mr. Causton earnestly to help our people secure their own land, and good land at that, prior to the arrival of a new transport and to desist from cutting off their provisions prior to the next harvest, for else their material want and misery could only increase and cause much damage to our cause. How much mockery and derision has not been heard in these parts concerning the descriptions of this country published by the late Purry, when they were brought here by the people who arrived here.[47] My only consolation is that the printed news was sent to us in time for us to prepare for all matters contained therein that might give rise to criticism and to pray the Lord for wisdom to deal with such matters in the proper fashion.]

N. N. [Cornberger] invited me to his hut for an important conversation. I found him and his wife engaged in the reading of the 5th chapter of St. Matthew, which afforded me some opportunity to speak to both of them according to their circumstances. For some time now, the couple have had misunderstandings and have borne ill will towards each other; and it was their desire that I should help them see the right way. After our joint prayer, God in his mercy gave me the right words to speak to them, and they thanked me most warmly, the woman with tears in her eyes.

Tuesday, the 5th of April. I talked to a woman from Salzburg, whose husband was not at home, and admonished her to take her faith more seriously. She not only recognized her lack of application but also assured me that her husband, in whom we had little confidence so far, was much touched by God's word and, after listening to His message, had taken to praying ear-

nestly in the cowshed. Some in our congregation pray from the
fullness of their hearts and are much pleased when we join them
for prayer in their hut. Such people, it is quite obvious, become
ever poorer in spirit but ever richer in God's mercy, even if they
may not perceive it. There is not much success with a few frivolous young people, despite the fact that, in the strength of the
mercy God has bestowed on us, we seek to work with them
publicly and with special care. A number of these have met in
the evenings and have sinned by useless talking and actions,
although such meetings have been terminated by God's grace.
As a warning, they have been told of the example of evil counsel
and wicked meeting of brothers in wickedness, Genesis 49:5–7,
and warned of the sinfulness and the resulting punishment incident thereto.

Wednesday, the 6th of April. This noon the unmarried men
and women in the congregation who will take Holy Communion
this coming Friday assembled in my hut for a brief discussion
of the Lord's word and for joint singing and praying. Tonight,
after the public prayer meeting, the married couples and widows
will come for the same purpose. May God, for the suffering
borne by His son, whose memory we celebrate this week, smile
upon this preparation of our souls. The good spirits among our
flock are much driven to prayer these days by the material want
we suffer. The other day I spoke to a pious man concerning the
benefit which, in God's wisdom, we receive from the experience
of such long and protracted suffering; and he replied that, if God
should free him of all his hardships, his heart might well become
so light and frivolous that he would lose the urge to pray. When
recently there had been much talk of the Spanish and their
threatened invasion of this colony, he had been full of fear and,
on his knees, had attempted many times to present to the Lord
the danger in which this region found itself. However, once the
danger and fear had passed, he had ceased his heartfelt prayers
almost entirely. He admitted this with much humility.

One of our young [Salzburgers] is now much beset in his
conscience, for the Lord is showing him the grief and heartfelt
pain that are the result of abandoning the Lord our God and
of ceasing to fear Him. It is almost a year since he defiled himself
with a certain sin against the sixth[48] commandment [peccato
onanitico]; and after clear signs of true repentance and grief had
been noticed in him, we attempted on several occasions to instill
in him full confidence in the unassailable merit and full redemption for all our sins of our Lord Jesus. None of this, however,

was to much avail, as our comfort did not reach his heart; he felt that he had sinned too much by defiling that body which was meant to be the temple of the Holy Spirit and the Trinity. I answered by confronting him with the powerful words: "If any man sin, etc.," "The blood of Jesus Christ, His Son, cleanseth us, etc";[49] likewise 2 Corinthians 7:1. Here, St. Paul demands that those whom the Almighty Lord, in accordance with Corinthians 6:16–18, has called upon to become His temple, His sons and daughters, should purify themselves of all that might sully their mind and bodies; accordingly, by virtue of Christ's blood, shed for our sins, it should be possible to attain purification. Vid: 1. Corinthians 6:9–11.

Thursday, the 7th of April. This morning between six and eight o'clock, as every year on Maundy Thursday, a sermon was held on 1. Corinthians 11:23 ff., that is, on our Lord Jesus' true and main purpose in setting the rite of the Last Supper. This might also serve our present confessors as a preparation for Holy Communion. We had assembled at such an early hour in order to meet the exigencies of the planting season, since at this time we have the most pleasant and promising weather for this purpose. Some of our people still have much work ahead of them with the erection of their garden fences. Tomorrow, the day of Christ's death, will be a holiday celebrating the most important day of redemption and atonement of the New Testament; and both the morning and the afternoon meetings will be based on the last part of the passion according to Luke 23.

Last night the boat came back from Savannah as empty as I had sent it, although Mr. Causton had asked for it to be sent at this time. Apart from flour, there are no provisions in the store-house in Savannah, and thus nothing could be sent to us. [In the meantime, the lack of food and provisions among us has become worse than at almost any other time, and the hungry bother me much with questions and complaints. Neither in Savannah nor in Purysburg can anything be had, not even for money. Mr. Causton has again failed to reply to my letter. If we had not recently purchased forty bushels of beans from Mr. Montaigut's plantation with our money, we would truly be suffering from worse than want.]

Friday, the 8th of April. [Bach[50] is a good-for-nothing, and all previous work with his soul has been in vain. This time he has been kept from Holy Communion in view of his obvious lack of repentance. He is not a Salzburger but was admitted to the 2nd Transport in Memmingen. There were four of these in all;

two, that is, Sanftleben and Zant, have adjusted very well; but this Bach and also Miggizer have remained as they were.]

All told, there were thirty-nine communicants at this communion. There are a few of the older children in the community whom I would have liked to prepare for the Lord's table, with much prayer and admonishment. However, the many material things which fall upon me, such as provisions and other matters, have prevented me. I only hope that after Easter nothing shall stop me from undertaking this holy task. If the provisions from Savannah for our people were to come all at once, instead of in the usual piecemeal fashion, I would have half the work with these matters. Instead of our customary repetition hour, we held a public prayer meeting tonight. For the sake of His promises, may the Lord lend His ear to all the requests that have been made for us and others in the name of His dear son.

Saturday, the 9th of April. N. [Ernst] came to see me this morning and presented me with a trivial complaint; he claimed also to have noticed something that would give me much sorrow, were I but to know it, in regard to a man who had taken Holy Communion yesterday, but whose name he did not wish to reveal. Ernst is a man who will quickly find fault, and serious fault at that, with others, whereas he will either ignore or belittle his own shortcomings. His neighbors, both at home and in the fields, have much trouble with him.

Toward evening, preparations for Easter were made on the basis of 2 Corinthians 5:19–21; and we showed that there is much and indubitable comfort in the example of the reconciliation between the deeply corrupted human race and the Holy and Just Lord according to the mercy He offered for that purpose. After the preparation, Christ, who was formerly a Jew, came to see me and told me that last night, when he had been on guard duty, he had on his rounds heard many of our people pray in the most heartfelt fashion. He had been much impressed with this and felt that God could not refuse His ear to such sincere and urgent prayers. He expressed his sorrow that he still found it difficult to pray from his heart, but he could only pray according to the condition of heart and as well as he could; he constantly implored the Lord for further illumination.

Sunday, the 10th of April. On this first day of Easter we have had, to be sure, raw weather and much rain; but these external inconveniences have done nothing to affect our glad and industrious proclamation and acceptance of the glorious gospel telling us of Christ, our resurrected and tender Savior, although the large hut where we hold our public services is quite uncomfortable in this kind of weather. Much singing and praying was heard throughout the day; and, on the strength of God's mercy as apparent from the gospel, we take courage that he may again bless our dear audience.

A Christian man from Switzerland, who recently arrived in Charleston with 170 of his countrymen,[51] has written to let me know that he as well as his two brothers and their entire family, eleven persons in all, had been moved by the printed news of our settlement and work to move to America. He now wishes to make our acquaintance, for his arrival here was entirely motivated by his wish to honor the Lord and redeem his soul. He did not add anything that would reveal the true intent of his letter. I believe that he shares the fate of many who, in order to work off the money for their passage, must indenture themselves in various places for a number of years.

Monday, the 11th of April. Yesterday Veit Lemmenhoffer's wife gave birth to a son who was publicly baptized today before the morning sermon. The mother is in pitiful physical condition, for she has been suffering from the fever for almost a year. Others who had been rid of the fever for quite some time have now suffered a relapse, which may be partly due to the poor care they receive, since even the most humble food is not available in sufficient amounts to feed them. The nights now are quite cool, but pleasant. May God be praised for having given us this Easter with much external calm and quiet and full of true pleasure and heartfelt edification. We had heard that 300 Indians had assembled in Purysburg; but we have received definite news that only 100 did in fact arrive there and have been taken by boat to Savannah, probably as a matter of precaution in the event of a Spanish attack. May Jesus Christ, the Lord of Peace and Victory, protect us and this entire land.

Tuesday, the 12th of April. Having received word that provisions have just arrived in Savannah, we will again send our boat down the river. May God guide the heart of Mr. Causton to help us in our great want, of which he has been informed many a time! The nights are again so cold that we have to fear for some of the plants in the gardens, especially since even some frost has fallen, something we had not feared at this time. The sun shines during the day to be sure; but, since there is a strong northerly wind, our workers are not hindered by the heat. By tomorrow or the day after, the hard work of putting up the fences will have been finished by everybody without exception, and some have already started planting the corn.

Wednesday, the 13th of April. Three people in our community, who have recently taken Holy Communion in great spiritual poverty and with much hunger and thirst of soul, have asked me to come to their house after school; for it appears that their spirits require comfort and help in prayer. God in His mercy has so blessed my exhortations and encouragement from the gospel and common prayer that they seem to have taken heart in their renewed belief in our loving Savior. If only our time permitted it, they would be most grateful to pray with me or my dear colleague every day. But they have resolved to come and see me as often as possible. If only we had more room in our hut, the pious and simple flock in our charge would join us there most gladly and industriously in prayer and examination of the Holy Word.

Thursday, the 14th of April. This evening five pious men and women of our flock met in my hut to join me and my family in prayer and edification from the Lord's words. These dear people were both hungry and thirsty in their spirit; and I sang for them the song, "You are Jesus, my joy,"[52] which is well suited for their circumstances. I also entertained them with the beautiful saying in Micha 2:13, "The breaker is come up before them," etc. We thereupon knelt down and united our souls in prayer, and the hour was spent in much heartfelt pleasure. A pious woman among them called me during the day and told me, with words both simple and convincing, how God in His mercy had helped her not only by bringing her to the realization of her many sins committed in the years of her ignorance, but also by giving her some reassurance, however remote, of His forgiveness. She had always been convinced of her standing as a good Christian, but she was now much surprised both at her own foolishness and at God's mercy in not letting her go into eternal life in such a state of self-deception. She truly felt as if a mist had previously shrouded her eyes and mind and thus she had seen only half of everything; for she should properly have felt the bitterness of her sins and realized that they relegated her to a life in hell, consuming all her body and vital strength. "Oh," she added, "if only all our people and our frivolous children would learn the true meaning of sin and how dearly we must pay for their redemption, they would change their lighthearted and frivolous ways."

Friday, the 15th of April. Out boat brought corn and beans from Savannah, and I immediately distributed part thereof to those among us who are in need. Mr. Causton is also sending us rice, seed corn, and beans with a subsequent pirogue.[53] He has shown himself to be most kind and has given us many promises concerning our situation. He is expecting large amounts of provisions in the near future, with which he will relieve us in our need.

A pious Salzburger came to me in tears to complain that his work in the fields had been for naught; both he and his neighbor had planted corn which had dried after coming up, while in his neighbor's fields, which has good soil, the corn was green and growing. He had even carried manure to the field on his back; but, since there was not enough of it and the soil is poor, nothing had availed. [He added: "Such poor land is not worth the tools which I have broken in tilling it. I am draining all my strength in working this land and nothing will come of it. It is now said that there will be no more provisions, and we have bad land. How shall we continue to live? If God will not send help, man's help will hardly succeed." I have tried to cheer and console him as much as is within my power.]

Saturday, the 16th of April. With God's help, we have finished the Book of Genesis in our evening prayer hours. We have not been able to hurry our flock in applying the divine truths that lie hidden in the Bible stories, because all these truths are so necessary for understanding the ways of the Lord and advancing our active life in Christ. Also, partly due to illnesses and partly for other reasons, we were prevented from conducting these prayer meetings every day. Furthermore, we have sometime felt it necessary to read edifying reports in these meetings or to repeat for the entire congregation matters discussed in school. Thus we have spent exactly a year on the Book of Genesis.

Sunday, the 17th of April. Kieffer from Purysburg is now sending four little girls to our school, the two older of whom shall be prepared for Holy Communion together with 6 grown children from the community. Christ is again suffering from the heavy hemorrhaging which afflicted him last year at this time.[54] There was no remedy available to arrest the flow of blood, and he must now have lost about 6 quarts in succession, being extremely weak and without any strength left in him. He takes this suffering as full proof of God's love as it will prepare him all the better for his blessed journey to heaven.

Monday, the 18th of April. Now is the most rewarding weather for planting, and our people are most eager and industrious in their work. Both worms and birds are causing much damage in the gardens and fields, despite the trouble everybody is taking to guard against the birds and remove the worms. Kieffer, who is leaving us today, would love nothing better than to move to us here if he could only be given some good land in our village. He is having a petition to the governor in Charleston prepared in which he presents the suffering which he and family underwent due to the fault of his superiors in Purysburg and especially of the deceased Mr. Purry.[55] Also, he is asking for some fertile land, several provisions withheld from him, and remission of the passage money. The gentlemen in Charleston are much inclined towards the poor people and thus he is hoping for a favorable answer and an improvement in his situation.

Tuesday, the 19th of April. In tonight's prayer meeting I again had occasion, when speaking on the remarkable and strange story in Chapter 1 of Exodus, to demonstrate the extent of God's mercy to the Salzburgers in having miraculously led them from Papist tyranny, their spiritual Egypt, and having bestowed on them complete freedom of conscience and in the exercise of their religion, a blessing for which many thousands still pine in their souls under the Papist yoke without attaining the object of their desires and heartfelt wishes. If these poor souls could but enjoy the spiritual benefits which our people have in this desert, thanks to the mercy of the Lord and our benefactors' providence, they would thank the Lord on their knees and count their physical deprivations for nothing as against the treasure of the free exercise of their evangelical beliefs. As an introduction, I felt compelled to remind my audience that many of the Israelites, despite all their pain and suffering, had soon after their miraculous delivery and exodus desired to be back in Egypt, as they had not found, while under the Lord's guidance, the gratification of their material desires regarding the good life and other means of well-being that they might have hoped for. However, history and 1 Corinthians 10 show what befell them because of it.

Wednesday, the 20th of April. The recently arrived provisions are far from sufficient to relieve our want, because we have many people to feed, whereas all that we received were twenty bushels of corn and twenty of beans. I only hope that the pirogue which is to come shortly will fill our needs. [Only I know how difficult the discharge of my office is rendered because of the constant want of our people. The worst of this is that, despite all appearances to the contrary, many members of the community have sinned against me by hasty judgments and suspicions and in other ways. Thus I have had to swallow a number of rude remarks and accusations of favoritism, etc. from some coarse and uncivil members of the 3rd transport.] Inasmuch as it is impossible to please everyone in taking care of the physical needs of man and since one is held to deal with some too leniently and with others too harshly, it is entirely possible that some among our people have secretly become embittered against our position and office, although this cannot easily be detected on the surface. But, once distrust starts to enter the mind of one's congregation, matters will rarely stop there. I urgently desire to be rid of this burden, and I will hardly be able to discharge my functions any longer if the matter of provisions is not settled definitely and satisfactorily.

Thursday, the 21st of April. The above-mentioned pirogue arrived here at noon, carrying both corn and beans and provisions, i.e., meat and rice. May God be praised for this blessing and strengthen our confidence in His future care and providence. I cannot but thank Mr. Causton for the provisions he has sent us; for, if our people had been forced to fetch them, they would have lost much time urgently needed for planting and tending the new crops. We now have sufficient provisions so that nobody will have to go hungry among us. I have not yet received precise instructions from Mr. Causton as to what provisions I should give to the 1st and 2nd transport until harvest time. However, since they can neither subsist nor work without food, and inasmuch as Mr. Oglethorpe has allotted a small advance to be refunded later, we shall give some provisions to those who request it.

Friday, the 22nd of April. Reck, the cobbler from Purysburg, now wishes to place his oldest son in our school, who will have to be entrusted to one of the Salzburgers for care and supervision. If only we were more convinced of the Divine Will and if a proper location could be permanently assigned therefor, we would have a spacious house constructed as a residence for such children, since this would make it possible to keep them under one roof. Also, we would be better able to care for their Christian welfare by entrusting them to supervisors appointed to this task. However, building is quite expensive here. We have fenced in the lot on which the houses for the preachers are to be erected so as to use it as a garden; and this has cost us more than 5£ Sterling. If we had used English labor, the expense would have been twice as high, without doubt.

Saturday, the 23rd of April. A married Salzburger has just told me, praising the Lord, that He had so blessed him in his supply of provisions and the fruits from a few plants in his garden that he was sufficiently provided for and could rejoice in his luck. During his meals he kept thinking of the words which he had heard in Old Ebenezer in a sermon from God's Word: i.e., that it is better to have little with the fear of the Lord than to have great treasure without tranquility. A dish of cabbage eaten in the knowledge of love was preferable to a fattened steer eaten in hate, and he felt that this wisdom fully applied in his case. He continued to speak of the certain help of the Lord, even where man were to refuse to provide for bodily needs; and I was much pleased in my heart at his words in our present circumstances.

Oh, if I could but visit our people more often! Both their duties and mine permit only infrequent visits in their houses, as I must spend three hours daily with the children in school and in their preparation for Holy Communion, in addition to other matters preventing me from exercising my spiritual functions. My dear colleague must spend four hours daily in instruction and has much other work; yet he finds many occasions for making house visits, which is also a blessing.

Sunday, the 24th of April. Last night after the prayer meeting Stephan Riedelsperger asked me for my opinion on his resolution to go into service for some time in order to gain some money. I told him briefly that he himself would have to examine his spiritual condition and inquire into God's will in this matter and that he should act accordingly. I could neither support nor advise against his wish to go into somebody else's service. Today, I found more time to speak to him on this matter and to point out to him the great danger he would incur both in his physical and spiritual well-being if he were to leave us. I feared that, being thus removed from God's word and in the company of unfit people, he would lose the little treasure of the spirit that he now might possess. And, even though he might turn over the care for his corn crop to someone else for a consideration, whatever care might be given would not be the same as if he were to do it himself. Also, there was not yet dire need for his departure from the community, for however short a time, firstly, since we now had some provisions and he was thus assured of food and, secondly, since I placed sufficient trust in the Lord to move the hearts of our benefactors to provide sustenance for the 1st and 2nd transports until harvest time. He knew full well from three years's experience that, although there had been need and deprivation many times, none of us had yet died for lack of food and that he should thus continue to place his trust in our Lord and Provider. The most important aspect of his conduct was to seek reassurance of God's merciful will, for no Christian should take a step in the absence of our Father's will, nor undertake any other action.

In this connection I reminded him of the events of a year past, that is, when many members of our community, forced by want and deprivation, had decided to seek work in Frederica for several months, where one of us would have accompanied them to serve our flock there in our ordained function. And, although those decisions had seemed well justified by our extreme need, and while Mr. Oglethorpe had quite clearly indicated a few weeks previously that he would have liked some Salzburgers there to help in the building of fortifications, the plan was abandoned after we seriously appealed to the Lord in our prayers for His guidance. That this change of mind was in accordance with God's will was made quite abundantly clear to us by subsequent events, for we all fell ill a little while later; and no doubt it was better to be ill here than in some other unknown and barren place. Moreover, the Lord so provided for us that nobody had to die of hunger, for which act of grace every honest soul among us still thanks Him from the bottom of his heart.

My preoccupation in this matter of Riedelsperger, and the many words I spent on him, are not without good reason: such separations can cause much damage both spiritually and physically. I gently chided him for his lack of zeal in the pursuit of his Christian beliefs, as well as for his desire to move away from Ebenezer altogether. The latter reproach he pretended not to understand fully; and, as to the former, he promised to seek relief with God's mercy. He acknowledged that his lack of faith and lack of application were due to his failure to pray earnestly and frequently. Whether he will now follow the above-mentioned work to another place, I do not know, although he promised to consider everything well before making a decision. Quite a few among our flock have had similar intentions in the past, but God has always miraculously prevented their departure, and in the end they have realized themselves how much their decision to remain has benefited them.

The children who are being prepared for the Lord's table give us much reason for hope that they will open their hearts to our Savior and become His faithful lambs. If only some good can be done to these souls through God's word, all the difficulties connected with our teaching duties will seem light and pleasant; this would be even more so if their souls could be entirely won over by His word.

Monday, the 25th of April. The cobbler at Purysburg, who has carried out his trade here for some time, has persuaded three Salzburgers to prepare and plant his land, which lies just across from us in Carolina, for a very modest consideration. Our people have accepted this work with great willingness, as this will permit them to come home every night and participate in the prayer meeting. Inasmuch, however, as these men receive their provisions in this colony and thus are bound to benefit our province by their labor, I have today written to Mr. Causton requesting his advice in this matter, so that nothing may be done among us against the will and without the knowledge of our benefactors and superiors. In my letter, I again pointed out how beneficial it would be for everyone if the land due to our community were to be fully surveyed and allotted.

Now that our people have finished their planting and will have time until the corn is hoed, they could do much useful work on their own plantations. Since the three aforementioned men would like to earn something, and since prior to learning Mr. Causton's will in this matter I cannot consent to their working on the cobbler's land, they have been hired as our woodcutters for several days, for which labor they shall be paid the same daily wages as the cobbler is prepared to give them.

Tuesday, the 26th of April. NB. The dear Lord will probably soon take our pious Mrs. Schweighofer to His kingdom and give her eternal peace, for which He has so magnificently prepared her by numerous blessed paths of the soul that I always am much uplifted by her words and listen to her testimony of the mercy of the Lord, which now fills her heart with deepest pleasure. Oh for the lessons to be learned by listening to such simple souls in whom the Lord has worked His mercy! I have become well acquainted with her. She is a faithful lamb of our Lord Jesus who does not take her eyes off her Shepherd and acquiesces entirely in His will so that He may only keep her under His guidance and care and not reject her for her many faults and defects, of which she is deeply aware. When He hides His face from her, oh how she prays and implores Him in her grief; and, in such hours of doubt and spiritual labor, the blessed Johann Arnd in his book on *True Christianity* gives her much help and succor, with God's mercy. In these hours of temptation and doubt He melts from her heart all impurities and leads her to the true strength

of her rebirth in the Lord. It is by His mercy that she finds herself
better than before despite her pitiful and poor material circumstances. "May God do unto me as He wishes," she said today,
"if He will only not refuse me His mercy and love for the sake
of my many sins. Oh how holy is the Lord! And who can stand
before Him? None of the saints could have been without Him;
when I consider this, all courage seeps away, but God be
praised! For we have our Savior," etc. My comforting words and
advice seem to have met her very needs today, and she received
them well. But she suffers much pain; and it causes her much
sighing and tears that her children do not wish to fear the Lord
as she does. We have placed the boy under the guidance and
supervision of the pious Kalcher, for he would not obey his
mother.

Wednesday, the 27th of April. Last night we experienced
heavy thunderstorms and sudden rain, accompanied by hail as
thick as a thumb. Those children who have been placed with
different Christian people for the sake of their guidance and
supervision are not faring badly, but not as well as we would
wish. These good people have much work, especially now; and
their time is taken from the early morning hours until late at
night. Thus, the children cannot be supervised constantly both
before and after school. For this reason it may be necessary to
build a spacious house of wood and clapboards, especially since
the bountiful and loving Lord has recently provided some funds.
Our poor people would gratefully welcome the opportunity to
earn some money in this way after they have completed their
work in the fields, for thus they would not have to look for work
elsewhere and with strangers. But we shall place this matter, too,
in the hands of the Lord. May His fatherly will guide us so that
we shall act to the glory of His name and the benefit of our
children and flock!

The wife of S. [Schmidt], a deeply pious Austrian, who until
now has secretly resisted the word of Christ and shown many
unpleasant traits, appears finally to have gained a better understanding of the need for a true conversion. I enquired into the
state of her soul while she was gardening, and her answer consisted more in tears than in words. She thanks God for having
brought her to Ebenezer, where she hopes that her and her
husband's souls may be saved. She told me she could not put
into words the good that God has wrought in her heart, and she
added that the prayer-meetings were especially blessed. In moving words she described how even her husband, who had al-

ready been grounded in the Christian faith, continued to be led on this blessed path by God's love, and how he praised the Lord's name for this.

Thursday, the 28th of April. Both S. R. [Stephan Riedelsperger] and M. R. [Michael Rieser] have left to travel to the plantation of Mrs. Musgrove, where they will try to earn some money in the next months. I do not object as much to M. R. [Michael Rieser]'s decision to thus leave our community as to S. R. [Stephan Riedelsperger]'s, for the former obtained only poor land for a garden, while the latter has good land and enough work on it. I remonstrated with his wife and showed her the danger into which he is throwing himself by thus removing his spirit from the Lord's word and Holy Communion, which he has not enjoyed for four or five months now, and all this for material reasons. She confided in me that he had refused to listen to her pleas and had offered many fictitious reasons for his decision. She even assured me that he is intending to leave for good, and for this purpose has already sold his best cow. I told her of the consequences which such independent action might carry with it and instructed her to pray sincerely to the Lord for his and her well-being.

I also spoke with a few other women (for, at this time of planting, the men can rarely be found at home); and, despite all material deprivation that they may be suffering, they told a quite different story. The honest souls among us rejoice at the smallest favors and do not consider themselves deserving of them. They thus think little of the complaints of the critics that are not lacking here as everywhere; and they feel that this is not a good sign.

In tonight's prayer-meeting I again had opportunity to speak on Exodus 3:21–22 and to show my listeners that God can direct the hearts of man like the water of a river: He had inclined the heart of many a benefactor toward us, who then had provided for our community in many ways. If He felt it to our benefit, He could not only increase the number of benefactors and well-wishers, but also change the minds of those who are not well disposed toward us and lead them to pity and good deeds on our behalf. This was quite evident from the sudden change in the Egyptians against His chosen people. If our ways please the Lord, He will make even our enemies approve of us and lead them to regard us favorably. However, despite the foresight and provisions made on our behalf by our dear benefactors, the all-knowing Lord has seen fit to expose us to much want and trial both now and in the past; and therefore it is obvious that He must have a holy purpose and a beneficial reason for this. And one of these has already been reached, i.e., there are some among us whose faithless and pleasure-loving hearts have become evident, whereas they might have imagined themselves to be strong in their faith and full of trust in the Lord and His promise. And it was this result, their recognition and renewed desire for salvation, which had been the Lord's intention. Contrariwise, the full treasure in the hearts of some of our brethern had become equally evident to all, to the glory of God and the edification of others.

Friday, the 29th of April. NB. In reply to my inquiry whether Mr. Causton would give permission for our people to seek work in Carolina, he stated that, while he was prepared to let the men have their freedom, he would prefer it if their work for remuneration were to be in the service of this colony. He himself would be willing to take some men on as workers on his plantation, if they should so desire. At the same time Mr. Causton has assured me that the land of the Salzburgers will be surveyed in the near future and that the great losses which they have incurred for lack of properly surveyed and allotted land shall be made good.

From P. [Purysburg], I learned through Mr. Z. [Zieblin][56] that the recently arrived Swiss, [having become wary of and dissatisfied with their preacher, a Mr. Zoberbüller,[57] had arrived in Purysburg without him. They had chosen this man for their minister in Rotterdam and upon their request obtained the bishop's confirmation of his appointment from London. They] have expressed their intention, [it is said, to continue in this country the exercise of the chaotic disturbing civil liberties which they practice in Switzerland toward their betters and superiors, and] to admit to their town only special compatriots from their own canton.

The location of their home will be far up on the Savannah River, close to a village inhabited by Indians and traders, Savannah-Town, and it is to be feared that they will have eaten up their provisions by the time they can travel there on the river. With a fully loaded boat it will take them at least four weeks; and it will be hard work upriver. The land there is reputed to be good; but the location is dangerous because of the Indians, and the lack of communications makes it a difficult place to live.

Saturday, the 30th of April. The public lots in our town have until now lain barren and deserted and much brush and weeds

are growing there, for [without recompense] nobody will take
the time to dig up the roots. So that the brush may be dug up
by the roots and the snakes and other vermin be deprived of
their habitat, our people have decided to fence in this land,
which covers more than four acres, and use it for planting corn,
beans, and potatoes. This they well deserve, for they had been
assigned only two acres for gardening plots, much to their detriment.

[An article has been found in the house of Mrs. Ortmann
which used to belong to a Salzburger and which had been taken
away from him secretly while he was still in Old Ebenezer; and
he had not been able to find his property despite his inquiries
about it. I had the woman come to me so as to question her in
regard to this matter, and she told me that it had been given
to her by a carpenter, in lieu of money, for some washing and
mending work she had done for him. As she was forced to tell
me the name of this man, whom I intended to have brought
before the authorities in Savannah, she returned after half an
hour had passed to pretend that she had been mistaken and had
not received the stolen article from the carpenter but that somebody must have left it in her house; and she did this after she
had made her first statement of her own free will and under
oath. Inasmuch as I now reprimanded her severely, in the presence of a Salzburger who had been a witness of her wickedness
and lies, for this theft of another's property and her shameful
contradictions, she again turned very hostile and abusive. Returning home, she even persuaded her husband to send me,
through one of the schoolchildren, a piece of paper on which
had been written all sorts of Biblical sayings and expressions as
to the bearing of false testimony, lying witnesses, malicious libel,
persecution, and envy. It is easy to see what and whom the poor
inconstant man wishes to attack with such misuse of the Lord's
word. Since his wife's return from Charleston, he has again
become evil and full of guile; and there is much to be feared
for the state of his soul. We do what we can for the material and
physical welfare of those poor people.]

MAY

Sunday, the 1st of May. NB. NB. A Salzburger woman who
has been earnestly striving for the remission of her sins and
God's mercy has told my dear colleague what our Lord Jesus
had done for her during this last week in his love and compas-

sion. She had gone to bed, filled with sorrow about her sins, and had fallen asleep with many sighs after having prayed to the Lord, fully realizing her misery but quite without strength, that He might preserve her from the temptations of the devil. And in her sleep it had appeared to her as if our beloved Savior had slowly approached her. She had at first been full of fear at this apparition, believing that He had come to punish her for her sins. But, since she perceived Him only as a very friendly and quite gentle figure, she prayed to Him and resolved to hold Him by the hem of his robe lest He turn from her as a great sinner. But He then merely started to talk to her in a most gentle manner, and in punishment only told her that she had been quite wicked. After she had promised Him to endeavor seriously to improve herself (which promise had gone like a flame through her body), He had fully absolved her of her sins and told her: "Take heart, my daughter, for your sins shall be forgiven unto you and all memory of them shall disappear." Words could not express her feelings when she heard these words of absolution. She now felt the power of His words and the forgiveness of her sins deeply and truthfully in her soul: and she was only fearful that after her promise she might not stay faithful to Our Savior. She felt totally changed, and she understood and comprehended God's word much more clearly and directly than ever before. She found more joy and refreshment in her prayers, and she could not help but believe that all this had been not an empty dream but the work of our faithful Lord, who searches and saves that which is lost.

After rising from her sleep, she took her hymnal and the *Cooing Dove*[58] so as to find edification in them. The first song on which her eye came to rest was: "Rise, morning star of my heart," etc.;[59] and the passage in the aforementioned book is to be found on pp. 64–65. She also told me about this delightful happening when she came to see me about certain matters; and her words were full of such tender emotion that it caused me the most heartfelt joy and made me praise the Lord, who so wondrously leads His children. She was much strengthened by this; and I demonstrated this to her by the example of God's guidance in the life of the late Prior Porst, and also by telling her about the sermon of the late Prof. Francke, which he had held at the court of Count Loberstein and which had been heard and repeated here. I also assured her that in the very same week our Lord Jesus had revealed Himself here in His love and gentleness to another repentant and struggling soul. If caution did

not restrain us, I could recount many more special cases of how
our dear Savior works in His secret ways among the souls of our
people, just as a good shepherd seeks out the straying and lost
sheep more than a wise one. May He be praised for His abundant mercy!

Tonight, at a meeting several of our people held in the hut
of one of the Salzburgers, I finished the story of the life of our
blessed Luther, which the Lord has filled with so much edification for all of us. May He alone be praised for this! We would
have finished this task earlier had we not been compelled to
explain a number of happenings so as to give our listeners a
better understanding of the strange circumstances prevailing at
that time and to apply such tales to the joint edification and
enlightenment of all. Also, it was occasionally necessary to discuss this or that point relating to the divine truths revealed on
a particular day, both for their and my own insight and edification. If God should now desire to have a spacious and well-
erected hut provided us for our lodging and for the better
supervision of the children entrusted to our care, such a hut
might offer a good place for meeting in prayer and private
communication, just as we did in Old Ebenezer.

Monday, the 2nd of May, [NB. NB.] B. [Burgsteiner] came to
have me compose a letter to his old father in Lindau; and I was
much edified by him and his wife, who was also present, because
of their good spirits and contentedness with that which the Lord
has given them here. He wished his father could be here, too:
for, while the work would be hard for man in his old age, everything would be made easier for him through God's word, which
he, who is hard of hearing, would be able to hear better here.
He assured me that, if he were to give an honest account to the
Salzburgers in Lindau of everything that happened here, both
the good and the bad, none would stay behind but all would
move here. I asked him why so few Salzburgers wrote to their
families, and he replied that this was due to their uncertainty
regarding their land; once this had been surveyed and assigned
to them, they would all write home.

Tuesday, the 3rd of May. The eight children who are being
prepared for Holy Communion have been coming to my house
between two and three o'clock in the afternoon. Since, however,
it is very hot at this time of the day and thus quite uncomfortable
and not conducive to our important task, I have decided to use
the hour from eight to nine in the morning for this purpose.
Ordinarily, I had used this time to study Bible stories with all

the schoolchildren, which lesson I will now give between ten and eleven o'clock. In view of this intended change in schedule, I asked the schoolmaster to come to me and informed him of the hours now assigned to him. Also, since things can no longer be changed, he might as well start giving a lesson in English.

I took this occasion to ask him for the meaning of the letter he had sent to me, in particular with reference to the passage: "He will save me from the snare of the fowler,[60] who says, 'Let us take for ourselves the house, the school, and the garden, etc.'" He gave a most pitiful and wretched explanation, viz., after his wife had traveled to Charleston against my wish, I had stated that neither of them would come to any good and that I would report this matter to London, etc. Also, I had given him only two acres for gardening, whereas, according to the assurances of the Honorable Trustees and the Honorable Dr. Gerdes, he was to receive a large garden next to the school in the settlement and fifty acres of land for his wife, who was to retain this property as her own after his death. This claim, however, cannot be but an act of despicable ingratitude: He received these two acres without drawing lots, as they had already been fenced in and cleared of trees. Not a single family had received more than that at the time. The second transport had cleared eight more acres in addition to those given to the schoolmaster; four of these were presented to the church as garden land, and the other four to me and my dear colleague. This was done against our will and wish and only because the people of the second transport could not have shared these commonly cleared grounds among them; and to assign them by lot would have caused nothing but envy, ill will, and disorder. However, so that the people of the second transport should not have worked in vain but would reap some benefit from their labors, we had left them the entire grounds for planting, excepting the two acres of the schoolmaster, who had done his own planting.

[Though the land in question was given to us freely and accepted only to forestall misunderstanding and discord, it is not our wish to use said land for our benefit, but for the future benefit of the community, e.g., so that they can make use of it to pay their herdsmen, or to provide better sustenance for the expected doctor, or to provide some advantage for the poor children in our school, depending on future circumstances and necessities. However, since the schoolmaster is so pressing in his demands and will not content himself with his two acres until all the land has been surveyed and assigned and can be expected to spread many lies and much slander in this respect, I have made him a present of the two acres which the second transport had given to me. Since, however, the land is planted, he cannot take possession of it until the coming fall, with which arrangement he was well content. If I had assigned the four acres to him at the time of surveying, the trees would have been left standing to the detriment of the neighbors and the land would have lain fallow, for he is not able to plant these additional four acres completely. The fieldhands of whom he speaks have yet to arrive, and the Salzburgers do not have the time to work his land, which he demanded quite openly in view of a letter received by him.

Wednesday, the 4th of May. [NB. NB.] A Salzburger woman told me how strongly she felt that she was totally lost to mercy; she often thought of her husband, now dead, who had on many occasions said to her that his sins were so many and his perdition so certain that he felt sure that God would send him to his damnation in hell. At the time she had not been able to comprehend this. Last night the devil had much tortured her with his temptations and she had been driven from her bed to save herself by praying, but the temptations had made prayer impossible. Thus tortured, she picked up her hymnal and, in the light of the moon, read the hymn: "Jesus, your holy wounds, etc."[61] While reading, her mind became calm and capable of prayer; and she now has found her peace again. I read her the hymn: "A mighty fortress is Our God,"[62] and prayed with her.

The shoemaker Reck of Purysburg has again come here to work for our community. More than eight pounds sterling are due to him for the shoes which he has made for those in want; part of this money he has received out of the poor box, part is still due to him and will be paid when the generous Lord shall provide again, for the funds which were given to our poor by some generous hearts have all been used up. It is true that the poor people mostly wear wooden shoes or go barefoot during workdays, but they must have shoes on Sundays and Holy Days as well as when they have hurt their feet, which easily happens in these hot latitudes, where there are many insects. Also, injuries often occur accidentally during their hard work. Had we tried to make do with the means at our disposal and refused their request for shoes, our people would quite clearly have been forced to seek income elsewhere and leave our community, to the detriment of their souls.

In addition to shoes and stockings, we have recently purchased some coarse linen for the poor, of which one piece cost more than 5 £ sterling, and the other more than 3 £ sterling; yet it will not go far in view of the many poor members of our community. It is nonetheless a great blessing, for which the honest souls among us praise our dear heavenly father. This year our dear Salzburgers have become quite poor for a variety of reasons and are unable to pay the herdsmen so that these might have their sustenance, however meager; and therefore it has become necessary to buy some articles of clothing, which would otherwise have been given to the poor from the poor box for the three herdsmen (for the cattle have to be kept in two different locations, and one herdsman would not be able to cope). Thus, the community pays a reasonable sum for every head of cattle, which is gladly done in view of the present satisfactory arrangements in this respect. Although nothing is left in the poor box, we have our God, the Almighty Creator of heaven and earth, from whom all blessings spring, I Kings 17: 14–16, and from Him we, too, shall expect that which is necessary and beneficial to us.

Thursday, the 5th of May, [NB. NB.] One of our schoolchildren has read to his mother and his sick brother some passages from a sermon of the late Prof. Francke,[63] which had been printed as a separate publication and which shows Christ as our true light and law. This reading seems to have been a true blessing for all three of them. May God make this blessing permanent. They showed me the passage which had gone to their hearts above all others, i.e., where it is said, among other things: " 'Because strait is the gate, and narrow is the way' (Matthew 7:14).[64] But, unfortunately, this truth is hidden from the eyes of most; they think that, if only a sermon is held and the churches are full, then all has gone well with the service and God has been served. But whether our hearts and minds are renewed, as God demands of us, that nobody seems to ask. Those who have gained understanding, however, see the light in Christ's tears which He cried for the blindness, stubbornness, and final punishment of Jerusalem; and they realize thereby and see clearly before their eyes the end to which we are all bound to come."

The sick boy told me in a sad voice and with moist eyes that which had appeared to him recently while he was lying on his bed, ill of the fever: He had been on his way to heaven; but all around him had been heavy, thick trees which were an obstacle to his path and to his passing through the gate of heaven. At the same time he had seen hell in all its vastness and had heard pitiful screams, which had caused him great fear; and he had cried to the Lord for help and salvation. Finally, our Lord Jesus had come to his help and had soon cleared the obstacles from his path, so that he could approach the gate of heaven. The mother added that, at the same time, he had been quite miserable in his bed and had asked for his brother. When hearing that he was not there, he had said that his mother should tell him to follow carefully all the teachings which his teachers[65] had told him from God's word, for that was the right and the only way to salvation. This matter gave me a good opportunity to speak at length with these souls, particularly with the two children who, until now, had been quite frivolous and slow in seeing the good life. I also read them Job 33:15-30.

Toward evening I was visited by an Englishman who is to survey the new town of the Swiss immigrants up the Savannah River in Carolina.[66] He is on his way from the settlement to Purysburg to find out why the Swiss have not yet arrived. He told me that there, too, good and bad land lie next to each other. The present settlers would probably be provided with good land, while those that are to follow would have to make do with poor soil. There was no danger from the Indians in that location, he said; but provisions would be hard to come by because the settlement is far removed from the present plantations in Carolina. He had occasion to see some of the work that our people have done here and was much surprised at their industry and at the solid, well-kept fences they have put up.

Friday, the 6th of May. This Wednesday evening two persons [a married couple][67] had started a serious quarrel, the noise of which could be heard in the entire neighborhood. The whole disorderly affair was the fault of the one person [the wife], who had so irritated the other [her husband] with her spite, accusations, and noise that he exploded in disgust and anger. At the same time I had been preoccupied with two other men [the cobbler, Reck, and Rheinlaender], who had gotten into a confused bargain due to uncertain payment. When the innocent party of the first pair [the husband] came to inform me of the story, however, he was so sad and choked with tears that he could not utter a word. He returned when I was alone and with many tears confessed and repented his conduct and admitted that he had not been sufficiently watchful of himself and had failed to pray so that he had let himself be goaded by the other party's [his wife's] anger and vicious manners into losing his temper. Yesterday morning I resolved to speak to both of them but was prevented in this by another's presence at their house. As the innocent party [the husband] had to leave our community on some voyage, I sent word twice to the other party [the woman] to come and see me. She failed to come, however, so I felt constrained to go again to her house this morning after the end of the preparatory hour. I found her alone and remonstrated with her for having failed through fear and flimsy excuses to come despite my request. On the basis of God's word, I endeavored to show her her divinely established duty in regard to the other party [her husband], and at the same time showed her the sins she had committed and the spectacle she had caused thereby, so that she might recognize the unrepentant state of her spirit and the resulting grave danger to her salvation. Finally, I joined her on my knees in prayer; and she cried steadily, both under my remonstrations and during our prayer. When the other person [her husband] returns today, I shall attempt to reconcile them completely.

[NB. NB.]

Christ has severely injured his right side in a hard fall, although there is no open wound. May God bless the application of the *pulvis antispasmoticus* which Mr. Zwiffler had prepared before his departure according to the instructions of Dr. Richter, so that the clotted blood may be dissolved. I have also given him some of the Schauer balm[68] to apply on the injured part which our people have used with much benefit for various injuries and for which the Lord may be praised. We shall pray that His blessing may devolve on our benefactor. True, Christ is faring poorly; but, as befits a true Christian, he is always content and grateful for the smallest favor.

Saturday, the 7th of May. NB. NB. A German captain from Purysburg, a Mr. Holtzendorff, who is well-versed in surgery, had several times offered to visit our settlement and bleed us. We therefore asked him to come yesterday evening, and he treated our people without asking for any remuneration. He offered to return and repeat his labors as soon as we should let him know that we thought it necessary. He is very skillful with a lancet, although he does not practice much in Purysburg, and we consider his willingness and kindness a great material blessing.

Sunday, the 8th of May. Last night a large boat arrived here

full of Swiss from the Canton of Appenzell, who stayed over-
night. [They are quite disgruntled and of bad humor in view of
Mr. Zoberbiller's[69] glowing letters, which are so different from
the situation they now find here. They claim that they had been
well off at home and there had been no need for them to emi-
grate. They also accuse their preacher, the old Mr. Zoberbiller,
but I would assume that some of the things they say should not
be taken for the truth. He, Mr. Zoberbiller, is still in Charleston.]
Among them is a man whom they address as cantonal governor,
who is said to be most skillful and is much admired by them.[70]
He has praised the land where they will settle, which he has
already inspected, in his conversations with some of our Salzburgers.

He also mentioned that one of the Salzburgers among us had
written a letter to Lindau in which he had spoken quite well of
our circumstances here. I assume that he is referring to the letter
by Ruprecht Steiner, of which we recently received a printed
copy. Upon rereading carefully the two printed sheets dealing
with our material and spiritual situation, and comparing them
with the reports we have now heard, we feel that neither our
present congregation nor those who will follow after them may
justly charge us with having painted too bright a picture in our
news. For, although we have constantly suffered much sorrow,
which we have not failed to mention in the aforesaid epistle, our
spiritual and material benefits have far outweighed all our trials,
so that we would have been quite wicked to forget our benefactors or to hold their deeds for little in view of our manifold
wants, as was done by the Jews in the wilderness.

I had intended to read the entire epistle to our flock, for it
would doubtless edify the honest souls among them. As for the
others, it might serve the purpose of preventing erroneous and
malicious interpretations of that which might read when a new
transport arrives. But I have changed my mind and decided to
leave this for an occasion which might truly warrant it, that is,
for the arrival of the fourth transport. For these people will
surely need an explanation and elucidation of such printed
news, which they all too often misunderstand and fail to interpret properly.

Meanwhile, I think that it may well be worthwhile if I were to
translate the aforesaid epistle, dealing with news from our community up to the 1st of September 1735, into English and to
forward it to Mr. Causton so that he may see that the good deeds
done for the Salzburgers for the glory of the Lord and the praise

of the Lord Trustees and the Honorable Society are not kept hidden and that he may also realize the high hopes held by our poor people in Germany concerning the actual provisions made by Mr. Oglethorpe.

Our boat will travel to Savannah this week, and I shall send the translation at that time. May the Lord guide us to do His will, and may all our writings truly fulfill the purpose for which they are intended. [If only our poor people were to obtain some good land from which they could gain their bread, it would surely be for the praise of the Lord. Should this not be possible, however, there will without doubt be many sad consequences. Our experience and the evidence of our senses clearly show that they cannot subsist on sandy soil. And, since the colonists in Carolina, particularly the first, like these Swiss, have the freedom to choose the best land, as there is not much settlement there at this time, our people are much aggrieved that they are not given similar freedom; and the surveying and titling of their land will be hard on them, even if it is finally accomplished in accordance with previous plans.]   ·

Monday, the 9th of May. Last year the first transport had not fenced in one side of the common pasture, since they thought that the water would serve instead of a fence; however, they suffered the consequences of this even then. And, as they did not know whether they would be able to use the pasture this year, or whether it would be subdivided into gardens, they did not finish the fence completely. Now that they are planting it again they will lack the time to erect such a large fence as is needed and, as it would be a shame to let the land lie waste, I proposed to the entire community last week, after the evening prayer hour, to help the first transport for one day in preparing the fence so that there would be some harvest for them from this fine plot of ground. God blessed my plan; and, although everybody has more work than he can handle, they were quite willing to agree to it; and thus they have jointly erected a sturdy fence which we both inspected today. In this country the fields must be quite carefully protected, for else not only the large birds and the squirrels but also the hogs will cause much damage. As there was no prayer meeting today, some Christian souls in search of the Lord came to our hut for prayer.

Tuesday, the 10th of May, [N.B. N.B. N.B.] A Salzburger who had come to speak to us of some affairs this evening told us in passing that some [of our people] are entertaining grand thoughts concerning the land that the Swiss are to get in Savannah-Town. He for his part was convinced that, if God had believed it to be to our benefit, He could easily have brought us, too, to such a good place. Did not the scriptures say: "He that overcometh shall inherit all things,"[71] and therefore we should attempt to face this trial with all our patience. The late Moshamer had given him this advice: If ever material needs and wants threatened to overpower him, he should but look at his hand and remember that our lives are not more than a handbreadth. For his part, he was prepared to bear all material want and suffering as long as his pastors felt that it could still be borne; he would not leave on his own; and, once they realized that it was impossible to continue living here without good land, they would surely not let their flock perish.

He himself would like to write to his cousin in Augsburg, as he had promised; but he feared that the account of his joys, despite all paternal punishments by the Lord, might be interpreted as complete happiness in all material aspects. Thus, if his cousin were to come here and not find everything as he had wished it to be, there might be quarrels and fights and recriminations. People always were solely concerned with their material well-being and happiness, and the last thing for which they asked was whether there would also be occasion for active Christian faith and the improvement of their souls. Nobody ever remembered that it was God's law that we shall pass into His kingdom through much misery, and that it was thus impossible to find a place in all the world where God would deviate from this rule and lead people to His heaven without the burden of the cross.

Wednesday, the 11th of May. [NB. NB.] The Haberfehner girl, a little orphan [who was placed with Pichler six months ago for care and supervision, is not well provided there; and Pichler himself has asked me to take her away. It seems that his wife, in his absence, has treated the poor child, which is suffering both in mind and body, in a most un-Christian manner which has caused the disapproval of the neighbors and others. For the time being,] we shall place [her] with Brandner, as both he and his wife share an honest and Christian spirit, until such time as a separate hut can be built for these poor children. The complaints in this respect have increased, and it will thus be necessary to start upon this plan as soon as possible, in particular as other causes related to the spiritual and material well being of these children and of the entire community urgently require the provision of such a house.

The aforesaid girl is among those being prepared for Holy Communion, and it appears that the Lord's word is blessed in her. We have heard her sing with much application; and she is often found engaged in prayer and in reading the Bible, in which occupation, [however, Pichler's wife is said to have more disturbed than encouraged her.] N. N. [The Zettler boy] was placed in the care of Kalcher some while ago, and he is well provided for there both spiritually and physically. Both the man and his wife hold him to prayer and the Lord's word and instruct him in his work. However, for some weeks now he has been spiteful and disobedient; and he may have thought to persuade me in this manner to give him freedom to live in his own hut, and thus without supervision, as some other young Salzburgers are doing. As he is not capable of controlling himself and hence would soon be in jeopardy in every respect, he cannot be given his way; I have therefore talked quite seriously with him and threatened to discipline him should he prove intractable.

Thursday, the 12th of May. [NB.] This morning some people from Savannah came here who also are on their way to Savannah-Town so as to build a new town and fortress in this colony, almost directly opposite from the Swiss who passed here some while ago. R. and R. [Stephan Riedelsperger and Michael Rieser], who recently went into service with Mrs. Mosgrove, are now tired of their work and life there and have let themselves been talked into joining these people on their voyage and want to work for them, against a consideration, for half a year. I seriously entreated poor R. [Riedelsperger] to reconsider, for I know full well that he is on a disastrous course, but he was defiant; and I fear that he is losing his Christian faith. R. and B. [Rheinlaender and Bach, two useless fellows], travelled with the last group of Swiss; we shall learn whether they will actually wish to move to their settlement. It seems clear that those who are still under the power of the flesh will reveal themselves.

I sincerely hope that God in his wisdom and mercy will bring everything to a good end, although matters are in a bad and miserable state as regards our physical sustenance and the land here. The song: "Shall I not praise my Lord in song,"[72] etc., gives us this message of comfort: "When the winter's snows have ended, beautiful summer will gladden our hearts, and thus pain will be relieved by joy, *for those who shall have the patience to wait.*" While our restless, wicked nature cannot bear this simple and trusting waiting for the Lord, we must remember that everything in the Bible teaches us that our dear Lord demands our patience for the fulfillment of His promise, and thus He will not change matters for our sake only. The corn looks poorly on some cleared lots where the ground is only somewhat sandy, and the owners of the land are about to lose all their courage.

Friday, the 13th of May, NB. NB. We have now embarked, in the name of the loving and almighty Lord, on the building to be erected for our poor children; and the people are quite glad that they will thus have a chance to earn some money in our community to alleviate their want. First, the stipulated place shall be guarded with a well-built fence so that some garden plants can be raised this year for the sustenance of the children, and it would be a pity if such planting should only be started after the planting season has passed. The lot has been surveyed in general only; we do not yet know the actual location of the roomy hut which will be erected, but we hope to be instructed shortly in this respect. May God accept this project and bless it.

This week it has rained constantly by night and by day, which is good for those whose land is high and dry. Those whose land lies in the lower portions will have to wait until the weather changes. In addition, it is quite cool and we will have to watch for our health.

Saturday, the 14th of May. [NB. NB.] Among the Swiss who passed here a week ago on their way to Savannah-Town, where they will settle, are several close relatives of the widow Helffenstein. They have tried to persuade her to join them, for she would have many occasions to find a living with them by sewing and similar female occupations. The governor of the Swiss, a fellow named Dobbler[73] who had also passed through here, equally offered to provide for her accommodations and well-being. She told me of the matter today, assuring me that she had no intention whatever to accept such a proposal, unless she should find it impossible to provide for herself and her family here. She added that she fully trusted God's will in this respect. She remembered her late husband on this occasion and told me many edifying instances connected with his illness and final leave-taking. Her oldest daughter is among those now being prepared for Holy Communion, and the mother spoke well of her industrious prayers and her good conduct at home.

The translation of the printed news concerning the spiritual and material condition of our Salzburgers has now been put in final form and will be sent to Mr. Causton at the earliest opportunity. In my accompanying letter I have mentioned that the document showed how almost everybody in Germany wishes our Salzburgers well and that our benefactors in particular hope that the generous care exercised by Mr. Oglethorpe on our behalf will ensure them such land as will permit them to gain their sustenance, which doubtless will redound to the honor of the Lord and the great fame of the Honorable Trustees. I also advised him that the document would show that his (Mr. Causton's) disposition and affection toward us were well-known in Germany and much appreciated by our friends.

I begged him to continue in this attitude and speak on our behalf to Mr. Oglethorpe so that the latter might order that land suitable for farming be allotted to the Salzburgers. I could say with certainty that our people are well aware of the fact that the tract of good land extending from our settlement to the so-called Indian Hut[74] is quite narrow and also that a large part of said land was still unsurveyed and thus left to lie idle, because the surveyor has orders to leave out 200 feet along each body of water on which canoes or some other small Indian boat could travel. Since the surveying lines have to run straight while the river's course is winding, many pieces of land will have to be left out (as was the case when the gardens were surveyed) and the Salzburgers will therefore be forced to accept useless land, a matter which is bound to have evil consequences. Our people have expressed the desire, I continued, for him to come here personally and inspect the cleared and planted fields, so that he might clearly recognize the difference between good and bad land and not take amiss our complaints about bad land and fruitless labor. The poor people would be content with ten or twelve acres of good land, and the rest could be as circumstances dictate. For, in the future, they might be able to improve such land with manure or compost, which at this time is quite impossible.

Sunday, the 15th of May. Next week we intend to celebrate Holy Communion; and those who desire to participate were asked to inscribe their names after the morning service. We prayed with them after a brief sermon. Those who neglect and ignore the means to salvation for their temporal desires, such as R. B. R. and R. [Rheinlaender, Bach, Michael Rieser, and Stephan Riedelsperger], shall regret their conduct soon enough, for on this path they shall certainly not find the material blessings which they so desire. Honest people would rather undergo the worst privations than forego the treasure of the gospels and of the Holy Sacraments, particularly for such a long time. In the private evening meeting I shall read from the news concerning the Lord's blessed footsteps in the matter of the orphanage at Halle, which will give me an opportunity to cheer our people by such evident examples of the paternal wisdom and care of the living Lord and thereby to encourage them to trust in His help in our miserable circumstances. Some of our community have themselves read the aforesaid book, which we had lent to them, and have been much edified thereby, as they have assured me.

Monday, the 16th of May. N. N. [Mrs. Rheinlaender] came to announce her intention of taking Holy Communion, as she had been prevented from attending services yesterday. She conducted herself quite seriously, shed her tears and, with many promises, begged my forgivance for the many un-Christian things for which she had to be punished and which had caused us much suffering. She feels that it was unjust to deny the presence of all spiritual good in her soul, as if she had not even taken the first step toward salvation. Should she attempt to prove, in fact and by a Christian life, that which she assured me her heart had experienced, I would be truly glad of it and praise the Lord. It is truly very difficult to convince a person from God's word such that he will truly believe (not only so as to please others or because religious principles require it) that Adam's fall has entirely corrupted man's nature and being[75] and thus demands a rebirth from the heavens.

Tuesday, the 17th of May. Some time ago Zettler was placed with Kalcher for supervision and care so that the latter might hold him to work and good conduct, but he has recently shown himself so obstinate and difficult that there is little we can now do for him here. I shall, therefore, try to place him with Hans Maurer, although, while his improvement in new circumstances is to be hoped for, it can hardly be expected. He deceives himself that I mistreat him by refusing to let him live and keep house for himself, as other unmarried people do. It is quite obvious that he would become a most disorderly person if he were given his will and desire. I have tried to persuade him again with much love; and I warned him in advance that sterner measures would have to be taken with him if he should again prove obstinate and wicked.]

Wednesday, the 18th of May. I was visited by three men from Purysburg who have worked for several months in Old Ebenezer and would have returned home with our boat, which left for Savannah yesterday morning to fetch provisions, had they not come too late. [It appears that these Swiss are badly off both spiritually and in material ways; and, unless they can receive true and effective help, they will have to remain beggars and use up their strength working for strangers.] While our people here also suffer much misery, they do enjoy many advantages; and it would thus be truly sinful if they were to count these for little. When we hear with our ears and see with our own eyes the fate of those who do not belong to our community and consequently to this colony, we feel it necessary to impress on our listeners the difference between their circumstances and those of other people. I gave a Bible and Arnd's *True Christianity* to these three men, for they told me of having lost all their books in Holland. They would also have liked to take some hymnals with them, but we are short of these and cannot spare any.

A father came to me with tears in his eyes and told me that his son had been accused of a misdeed, which he is said by the Salzburger in question to have committed while still in Old Ebenezer. Both the father and mother were much upset by this. They had severely disciplined the boy; but he could not be moved to confess to the deed, and I was asked for my advice on how to proceed further. I promised to have the boy brought to me as soon as current business would permit it and to question him in this matter, with God's help. I spoke to his heart as much as was in my power, for which I relied on the sweet gospel, which has a peculiar power to soften the heart, but also made him read some passages from Acts 5 and the saying in Proverbs 28:13. He wept bitterly throughout our talk, but he could not be moved to confess his sins. I prayed with him and sent him home for the time being, admonishing him to reflect carefully on his life and ponder the aforementioned saying: "He who covereth his sins shall not prosper, etc."

I have talked to the Salzburger who knows of this matter; and he has assured me that he had met the boy on his sinful path. He regretted not having talked about the matter at an earlier date, so that the boy might have been convinced. This matter has persuaded me again to see to it that those of the schoolchildren who are orphans or strangers be placed under strict supervision, for it was said that an orphan had taken part in the sin in question. Those of our people who are in charge of such children must attend to their work during the day, so that outside of their school hours they are alone and tend to stray around.

Thursday, the 19th of May. [NB. NB.] At this time I shall

admit to the Lord's table only four young girls who show clear sign of a true and good beginning in the Christian faith. I have learned that they pray sincerely when alone and join each other in prayer or come to me jointly for this purpose. The other four children who have been included in the preparation until now will have to wait for the next time, which will give us more of an opportunity to work with them. [The two boys among them, Zettler and Balthasar Rieser, are not worth much at this point, though I place more hope in the latter than in the former.]

[NB.]

For some of us, this Ascension Day has been a new day of blessing and salvation, on which our dear Savior in His great kindness has been able to do much good by the revelation of His word. Prior to repetition the married couples and unmarried women came to me; and I tried to awaken their spirits, on the basis of Colossians 3:1-2 and Acts 4:31-32, to the matter which is essential in our Christian belief and also in the preparation for Holy Communion. We then bent our knees before our Lord, and some of those among them who eagerly seek salvation shed copious tears. It would seem that Kieffer's two daughters from Purysburg show much obedience to the gospels; and, if they will let themselves be truly grounded in the faith and in what is good, they will be as salt and light in their parent's house.

Friday, the 20th of May. Kieffer of Purysburg and his wife have arrived here on our boat, which had fetched molasses from Savannah, so as to join us in Holy Communion this coming Sunday, which is particularly appropriate since two of his daughters shall be admitted to the Lord's table for the first time, after they are confirmed . . .

Inasmuch as Mrs. Rheinlaender has not revealed any sign of even the beginning of redemption, but rather the contrary, I had again asked her to come to my house to speak to her of the state of her soul and to convince her of some offences that have only recently come to my attention. However, as before, my words seemed only to pour oil into the flames and created in her such a terrible rage that I again became the subject of much brutal accusation and insult. She cried much at the malice of others, cleverly excused all her misdeeds, and denied all of them, in some cases against all evidence.

I cannot admit her to Holy Communion in this abominable

state; and she has again earnestly resolved to move away from here so as to find what she desires, both spiritually and materially, at some other place.

They had met many preachers all over the world, she claimed; but none had treated her as we had, in particular I, at which point she had the effrontery to call me her worst enemy, adding that, if I could throw her into utter perdition, I would surely not hesitate. And this despite the fact that the entire community, particularly those who are always with us, know full well from their own experience what good we have done her and her family in the sole desire to pave the way so that we might work with their souls and prevent all suspicion and ill will when we are forced to remonstrate with them seriously. However, all effort is for nothing in this matter. The neighbors have much trouble with this obstreperous bunch.

[Saturday, the 21st of May. This morning a captain came to ask me whether I would object if two of our men were to take service with him for six months to work on the small fortification which is to be built above Savannah-Town.[76] Both men, Rauner and Leitner, came to see me and tell me of the plans; they claim that they are driven to this course, the one because of his useless land, which is now flooded by the heavy rains, and the other, Rauner, by the extreme need of his family, which lacks both food and clothing. Two other men, Muggitzer and Bruckner, have left to go into service with Mr. Causton. These are in addition to the four men of whom I wrote under the 15th of May. They are all people in whom there is little, if any, good. Honest Salzburgers need much motivation to leave our place. Nonetheless, the continuing privation will not be without consequence, particularly if matters should get worse.

[NB.] Sunday, the 22nd of May. This morning four young girls, two from Purysburg and two from our community, have joined the others in Holy Communion. As is customary, they were first examined in the catechism and then formally confirmed in their baptismal compact. I based my examination on the questions at the end of our catechism, which are of great importance if properly evaluated. As the examination and the entire act of confirmation required much time, the text for Sunday, which is ordinarily explained in the morning service, was taken up in the afternoon. By God's grace, the entire ceremony was so conducted that it made an edifying and deep impression, not only on the four aforesaid children, but also the entire parish, all members of which were present. Our gracious Lord has certainly started his work with these children; and, if they will watch over themselves and seek to gain strength from the Lord's wounds for growth and constancy (as we have always seriously admonished both old and young), we may hope to gain a rich harvest of godliness in them.

About an hour after the afternoon service I started out to visit a married couple. When I did not find them at home, but heard that the woman had gone to see another woman who also loves her Savior dearly, I went to meet them at her house. However, I met both of them of the road, sitting on a fallen tree and discussing the state of their souls. One of them was crying bitterly; and, when I inquired into the reason, she said that the dear Savior would surely lose His patience with her; He had always taken pity on her, and even yesterday had given her His comfort, but she was aware of the imperfections that were still in her and, since this would not change, she was convinced that the dear Savior would lose His patience and finally reject her.

I talked to them seriously and tried to show them that all children of the Lord suffer such doubts and that they should continue in their faith even though this would mean a continuing struggle. We finally encouraged each other to use the time for prayer and thereby fill our souls with the Holy Spirit, who would lead us to the truth and comfort us and bear witness in our souls of Christ our Savior.

In the evening some hungry and thirsty souls came to us in our hut, and we sang together and rejoiced in the preparation of the holy feast of Whitsun on the basis of the text of the late Prof. Francke on Revelations 22:17. Finally, we prayed with each other in the manner in which we were instructed; and this caused a great revival in our souls.

Monday, the 23rd of May to Thursday, the 26th. The condition and circumstances of our community have again required me to travel to Savannah. Mr. Causton again showed much love to me and our people; and, if it were but possible, he would gladly help us out in our need with whatever is necessary. There is such a dearth of money and provisions in Savannah as has never before been experienced by the people there. God in His wisdom arranged for the arrival of a sloop from New York laden with meat and flour, while we were there; and I was given some of these provisions to carry home.

A man from Purysburg asked me to accept his eight-year

old son for schooling and care. However, with provisions quite scarce and little actual means for proper supervision and care being available, I had to refuse his request. He himself is not in a position to provide for the child here. Kieffer of Purysburg had to take home all his children because he no longer could afford to furnish food and provisions for them, but he would have much preferred to leave the two smallest girls here. Once God provides again, he intends to send us not only the youngest children but also his oldest daughter. He has seen how much has been learned in a short time, with the grace of God, by his two other daughters, who went to school here and were prepared for Holy Communion. Reck, the cobbler in Purysburg, has asked me to intercede on his behalf with Mr. Causton, so that he may be allotted a place to live in our village, for he would like to move here. However, I shall not waste a word on his behalf, for his is a most disorderly life.[77]

Friday the 27th of May. Our people have recently lost a number of pigs and have only now noticed that the source of our trouble has been a large bear that is roaming close to our village. He was observed killing a pig yesterday, but it was impossible to shoot him then. There are many bears in this country, and the Indians and others hunt them. Since these bears are usually quite fat, their rendered grease is often used not just for greasing and lubricating but, instead of olive oil, for preparing salads.

We have had a pleasant and cool spring until recently, but now the heat has become quite bad during the day. In previous years we had numerous heavy thunderstorms at this time and even earlier; but we have not had any this year.

Saturday, the 28th of May. A few of our people cause me much grief with their improper conduct and render the burden of the many material matters in my charge even heavier. If I cannot agree with their importunate demands and sometimes must even speak quite seriously to them, they become embittered; and this makes it even more difficult to bring God's word to them. Last night, before the evening prayer hour, I had another example of this difficulty, which caused me to keep the men with me after the prayer hour. I told them my opinion in this respect and said that, for the reasons mentioned, it would be impossible for me to take care of the provisions and other material matters any longer than, at most, until the arrival of Mr. Oglethorpe and that I would

therefore advise those among them who could to pray warmly
that God might send them a magistrate and store-house manager who would serve their purposes, etc.[78] My presentation
caused much grief among the more honest members of our
community, as I have learned today, and four men came to
speak to me on behalf of the parish to ask me to change my
mind.

I shall convoke the community after the holidays to talk
more specifically on this matter. I would not mind the work
and the many worries which such tasks bring with them, were
it not for the interference which they cause, if only by accident,
with the spreading of the gospel and the blessed execution
of my spiritual office. To be sure, many urgent matters have
to be taken care of and there is far too much want, which may
admittedly get much worse if a stranger were to be sent here
as store-house manager and general supervisor. May God
have mercy on us in this pressing need and bestow on us the
wisdom and His blessing so that we may only recognize and
execute His will.

A man has confided in me that he is little troubled by material wants and is only concerned with recognizing his Savior
and increasing his faith. He continued that in recent days God
has bestowed on him much joy and happiness in his prayers.
Upon going to bed and preparing for sleep after these experiences, he was convinced that his heart and soul would be more
than usually filled with nothing but sweet and pleasant
thoughts of our Lord Jesus. However, the very opposite has
been the case, and this has taught him that he should place
his confidence in prayers alone but that, like a miserable
worm, he should continue to bend his knee before the Lord,
in the name of His son.

Sunday, the 29th of May, the feast of Whitsun. Both yesterday during our preparation and today, on His lovely feast of
the Holy Spirit, our dear Father has given us much edification
through His word. Last night, prior to the repetition, something happened that almost spoiled my joyous mood on the
occasion of Whitsun; but I shall consider it as a lesson from
which I will have to benefit.

[In short, the schoolmaster Ortmann sent me, through one
of the schoolchildren, a long rambling letter in English, running over two full pages, in which he went to great lengths
to complain of my behavior toward himself and particularly
toward his wife. He not only repeated, as he has often done

before, old and forgotten matters relating to our sea voyage and the period subsequent thereto, but let himself go with the most brutal and defamatory accusations against my person and my office. He uses these deceitful and quite unfounded charges, many of which are out of context and quite wilfull, as an excuse for his own and his wife's refusal to go to the Lord's table, a matter of which I had in the kindest possible manner reminded him recently at his house, when I tried to impress on him the scandal caused in our community by his negligence in this respect, considering his office as schoolmaster. It would go too far to insert the contents of this miserable letter here: nonetheless, my conscience forces me to take the next opportunity to forward it to the royal chaplain, Mr. Ziegenhagen.

[I had taken the opportunity during our recent meeting to impress on Ortmann that he should not permit his wife to set up quarters again for passing Englishmen, bearing in mind the inconvenience, scandal, affront, and serious consequences it had caused in Old Ebenezer and how ill this conduct had been received by Mr. Causton and our benefactors, etc. I demonstrated to him the objectionable and suspicious impression left by the fact that his wife had stayed away from church throughout the entire Sunday of Rogate and instead, while the morning and afternoon services were conducted, had entertained a young Englishman of quite horrible reputation in their hut. I also added that our people were quite shocked by his constant reading of the English Bible during our sermons, etc. At the time it seemed that he had not taken any offence at my friendly remonstrations (and I know that he can put on a friendly mien if he so pleases); but he has now fully revealed his mind and soul, which are full not only of great simplicity and lack of understanding, but of a deep-rooted wickedness. Being so deeply prejudiced against my dear colleague and myself, he will hardly be amenable to reason, and I fear for both his and her souls.

Monday, the 30th of May. I had wanted to visit some of our young people; but wherever I went only a few were at home, whereas the others had largely gone out in the pursuit of material and outward matters. Considering that much damage can be caused by such behavior, particularly with regard to the Lord's word as publicly read, I took this point up in our repetition and reminded them of the duties incumbent upon parents, married couples, and other listeners when returning from public worship.

A Salzburger woman was much worried about her children, who do not seem to be doing as well as they should; and she felt guilty for their behavior, thinking that it was due to her lack of supervision, remonstration, and prayer. She also complained of her husband's leaving the care for the children more to her than taking their well-being as his responsibility; and she added that, whenever she reminded him of his omissions and of the heavy burden which this failure in his duties might impose on him in the future, he was ill prepared to accept her criticism. She asked me with tears in her eyes not to fail to bring to her and her family's attention all matters to which I might take objection.

While this holiday has surely been marked by many unpleasant and sad occurrences, there has also been no lack of joyful and rewarding experiences, which have strengthened our hearts. Firstly, the Lord has refreshed us with His sweet word and given us many blessings on this feast of the Holy Spirit; also, He has awakened and edified many of those in our community, as we have been told by several of our listeners.

When we go to the houses of the Salzburgers after the sermon and inquire into the state of their souls, we learn many things that are of much importance to us. Occasionally, we realize that they have failed to understand this or that part of our sermon or have applied it incorrectly, or they are convinced that they have not yet reached that state where those glorious promises will come true for them but rather they would have to reach yet another stage in their Christian beliefs. In such cases we can help them by our instructions and advice, which constitutes a great help and unburdens their spirits. They are also very fond of singing and praying with us, and it is often very helpful to repeat the Lord's word in our prayers to Him. It gives us much pleasure to participate in such meetings, for there we find only such souls as are exclusively concerned with finding edification and gaining an ever better understanding of their sweet Jesus. Praised be the Lord, therefore, that He has not refused us His mercy during these days; may He teach us every day truly to celebrate the feast of the Holy Spirit and constantly to drink from Christ, our living source, which yields the water of life.

Tuesday, the 31st of May. Last night, during our repetition, when speaking on the words in the gospels: "Men loved darkness rather than light," etc.,[79] I felt constrained to mention to my listeners the matters that befall us in the execution of our office. I told them that many of them could not stand the truth and that, when we felt it our duty not to leave them to their wrongheaded and unenlightened opinions, they would become hostile and treat us quite irresponsibly.

[In this connection, I could not but mention the letter which the schoolmaster, Ortmann, had sent me on the first day of Whitsun, Hōs en Parōdía[80], although I took care to speak of it in such a fashion as to hide its author's name. This morning the schoolmaster came to see me, quite embarrassed by his letter, and tried to make me believe that he had written it in a fit of melancholy and scruple. He was much aggrieved that his wife should have been so blamed and accused, for she was truly a woman of good disposition. However, he was sorry for his conduct; and he asked me for my pardon, adding that Christ our Lord had also been maligned and persecuted but had forgiven and suffered, etc. I asked him to explain the worst parts of his letter and give me proof of his accusations, but his attempts were quite miserable. I have again asked both him and his wife, with much love and sincerity, to see the evil of their ways and to make amends therefor, so that God might forgive him for this and other sins.

For my part, I would gladly forgive him that which he had perpetrated against me and, in particular, my office. The poor man and his wife are much prejudiced, not only against me and my dear colleague, but against all of the Salzburgers here, although everything possible has been done for him. He had been given two acres for garden land, which was cleaned of trees and bushes by the joint effort of our Salzburgers; and, since he was not content with that but insisted on also having land for his wife's garden (claiming that she had been promised land in her name in the case of his death), I had recently ceded him my own garden plot, which has also been cleared. But none of this is to any avail, and he is content neither with us nor with the Salzburgers. He has not even been able to plant his own garden but has assigned half of it to the watch-maker,[81] as I have just learned. He would never have done this for any of our Salzburgers, although it was they who cleared and prepared the land for him. We have done this and other things for such ungrateful people, if only to shut their loose mouths with gifts and favors. They do not know how to man-age their households or to husband their resources, and there-fore they will never have enough, even if there were more cleared land for them.]

N. [The shoemaker's wife, Mrs. Arnsdorff], and her family[82] live in much poverty, but she never complains. Instead, she thanks the Lord that He has led her and her kin to this place and has helped them through all their trials and has given them edification in His words. She has confided in me a few of her thoughts and special circumstances, which clearly show me her living faith and confident belief in God's paternal help. There are several women in our community who would offend the eye of the Lord; but of them the Ortmann and Rhein-laender women are the very worst, and they continue to deteriorate.

JUNE

Wednesday, the 1st of June. Late last evening I was again visited by a number of souls eager for their salvation, who wished to pray and be uplifted by the Lord's word. As is often the case at such meetings, we entertained each other with great simplicity of heart and mind; but it has pleased the Lord so to bless this brief hour that we were all awakened to the Lord's praise, and my flock took leave from me with much pleasure and many expressions of gratitude. Those in our community who are not like these simple lambs of our Lord Jesus but think it enough to attend the public services in church will hardly equal their serious understanding of the Christian faith. We do every-thing in our power for our parishioners so as to contribute to their salvation, and the Lord has indeed not withheld His bless-ing from some of our efforts.

While there are many among our flock who are ungrateful, spiteful, and quite hypocritical, and who in many ways render our life difficult and unduly burden our office, there is also no lack of honest souls among us, praised be the Lord, who faith-fully follow our Lord Jesus and show their belief by shedding their sins by virtue of the grace bestowed on them. It is for their sake that we continue to carry the burden of managing the material affairs of our community. [If these were to be handled by a godless administrator, the wicked among us would soon gain power and render the lot of the believers much harder. Now, however, they dare not raise their heads, although they spread much malicious gossip about us, if secretly rather than in public. Ortmann, the schoolmaster, will not admit to the presence of honest and pious men among us; just as he holds me to be, in his letter, a godless man unworthy of the task of preaching the gospel, so there cannot be any but godless men among my flock, whose side I am accused of taking.]

Thursday, the 2nd of June. For the last few days rains and

thunderstorms have threatened, but they have always passed over us. The recent beneficial period of rains has been followed by very hot days, and the land is much in need of rain. In some of the fields where the corn had at first done very poorly, it has now caught up and is continuing to grow rapidly, much to the joy of our people.

My physical health and my circumstances and tasks make it impossible at this point to spend more than one hour on teaching and informing the children. God will give me the strength and the time that will permit me to resume this pleasant work with greater energy. My dear colleague is fully occupied with his schoolwork, inasmuch as we cannot use the schoolmaster for anything else but teaching spelling and reading to the small children. In this he has so far proved his industry and application as much as his power and gifts permit him.

Friday, the 3rd of June. At present Mr. Causton is sending the third transport the same amount of provisions as was formerly allotted to the first transport. He would send more if it were not for the exceeding scarcity of supplies even in the store-house in Savannah. Last night I received molasses, vinegar, and flour, which I distributed very early this morning and also after lunch. [Since the accounts for the first and second transports' provisions have not yet been audited, despite constant reminders to this effect, these two groups are suffering much want. It is without question that Mr. Causton owes several sums to our people, in part for harvested produce and grain, in accordance with Mr. Oglethorpe's instructions,[83] and also for miscellaneous work done by them. He has promised to pay in provisions as soon as the bills have been audited. No doubt this difficult and confusing task will fall on me; because he will do nothing but advise me of the entire sum that our people are entitled to, leaving me with the job of satisfying all demands on the basis of the work done by each man and considering the provisions already received as well as other items distributed from the store house.]

The surveyor, Ross, who contrary to Mr. Oglethorpe's instructions has failed to survey our land until now, has now written me from Purysburg, excusing his long delay with the threatening Spanish war and stating that he is now prepared to come if we so wish. However, I shall instruct him to get new orders for surveying, inasmuch as his instructions were valid only until the first day of this past month of May. Having waited for so long, our people can now well afford to wait until the arrival of Mr. Oglethorpe, who is expected shortly. It is possible that we may even receive welcome news from the Lord Trustees or the Honorable Society concerning the good land across the Ebenezer River.

Saturday, the 4th of June. Last night I considered it advisable to cancel the usual evening prayer hour in favor of a meeting, in which I was again forced to take up the conduct of some spiteful people against me in regard to our material situation. I impressed on them the good will which our benefactors had shown in refraining from setting an outside administrator over them but instead imposing on me and my dear colleague the additional burden of discharging such matters as are necessary for the maintenance of order and proper management. They knew full well the benefits that had accrued to them by this arrangement. However, because some among them were full of suspicion and were making contradictory and rebellious statements in their anger and sufficiently demonstrating their ill will, dissatisfaction, and disobedience so as to render our life miserable and impeding our task of working on their souls with God's word, I pleaded with them again to see to it that some solution were found in this matter. For, if this improper and confusing situation were to continue unchecked, I had decided to relieve myself entirely of these unnecessary burdens. If, however, they were prepared to acquiesce in the order of things and be instructed by God's word, we would not refuse to continue carrying our burden. Such remonstrations usually have much effect on our flock, as I did not fail to notice. May God support us with the spirit of wisdom, good counsel, and strength so that everything shall work for His glory and our blessing.

Sunday, the 5th of June. Last night, during our prayer hour, a boat full of Swiss arrived here from Purysburg; they, too, are travelling to their settlement near Savannah-Town. They have spent the day here to attend divine services and were put up with some of our Salzburgers; they have been as well-treated as our circumstances would permit. Who knows but that the Lord in His limitless wisdom has bestowed His blessing on them by His word as heard in the services. We spoke on the customary text for Trinity Sunday, from John 3, treating of the only and correct way to salvation and glory. In our repetition we read from the life of a burgomaster in Erfurt, as chronicled by the deceased Dr. Joch, and thus illustrated and supported the important reading from the gospel with this exceptional example, which clearly demonstrates both the wrong, independent way of self-sufficient justice and piety and the true path of full conversion.[84]

[Inasmuch as I have learned that Pichler intends to travel with these Swiss tomorrow and help them transport their belongings to their destination, and having noticed a number of instances which do not conform to his pretended Christian faith and condition, I asked him to visit me this evening; for I wished to call these matters to his attention. However, I have observed an obvious decline in the good ways which he once recognized and pretended to have made his own. He insists on having chosen the right path in his dishonest ways and in his concerns with matters of the flesh, and I can only look upon him with pity. It must be said that his unreformed and selfish wife bears much of the blame. At this time of trials and need, many will become revealed to the bottom of their evil hearts. However, in all truth it must be said that there are also true children of the Lord among us.]

Monday, the 6th of June. I have visited N. N. [the Kalchers], who have much refreshed me with their Christian talk. Yesterday's sermon has left her in a state of great and heartfelt sadness, which, however, has the sole purpose of cleansing her of all remaining earthly faults and leading her to the true state of blessedness.

[Today, Pichler and his wife have so sinned against me and my office that those who did not hear and see us here would find it hard to believe. The following occasion gave rise to this outrage: Not only his wife but he too had sold something to the English at a price far in excess of that demanded by the rules of common decency. But that was not all: he received flour instead of money in Savannah and has sold it here to our poor people for a higher price than that for which he received it; and this has caused much ill will with those who knew of this matter. Furthermore, this Pichler is willing to accompany the Swiss to Savannah-Town, and he is making the poor people pay him for this service at the same high rates as the English demand, if not higher. We, who so richly benefit from God's word, should neither in this nor in other matters act as others who have only earthly concerns.

[And, as far as his forthcoming voyage is concerned, he should not ask for high pay but rather serve these people with love and brotherly generosity, for it is God's will that poor strangers should be thus treated; and, inasmuch as the Salzburgers have received everything for nothing and been given much, it is God's demand that they should show their gratitude in their treatment of their poor brethren. I admonished him to examine carefully his selfish behavior (for thus I had to call it) and include other Christian people in his plans. If he should find that he could keep a clear conscience, I would be only too content, etc. Instead of accepting my words in the spirit of love, he grew full of suspicion against me and some others and flew into a shocking rage and uttered many insults. He has now turned both the Swiss and those to whom he sold his flour against me, and both he and his wife have revealed themselves to our community in their selfish and unredeemed state.

[After both had dealt me what should have been a full measure of sin and insult for this day, God in His wisdom ordained that his wife should utter such horrendous and frightening words against me and my office, in the presence of several pious Christian as well as of some wicked people, that even her husband grew utterly confused and administered a timely punishment. The men in question soon afterwards met in the house of their leader and asked Pichler to come there; they called his wife's wickedness to his mind and told him that their conscience demanded the revelation of these occurrences. Pichler recognized that I would have to be informed, and he tried to persuade his wife to come to me, together with Pichler himself, to show their remorse. However, all was in vain. We conducted an evening prayer hour which was directed, without my prior knowledge of this matter, against the very existence of these sad but heretofore hidden circumstances, and in the course of which Pichler, as he later confessed, was led to greater reflection on and recognition of his wrongs.

After the prayer meeting I was informed of the aforementioned calumny, and I sent for Pichler so as to take this matter up with him. He was much aggrieved by this affair and could not but assume but that I would inform Mr. Causton of it. I told him that the present matter worried me much less than what had passed before; because from it I recognized the Lord as a holy, wondrous God who, in His great justice, had thus let the woman fall into her own trap in such a manner that now everyone realizes her wickedness and is much shocked by it. I also told him that I had heard that she had given the malicious Mrs. Spielbiegler occasion for slanderous remarks, which reflected badly on her. I pitied her poor soul; for, as she could not in any way be moved to true recognition, remorse, and satisfaction for this affront, she *eo ipso* excluded herself not only from Holy Communion but from all other privileges bestowed on true Christians. I am not yet quite certain in my mind whether I should reveal this matter to Mr. Causton. I would prefer it if the woman could be made to improve her conduct without it. Her husband will depart tomorrow morning with the Swiss, and his wife will not be pleased by this.

Tuesday, the 7th of June. As I had heard that Mrs. Ortmann is again using her libelous and untruthful tongue against me from time to time among our community and also boasts of the previously mentioned letter her husband wrote to me, in which, as she claims, he did not hesitate to let me know the truth, I made the schoolmaster come to me this morning. However, he did not conduct himself as humbly as on the last occasion, but spoke so bluntly and spitefully that a schoolmaster could hardly address his minister thus. He was in quite a temper; and it was impossible to speak with him in a reasonable, let alone Christian, manner. After he had given vent to his wickedness, he left me without taking leave and without having given me a chance to say anything. His old soldier's mind is now even more clearly revealed than before.[85]

[Ortmann recently had someone bring him two barrels of flour from Savannah at one time; and, since his wife, as is her habit, did not economize with it (a fact of which the neighbors are well aware), she has, now that the flour is almost exhausted, claimed that during a prayer meeting somebody had broken into their hut and taken about 50 pounds of flour and some soap; and her poor husband must believe what she says. She did the same thing when their belongings were still stored in Aberkorn, and she cried about theft and robbery although it had been she who had taken articles from their boxes and sold them in Savannah.]

Wednesday, the 8th of June. I have visited a few people, who, I knew, were in need of spiritual help and advice in their prayers. I found a few dear souls, whom the Lord is purifying in secret by hidden trials, in one of the huts, where they were sighing not only about their own perdition but also about the matters that had transpired in our community. We spent an edifying half hour together. May the Lord be praised for His inexpressible mercy in that he so reveals their perdition to some of our listeners that, while they may be deeply bowed down and grieving, they are bowed down and grieving in a divine way and for the good of their souls. One of the women followed me from the house into the street and told me how the Lord had recently granted her such a certain knowledge of the forgiveness of her sins that she could not possibly attribute it to her imagination or hold it to be a self-fabricated consolation, whereas, since then, He had led her into such arid deserts of the soul that she could see nothing in herself but lack of faith and sin.

Because of this feeling of perdition she often wished to stay away altogether from the preaching of the gospel, since she felt unworthy of this precious blessing and, in view of her heavy sins, did not wish to impose her presence on the church and the other Christians there. During the sermon she often felt a strong inner urge to follow me right after the service and confess from the bottom of her heart all the sins she had committed since her youth, but she was afraid to burden me with such talk, etc. I recently spoke with her and inquired into her situation, and I told her of several other women in the community whom God was leading along many strange but blessed paths. I suggested that she join these women often for enlightening conversation and prayer. I have in general found that our dear Lord has splendidly blessed several souls from our recent sermon on the one and only true path to salvation, as well as the relevant examples which we presented in the repetition. However, some among us get no better as time goes on, which sadly affects not only us but our honest listeners, who therefore strongly help us in our prayers.

Thursday, the 9th of June. Last night Mr. Causton sent us a large bundle of letters, which had arrived with a boat from London. The content of these letters is most enjoyable; in particular the many edifying and cordial communications from our worthy benefactors in London and Germany have caused us to praise our Savior and have fortified our belief in the living God, as one who has looked graciously on our misery and also, as we have gathered, is willing to send us new help.

As we learn from the letter of Mr. Verelst, the comptroller, the Honorable Trustees have well received the presentations made by the royal Chaplain, Mr. Ziegenhagen, on the basis of our letters and diaries; and Mr. Causton has been instructed to assist the Salzburgers in their circumstances with true and substantial help. Furthermore, our dear benefactors in England and Germany have sent a number of substantial presents to us and the members of our community in the form of money, books, medicines, and other items necessary for housekeeping, of which we recognize ourselves as truly unworthy. At the same time, these gifts lead us to realize clearly the beneficent providence of our Heavenly Father, who has thus, contrary to our expectations and hopes, relieved much of our previous wants.

May He be praised for this in all eternity and may He instil in our hearts deep and honest gratefulness for Him and our dear benefactors. The Honorable Society[86] has again sent us a considerable quantity of good madeira wine for our use and that of the sick among us, for which, as well as for the other gifts and benefactions, may God repay them and return to our benefactors a thousandfold blessing!

Circumstances required my early departure this morning for Savannah, partly to speak to Mr. Causton concerning the letters received by us and partly to collect at least part of the articles which have arrived. Mr. Causton was much pleased by my arrival and informed me of having received favorable instructions, so that he hoped to render the Salzburgers happy in a short time. The accounts will be brought up to date shortly, and the Salzburgers will receive provisions until next September. He also is looking for a reliable surveyor, who will allot the land in the manner which we think fit and beneficial. He also informed me that the royal chaplain, Mr. Ziegenhagen, had addressed to him a very cordial letter, which had pleased Mr. Causton very much and of which we have received a copy by the hand of Mr. Ziegenhagen himself.

Friday, the 10th of June. As I had some time on my hands in Savannah, I went to visit Mr. Causton's plantation in the company of the preacher at Savannah, Mr. Wesley. This offered me an opportunity to comment on a number of matters on which he wished to be informed and enlightened: e.g., he was doubtful concerning a number of points in the journals by ourselves and Mr. von Reck, which have been printed in London;[87] and I attempted to explain these points to him on his insistence, without, however, being able or willing, to defend the statements made therein by Mr. von Reck. It would appear that the esteem he previously had for the N. N. [the Herrnhuters] has somewhat abated. Among other things he told me that, while he had not caught them in any untruth, he could not divine any truly felt and expressed honesty in them. Instead, they hesitated making a full basic revelation of their belief and, when he inquired into the meaning of their teachings, they would only refer to the Bible, which, he added, both old and new heretics are wont to do.

He was also not much pleased with a letter which he had received from a person [close to the Herrnhuters] in Germany, in which it had been argued that the time was approaching when a greater holiness and purity of Christian dogma and life would be established; whereas it was his (Mr. Wesley's) belief that the truly holy dogma and truly holy life was that which is described and presented in the writings of the prophets, evangelists, and the apostles of the Lord, and that no greater holiness and purity than that stated there could be expected in this life. [He also confirmed news I had previously heard, i.e., that the Herrnhuters now in Savannah intended to move to Pennsylvania in the fall. They complain that they suffer much at the hands of the English, and that they are hardly considered as Christians by them, etc.]

Saturday, the 11th of June. This noon I returned safe and sound to our dear Ebenezer and brought with me to everyone's joy a portion of material blessings which we have received from Europe. God willing, we shall send the boat back to Savannah next Monday for the remainder. May the Lord grant us mercy and wisdom to distribute the benefits received for the best of our community and in such a manner that the salutary purpose for which these gifts were intended may in fact materialize in all their recipients! I was somewhat weak from the voyage and the lack of sleep caused by it and therefore somewhat tired and incapacitated. Otherwise, I would have begun this evening to read to our congregation from the many edifying letters which we have received from England and Germany, as is my customary habit; for the good souls among us look forward to this with great anticipation. With God's blessing, I will make up for it partly tomorrow, during the repetition, and partly in the subsequent prayer hours.

Sunday, the 12th of June. Through a number of Christian people, our heavenly Father has bestowed a gift of money on dear Professor Francke for the benefit of some of our poor Salzburgers; and with it a supply of linen, which is very expensive here, has been purchased and sent to us as part of the recent shipment. It is our urgent desire that this blessing, as well as other gifts which have been sent here previously and now, may accrue to the benefit of our congregation not only in material respects but also for the spiritual purpose for which Christian gifts are intended. Therefore, today in my sermon on the regular gospel for the First Sunday after Trinity, I have thus taken the opportunity to show my listeners that they should be the Lord's true stewards of whatever He may give them in temporal goods and blessings, be they gifts for their bodies, minds, or souls, for fear of abusing temporal wealth, like the rich man in the gospel, and thus run the risk of eternal perdition.

After warning them against the spirit of material wealth, I admonished them to follow, in Christian contentedness, tranquility, and acquiescence in God's will, the example of Lazarus, who had asked only to still his hunger with the crumbs from the table of the rich man, which are otherwise thrown to the dogs. I then proceeded to inform them of the bountiful material gifts which the Lord, notwithstanding our lack of merit and worth, had again bestowed on us from London and Germany. I implored our honest listeners to help us pray that our dear Lord should give both of us wisdom to distribute these gifts, not according to our will, but according to His desire, and that the dear Lord might prevent all envy, suspicion, and discontent such as had not been lacking among us the previous time. For such behavior would act like a dam to the freely flowing river of God's blessing.

After the sermon I had heard someone remark that this admonition had been much needed. Some of the members of our community are of such nature that they have not been improved by the benefits which were given to them as well as to others. We have even come under judgment in the distribution of some former gifts, and I feel that it would not be against the wishes of our benefactors if we were to think first of all of those Salzburgers who are honest and praise the Lord for what they receive and pray for the Christian givers. Nevertheless, we do not intend to exclude the others, even those of a malicious mind; and we wish to wait for their repentance, or even the first beginning of such repentance, and we shall thus let them participate in our blessing with all the more joy. We shall retain some of our gifts for this purpose.

After the afternoon service, our schoolchildren edified me profoundly in my hut. Almost all of them came to my door and asked to be admonished. I first told them that a benefactor in Germany had sent presents for three children of whom he had been told, but that I would not give these gifts to them now but would keep them, as they had not continued in a consistent manner on the good path, etc.; and I therefore wished to wait for their improvement. I indicated what it was that pious persons in England and Germany wished of them, namely, that they might open their tender hearts to our Lord Jesus and that, if these people would hear such news, they would praise the Lord and give signs of their joy by new gifts. In this manner it would come to pass that the Lord's name should be praised through them also, as they had been catechised this afternoon on the first petition in our Lord's Prayer, which, to be sure, was a right angelic business.

Next I undertook to remind them, among other things, of what was told them this morning with regard to the lesson of the rich man who had used some of his temporal wealth vainly and to adorn himself with rich clothes. We had talked about this as a warning both to parents and children not to commit such a cruelty toward their children's souls as to tempt them, by clothes and other fancy furnishings and temporal goods, to become even more ensconced in pride and love of the world. I read some passages to the children, catechised them on their contents, and finally summarized these teachings in our prayer. When we had risen from prayer, I admonished them again to give their love not to the temporal world, but to their loving and deserving Savior; and, seeing that their minds were touched by my words, I asked them most lovingly whether there was not among them at least one child who would open his heart to Jesus and give himself to Him in the truth. That child should give me his hand as a sign of this promise and pronounce such love before the face of the Lord. This request caused much emotion and tears, as I sought to move their hearts further with gentle urgings and inducements.

B. [Bacher's] oldest daughter was the first to offer me her hand with a pleasant and charming gesture and to promise her sincere love solely to the Lord Jesus. I reminded her in the presence of all other children, who were generally standing about in the room crying, that she had made many previous promises and good resolutions; and I reminded her that God had wished to work on her soul by means of dreams, which touched upon the content of today's readings from the gospels, and to move her from the love of the world to the love of the most beloved son of God and man. There was no child present who would not dedicate himself by word and thought to our Lord Jesus. Oh! If this would only become truth, and if only their parents and the other people around them would watch over them! How beautiful are the words in Isaiah 44:3–5. [So as to ensure their continued revival, I gave them five copies of the printed life of Pastor Henning Kusen, which they might read at home and thus be led to read together.]

Instead of the repetition, I read to our congregation the edifying letter of our esteemed Senior Urslperger of the 7th of February and impressed on them his most tender love for us and his great concern with our temporal and spiritual well-being. Seeing that not only he, but also many other beloved servants of Christ are fervently praying for us, as the letter tells us, what a blessing this is (Luke 18:7–8);[88] and who would be so foolish as to forego such blessings by moving away or through some other action. The Honorable Senior acknowledges his pleasure that we have been able truthfully to report that we knew of no one here who was sorry at having been led by our Lord from the cities into this desert, for none of us would wish to exchange the spiritual and temporal advantages which we enjoy here for any others. This gave me a good opportunity to make some comparisons between the former attitudes of all our people and the present attitudes of some of our members, showing them that their Christian spirits had quite certainly regressed. The only point which does constitute a grievance is the lack of good land.

Discussing the request for a second continuation of the reports from Ebenezer, I impressed on them how the name of the Lord, and the honor of our King of Mercy, Jesus Christ, and the edification of our brethren might well be augmented if they would continue to bear their cross faithfully. For one thing is certain; the name of the Lord is honored not so much in pleasant days but rather, among us and for us, in the sign of the cross, a sanctification to which we are bound as baptized Christians, as shown in today's reading of Peter 1. Referring to the mention in the letter of the temporal gifts, some of which have arrived here and more of which will be sent here in the future by a prominent lady and her family in A [our dear Mrs. von Haesslin], who is well known among us for her dear and honest love of Jesus and his poor children, we took the occasion to impress our listeners with the providence of the Lord and to encourage them to gratefulness both toward our Father in heaven and to prayers on behalf of our benefactors.

On the way home we were joined by a pious Salzburger who wished in the presence of Mr. Gronau and myself, to thank the Lord for His overwhelming generosity. A few others felt sufficiently stirred to promise to write to Germany so as to express their gratitude. [There was one among them, however, who was much worried, since he had gathered from our reading of the letter that one among us had sent an uncouth and angry message (it was Mrs. Holzer); he was much concerned that he, too, had written but could not clearly remember the contents of his message and whether he too had made an inappropriate statement. The man was Ruprecht Steiner, an honest soul; and I

quite honestly could absolve him of such fears and urge him to
write. He would like to have his brother here.]

Monday, the 13th of June. I had learned that N. [Mrs. Rhein-
laender] was ill but could occasionally leave her house none the
less; I therefore sent word asking her to come and see me, since
I had reasons not to pass by at her house myself. I told her that
I had heard that she felt that her bodily strength was progres-
sively weakening, and that she did not expect to live much
longer. I enquired from her as to her feeling towards the Lord
and whether she felt she could stand before the throne of justice.
Her reply at first consisted more in tears than in words, and she
begged my forgiveness for having borne much animosity toward
me and having said many things against me whenever I had tried
to reveal to her the bottom of her heart. She had not understood
but had thought herself a good Christian for a long time, but
now she would only cry and pray that she might be led to the
true recognition of her sins and thus be prepared for eternal
salvation. She also agreed readily, as soon as I would like, to
reconcile herself in my room with the Salzburger with whom she
had recently quarreled, for in truth she held no grudge against
him in her heart.

The occasion for her being seriously concerned about her sins
was a dream that had come to her just before Whitsun: Satan
had appeared to her with a big chain and had come towards her;
she had tried to escape but found herself so deeply mired in the
filth of her sins that she could neither advance nor recede. As
soon as she had awakened from her dream, she had thrown
herself on her knees and cried for mercy and help from the Lord,
who had let her feel His strength in her heart. The following
Saturday, after the preparations for Whitsun, Mr. Gronau had
come to see her and told her what he recognized her to be. She
had failed to understand this at the time, but it was clear to her
now. She asked me for a book that would clearly show her the
way to recognition of her sins. I referred her to prayer and to
the first book of Johann Arndt's *True Christianity* and read her
its entire forty-first chapter. I took the occasion to repeat to her
my words during a recent evening prayer meeting, namely that,
for her repentance to be of the right kind, it should not lack true
humility before the Lord, as was the case for Pharaoh (Exodus
10: 3; cf. v 16, 17; 9:27). I explicated this to her with the example
of the publican.

I also recalled to her the merciful act of the Lord toward her
husband in Old Ebenezer, where He had spoken to his con-

science and humbled him for his sins, which she had not been able to accept, as she now realized herself. But her husband too had not remained faithful. I also prayed with her. May the Lord finally show the truth to her and her husband. [The latter went this morning with our dear colleague to Savannah to fetch our goods and money.] She told me that he had been moved to tears last night by the difficulties caused us by some of the people, whereas only good was being meant for them. God has led many of those among us to reflection and to the path of truth; He will also show mercy to the others. We shall tolerate them as long as the Lord will tolerate them. However much wrong and insult they may heap on us (and such has happened since Whitsun), we shall bear it with God's will, for this will impress them more strongly than any recriminations.

[Rauner wrote from Savannah, where he has gone to work, concerning some affairs of the world; and he also let me know that he had never in his life witnessed such licentious and evil doings as were going on in that town. A similar tale was told me recently by the surveyor, Jonas,[89] from Savannah; and I repeated these stories to some of our people, not without purpose. This Rauner, as well as Stephan Riedelsperger, Michael Rieser, and Leitner, who have all gone to Savannah,[90] may well be pitied.]

Tuesday, the 14th of June. Some of our children and older people have had strong hot spells, such as were observed last year as the beginning of the fever. May God in His mercy turn all evil away from us and give us patience to accept all trials willingly as coming from His fatherly hands. It is very hot now during the day. Last night we had heavy thunderstorms and cloudbursts. [Several days ago I had the watchmaker, Mueller, come to me to warn him not to take any part in the calumnies against me by Mrs. Ortmann, who is constantly in and out of his house. I gave the same advice to his wife when she came to seek counsel and help from me. Both had to admit that Mrs. Ortmann had uttered many irresponsible things, but they assured me that they had attempted to admonish her and bring her to reason.]

M. [this couple] has a daughter who recently took her first communion, having been previously confirmed with three others; in her soul, the influence of the Lord's word can be well observed and shines forth so as to reflect on her parents and sisters and brothers. We have also reminded the parents of their duties regarding the recently confirmed children; and, when I visited their house and thus had both parents and children around me, I did not fail to address them according to their needs. In their home they are all good listeners of the Lord's words, although, with the exception of the aforementioned daughter, none of them has yet reached full conversion.

Wednesday, the 15th of June. Today our time has been taken up with the money sent to us, partly for our own sustenance and partly for the poor box and the support of the school. In addition to our stipend, our benefactors in London and Germany have bestowed on us extra generosity, of which we must hold ourselves quite unworthy. We shall accept this gift with deep gratitude as coming from our generous Father, who has always helped us in our circumstances; and we shall not hesitate to share with others of our poor people that which is bestowed on us, whenever it should be possible. The schoolmaster, Ortmann, has received 5 £ sterling as a gift from the Honorable Society, which also has presented me and my dear colleague with twelve dozen bottles of good madeira wine, intended also for the benefit of our sick. The merciful Lord has always provided so well for us that up to this day we have always been supplied with the means of comforting and strengthening our sick and our women in confinement.

[I have sent word repeatedly to Mrs. Pichler to come and see me, but she let me know that she would not come. I would well have gone to her myself if only I could achieve in her house what I can hope to achieve in my quarters. When one has to speak to her conscience and ask her about a number of things, she acts as she were dumb and finds much to do for her infant. After dinner she finally came; but I cannot find any repentance in her, and I was forced to tell her clearly the probable result of her recalcitrance and disobedience of the divine order. I repeated this statement to her several times with all necessary seriousness. I also told her that many in the community who knew about the wickedness she had spouted forth against me were convinced that the temporal powers would punish her therefor. This, however, was far from my concern; and I told her that, as long as the Lord would bear with her, so would I, and that I would implore the merciful Lord to bestow repentance on her. This would delight my heart and make me forget all the insults she had heaped upon me. If, however, she were to insist on her lack of repentance, this would not only wring from me many unhappy thoughts about her and her husband, but would also bring upon both of them much evil. I had heard her sing in her hut, "What God does, is well done, etc.",[91] and asked her whether she could sing this in all honesty. I admonished her that she should sing and pray in accordance with her circumstances and should start an honest prayer of repentance as soon as she returned home.]

At last night's prayer meeting I informed my flock of the contents of the letter the Honorable Trustees had conveyed to me through Mr. Verelst. The letter is in reply to the remonstrances made on behalf of our Salzburgers by the esteemed Mr. Ziegenhagen to the Honorable Trustees; and the latter have ceded some of the points made, e.g. that the first and second transport should continue to receive the reduced provisions without any payment until September of this year. However, the corn harvest in Old Ebenezer and what had been advanced to us when we moved from there to New Ebenezer would have to be counted as part of these provisions. Also, our new boat is to be paid for by Mr. Causton at the expense of the Honorable Trustees; further, Mr. Causton has been instructed to help the third transport with provisions, tools, and other necessities such as were provided for the first and second transports. The failure to do so until now should be attributed to the original intent of the Trustees to send the third transport south, with Mr. Gronau as their preacher. As a result, their provisions and tools, an ample supply of which had been loaded on the boats, had travelled to Altamaha.[92] Also, each family of the third transport should receive a chicken and a rooster, and every five persons one sow, one turkey, and one goose, no mention being made of cows.

The letter also promised that all the land due to the Salzburgers would be surveyed and allotted as soon as possible, in connection with which the surveyor would exercise "equal justice" (as the expression goes), but that the people would then have to be content with what they received. It is to be hoped that everyone will receive some good land. Finally, the letter explained the reason why Mr. Oglethorpe or Mr. Causton had failed to pay our stipend; and mention is made of the fact that 16 £ sterling were being transferred to me for the building of a house and school. I read this letter to our dear community, translated into German. I spent much time on each individual point, partly to make its meaning quite clear to them but partly also to guard their minds against improper schemes and thoughts, as much as is possible by explanation and suggestions.

Although not everything was according to wish, we did find

examples of the paternal providence of the Lord, who has again inclined the hearts of the Honorable Trustees to our needs. And, since it is always the good Lord's way to deal His temporal gifts to His children bit by bit and in crumbs along the way, as it were, so that they may praise Him as David did with a pleasing song for each of them, I reminded them of their obligation not to make temporal judgments and criticisms and ignore the true evidence of divine providence just because some things might not be to their liking, but to praise the Lord for each and everything that they may have received. As for the rest of our needs, they should await their fulfillment in peace and quiet, as did Abraham and all those faithful people who also had not received everything at once but bit by bit, often after long waiting, so as to support them constantly in their faith. The letter also promised that our four carpenters who built Mr. Gronau's house would be paid, since they had been properly hired by Mr. Causton under some kind of contractual arrangement.

Tonight I put Mr. Urlsperger's very evangelical letter of 11 February of this year to good purpose with our dear congregation. His love for us is most fatherly; may the Lord in turn bestow on him His fatherly love in rich measure. Although I was of feeble health, God gave me rich material of which to remind the congregation for their edification. The fact that God is still helping some of the Salzburgers to escape from their dark fatherland can only be a joy to those among us who still have some of their loved ones over there. One of our women hoped with tears in her eyes that some of her family might be among them and come to join her here, and she declared she could not wish for greater happiness here on earth.

Thursday, the 16th of June.[93] [Mr. Causton requests my presence in Savannah to discuss the accounts, which reached him long ago. However,]because I am in a feeble condition and also because the men do not wish to lose an hour of their time at this fruitful season of the year, I shall not travel this week or next, the latter being the preparatory week for Holy Communion, which was announced last Sunday for the third Sunday after Trinity. In previous times we have always observed, by God's grace, a marked revival in the souls of our flock at this occasion; and we shall therefore not miss this opportunity. Also, examination of the accounts will not do much for our people, inasmuch as there are no provisions whatever in the storehouses in Savannah.

If our boat had been sent down again to Savannah this week,

the preacher there, Mr. Wesley, would have come up to Ebenezer yesterday or the day before in reply to my recent invitation and would have returned with that boat. Mr. Wesley takes much interest in the good reports he has heard about our people and only wishes that he could achieve more in Savannah than is the case. He was most pleased to hear of the manner in which we conduct our visits at the homes of our flock and of the blessing that the Lord bestows on both teachers and listeners on these occasions. However, he complained that such fruits were still far away in the case of his parishioners. He cited some examples why the people in Savannah would not pay greater heed to the gospels, among them the ridicule and persecution suffered by those who give sign of a revived spirit, matters which did not touch us here. I pointed out to him though, that in my experience even in our place God would lead the souls in His customary way, i.e., those who wish to live in the blessing of the Lord and in Jesus Christ would have to suffer persecution, although it might not be so obvious.

[Since his own congregation offers him so little opportunity for edification, he often visits the Herrnhuters and attends their prayer meetings, where he has learned to read a good amount of German so that he can sing German songs and their tunes.] He finds it suspicious, though, that N. N. [these people] have no creed[94] but, like all heretics, simply rely on the Bible. He has again resolved to read the New Testament with them and to concentrate on important passages which contain the major tenets of Christian belief, so as to divine the basis of their creed by these means. However, he has not yet been able to realize this undertaking.

Friday, the 17th of June. A misunderstanding had arisen among four men whom I asked to come to me today in order to rejoin them on this day of reconciliation, which our Lord Jesus Christ has achieved for us by His death on the cross. The one who had given the least cause for quarrel was also the one who first offered his hand to the others. May God grant that this gesture is not all that there is to it! This afternoon I gave much joy to our schoolchildren by the gift of some linen, which was forwarded to us from some benefactors in Germany through the good offices of Prof. Francke. I first sang the song of praise, "We praise you in the quiet of our hearts, etc."[95] I thereupon catechised them upon the occasion of this Friday, reminding them that on this day our Lord Jesus was suspended, from the cross, naked and without help and in such a condition that it was actually the way it was reported of Him in Psalms 22:6. "But I am a worm, and no man, a reproach of men and despised of the people."[96] I asked them why our Lord Jesus would have made such a spectacle of himself. Reply: Not only because of the pride of men, evidenced among other things by their pride of dress, which extends even to the children, but also to atone for our fall from grace, whereby we had been deprived of God's likeness and had been clothed from inside out with the likeness of Satan, and to restore to us the beautiful likeness of God, or the dress of salvation and the robe of righteousness, which effort on our behalf had cost Him much pain.[97]

How well it becomes a man if he receives these vestments in God's scheme of things, and all other precious clothing is but a poor rag compared to it. The truth of this had been well understood by that blessed princess who, upon the question of her chambermaid as to what she intended to wear that day, had replied: "It matters little what rag I shall use to cover this sack of worms." I told the children that they could all easily acquire this precious vestment if only they wished to, for God is a thousand times more willing to give them such treasure than I am now willing to distribute among them the material gift in accordance with the dear wishes of our benefactors. And those who had the greater treasure, that is, the so dearly bought robe of salvation, should not have to worry for the lesser gift, that is, our daily support and clothing, for would He not give us everything along with it? For the 23rd Psalm begins, "The Lord is my shepherd, I shall not want." They should think what the Lord does for the sheep, for He not only feeds them but also clothes them several times a year, although man borrows their wool for his use and clothing. Oh how blessed a state if they were to believe in Jesus and also could say, "Our Lord Jesus is my shepherd, I shall not want either spiritually or materially."

After I had praised to them the sweet love of Jesus and the blessed state of His children, I asked them which of the children would like to become such a dear little lamb of our Lord Jesus. When some of them extended their hands to me with pleasant gestures and bespoke themselves for the Lord Jesus and some of them cried, even some of those who were normally obdurate, we fell to our knees and thanked the Lord for his gift of linen and prayed to Him for our benefactors. That this entire store of linen should have passed over such a long path, over both land and water, and reached us here without any damage is another sign of God's paternal providence, which I would not let the children forget, especially since they know from experience what happened to a large part of their families' linens and belongings during the voyage across the sea. Upon leaving they promised me to keep their vow with God's grace and together with their parents to send their praise to heaven for the gifts received.

After they had gone, a certain mother came to my hut; and I told her that her children had promised me to pray with her and that she should remind them of it. She was much pleased and assured me that she accustomed her children to praise the Lord for every bit of greens that they fetched from the garden for their meals, so how would they then not thank Him for this great and unexpected gift? Another said that there will be great joy in heaven when we finally meet our unknown benefactors there face to face. "May my dear God help me," she added, "to reach heaven." Two other pious women join this one every afternoon for prayer during school hours; and she said that they would all praise God and pray for our benefactors.

Both yesterday and today I used the prayer meeting to read from several letters of Prof. Francke of various dates on some points I considered well taken for the instruction, edification, and comfort of our listeners. May God be praised for filling the dear Professor's heart with love and affection for us; and it gives us no little comfort that he, as well as the Honorable Senior and Mr. Ziegenhagen, takes our sufferings and trials to heart as if they were his own. As we can see from the attached reports from the year 1736, our institution in Halle is also suffering its trials, yet God has given him His comfort and aid in this respect. Therefore, God can also comfort us who are bearing our share of suffering, with the reassurance that he[98] and other honest servants of the Lord are being comforted. I do not doubt that the Lord, as always, will bless in our listeners' hearts what we have read to them and impressed upon them. We were much comforted that so many of God's servants and children are praying for us in Halle.

I could tell my listeners how the beautiful custom was introduced into the orphanage that every night after supper more than 500 souls pray jointly in one room for the entire Christian flock, i.e., for the institutions, for the conversion of the heathen in East India, and surely for us too, inasmuch as the Lord's work with us here is well known in Halle. In view of this beautiful example, I also sought to arouse our listeners to pray from their hearts for our benefactors and for each other and to do as much for the need of their neighbors as others are doing for us, i.e., that each among them should regard his neighbor's needs as his own and assist him with intercession, counsel, and deed. It is not a sign of brotherly love and righteous behavior, I continued, if people either stay indifferent to the need and wants of their brothers or depress them even further with worrisome remonstrations and warnings of things to come.

I followed this up with examples of the behavior of some here against those who had received only barren land, on which nothing or only little will grow. I also had a good opportunity to remind them of the grace which the Lord had shown to their souls in their illness and touched upon a few details serving for their edification. We have received much joy and we praise the Lord for the great trouble taken to provide us with a doctor and because our dear Mr. Thilo,[99] through the grace of God our Physician, is prepared to deny himself in his practice. Is there anywhere else in the desert a group of people for whom the Lord cares in so many ways as He cares for us? May He be praised for His ineffable grace. By His blessing we have also availed ourselves of the lessons given by the inundations in Germany, the special example of His protection of His children in the disturbances of the Polish wars,[100] and also in respect to that which has been reported about Tranquebar.[101] All the letters and gifts from Germany which have reached us through the hands of our dearly beloved court chaplain, Mr. Ziegenhagen, are ample witness that our dear patrons and friends are more than willing to further our spiritual and temporal well being. If their will and desire were done, we should be well provided for in material things; but, since this is not so and God has chosen to lead us through many rough thickets and paths, we must believe that these trials of our flesh are of greater benefit to us than the former.

Saturday, the 18th of June. Today I distributed the large store of linen among our people. Half of them came in the morning at ten, the others in the afternoon, towards two o'clock. Everybody was treated in the same manner. First we sang, "Praise the Lord, the powerful King of Glory."[102] Then I briefly showed them from Biblical history that what God had done for His people in the desert, He was now doing for them. He had led the children of Israel into many dangers, trials and sadness; but at the same time had shown them His blessed presence and proof of His providence and love. Hardly had they left Egypt before they were endangered by their enemies, whereupon they had revealed their careless and faithless hearts. God showed them a path through the sea, but He also let them wander in the desert and imposed many trials and dangers upon them. For four weeks they ate nothing but their unleavened bread made of water and flour without salt and lard, and they had to suffer thirst for three days during which there had been much grief among children and adults. To be sure, if He had wished, God could have led them to the land of Canaan without much tribulations and given them all the splendors of this life, and they might have expected that rather than the conditions of want in which they found themselves. However, He felt it necessary to try them thus to make them examine the depths of their hearts and to make everyone realize that it was not their piety that had merited God's releasing them from bondage and showing them such signs and miracles and so that they should be convinced of their need of conversion.

God would not have merely led His people into trials, but would have let them experience His faith and providence, if only they had wished to wait for the help of the Lord. We well knew their behavior in times of trial and in the face of His blessings from Biblical history; and their example should instill in us a beneficial vigilance, fear, and caution. In time of need they murmured, listened to others, made life difficult for Moses and Aaron, regretted having left Egypt, and desired to return there, at which the Lord was much displeased. When experiencing God's help and grace, they were well content, praised the Lord, and made many good resolutions; but they failed to turn to Him in true conversion. Also they had not learned to keep trust in Him and failed to believe that He would help them again as He had helped them before. Instead, when new trials came upon them, they would again complain; and the old impatience and material concerns would appear, for their hearts were not steadfast with God (Psalms 78:8), for which reason they were cast down in the desert and did not reach the Promised Land.

In the application I showed our listeners that this was the path along which God had also led the Salzburgers (as was illustrated step by step), but there had been many among us who resembled the old Israelites, etc. Now God was showing them a new blessing, in that pious people had sent us such a generous gift of linen across the ocean, such that both old and young could be given more than just a shirt. I did not doubt that they would rejoice with us, praise the Lord, and pray for our benefactors. However, I admonished them to use the experience of these blessings in times of trial to protect themselves with this sign of divine providence against all complaints and objections of their reason, and to trust instead that our almighty God and heavenly Father, for whom nothing is impossible, will also provide for all else and end all our sorrow, if this be for the benefit of our souls. Inasmuch as the faith of our benefactors shone into our eyes so clearly from this real and true act of brotherly love, this should lead us to become true successors in the living faith of the living Lord so that we should want for nothing. We thereupon fell to our knees and prayed to our dear Lord for forgiveness for our sins, committed in times of trial as well as in times of blessing, and begged for abundant repayment for so pleasant and so necessary benefactions. May He accept our prayers for the sake of His son. Amen. [Nothing was given to those who have left God's word and have travelled to Savannah or even Savannah-Town for the sake of some profit; *absens carens*.[103] Also, Mrs. Pichler, Ernst, and Mrs. Ortmann, who had come uninvited, did not receive anything on this occasion; instead, we put their share aside without telling them so, until they have cleansed themselves of their outrages and offenses by true conversion in the blood of Jesus Christ.]

On this so pleasant Saturday, when doubtless God has received much true and humble gratitude, I read part of the letter by Court Chaplain Ziegenhagen during the evening prayer meeting; and I must confess, for the praise of our loving and generous Lord, that my heart was much enlightened by the letter's instructive considerations of the beneficial and secret paths of the cross which He has travelled and is still travelling with the believers of the old and the new covenant. I feel encouraged to follow my Blood-betrothed, with the strength which He won so abundantly for us, on the path of the cross. Such periods of trial and suffering signify but a short hour and are only the blink of an eye in the face of the eternal and immensely important glory of the Lord which shall be given to us, free and forever, after a few short periods of suffering, struggle, and victory. Here in the face of the Lord we give thanks for the paternal love of the court chaplain for us and our flock.

May He, our true God, set His heart to a gracious reward for this and all similar evidence of charitable love, which, as we know, He has blessed previously for our material and spiritual well being. May the blessing which our dear St. Paul asked for his benefactor, Onesiphorus,[104] be bestowed on him and on all our benevolent friends and benefactors and grant them eternal reward of grace from the hand of our Supreme Sovereign, Jesus Christ. I always think it is not without cause that the dear Lord has proclaimed so much to us through news from afar of the necessity and benefit of the cross and has, through His constant admonition, given us courage to bear it. Maybe He has, in His wisdom, decided to burden us with another trial of which we still know nothing. May He make us prepared and ready for everything. "It cannot last forever, he often has dried our tears before we knew it. Whenever we say, 'How long shall I fear and tremble?', He has already refreshed soul and body."[105]

We have received several edifying books, but we have little time to read them now, since next week we must prepare ourselves from His holy word for Communion.

Sunday, June 19th. A young Salzburger asked me last Friday to stop at his house, if I had an occasion; for he wished to speak to me about his soul but was too bashful to do so in my hut. I had forgotten his request; but I remembered him today when he, along with others, registered for Holy Communion. When I came to him, he revealed his grief to me and told me he felt as if God had left him to his judgment. He had previously sinned much against our dear Lord, as he had told me before, and could not rid himself of the memory of his transgressions.

[N. B.] Since God had shown some examples of His grace with our school-children last Sunday, the benefits of which I have noticed throughout the week, I used this method again when they visited me this afternoon so as to excite their tender hearts to follow such beautiful examples, and it was not without benefit. After they left me, I learned that some of the children assembled among themselves for further edification. The hymn which we had sung during the service and afterwards with the children, "Good night, you vain world, etc." impresses them greatly. Upon closing I had pointed out for their use the last words of this song: "Should I then forfeit my own happiness? I should never cease grieving for it if I did."[106] We urgently need the little book of exempla for the children, as well as some other good reports and booklets, which would edify us, as our friends in England and Germany know. Much is needed in the building of the Lord's house, and even little things should not be missed. All in the honor of our Lord the King.

Monday, the 20th of June. After all the joy that our Lord gave our whole community last week with the gift of linen, He now has filled our cup with sorrow and suffering in that He has suddenly let one after the other of our flock fall ill. The same fever that afflicted them last year has returned, and we must hold still and accept the help of the wondrous Lord. Although we have been sorely afflicted with this fever previously, He has not tried any one among us too severely or let him suffer damage to his soul. Honest souls recognize the need for this chastisement, which is after all but a rod and not a sword. Our dear Lord does everything in His time; and only recently He has sent us a store of well tried medicines from Halle, which shall be used for His glory. The people know the blessing of the Lord which is to flow from this and take the medicines without fear and certainly with praise for the Lord and to good effect.

Good R. P. [Ruprecht Steiner's]wife has been in a dangerous way during her pregnancy, but with God's help a few doses have prevented damage and the miscarriage which had been feared. It was a joy to hear how both these good people praised the Lord in true poverty of the spirit and have wished spiritual and physical well-being for their benefactors. Another woman came to me this afternoon and fetched some wine for her sick husband, and at the same time she brought me her thanks for the linen she had received. She remembered how, in London, she had received some linen as a gift from a woman through the good offices of one of the court chaplains, for which she had wished all blessings on the benefactress. She said that it was quite true in our case that, as the proverb says: "God lets us sink a little, but not drown."[107] He always shows us His help and providence even in times of want. He wishes to try us and our patience and the depths of our hearts by such want; and, if we become impatient and malcontent with God's guidance, it can only get worse. What good would it do her if she complained that her husband had fallen ill, that they had lost a cow, and that they suffered want here and there. It is said, "To be sure, He will tarry with his comfort, etc. But if it comes to pass that you remain true to Him, He will release you, etc."[108] God had apparently shown her in her garden that He was a Lord of blessings and could make much of little. She had had only a single grain of wheat, which she had planted, and now ten full ears of wheat were growing and, if God blessed them, she would give them to others as seed.

I took the occasion to show her that this had always been the Lord's way, to start with small and lowly things and to bring them to glorious ends. Although he now humbles us, He will continue His work such that one will have to say, "God has done that." After all, everything must serve for our good, our perfection, and our glory, just as all kinds of contrary weather, such as rain, sunshine, cold, and wind, must serve for the growth and ripening of the fruits of the earth; for, if there were only one kind of weather or, if one of the mentioned elements were missing, there would be no harvest.

Veit Lemmenhofer's child had been sickly and miserable ever since his birth and finally died yesterday and was buried today. Ernst too has a sickly child which will likely not grow up. Since its mother cannot nurse it, its milk is bought from the poor box. I had Mrs. Ernst come here this morning and told her that the milk for her child will be continued, [and she used the occasion to complain about the malicious and cruel nature of her husband, with whom she could not live in peace. He demanded and insisted that she go into the field like other Salzburger women and work the ground, but that she simply could not do that in view of her two sick children. The woman herself is not worth much, and she as well as her husband are at fault in all the disorder and unpleasantness, of which even the children are aware. She had complained about him before; and, when we talked to him and showed him this or that fault and tried to demonstrate the wrongness of his heart, she herself has excused him as much as possible and belittled his misdeeds.]

Tuesday, the 21st of June. It has pleased the Lord to let all the members of my family fall ill of the fever, so that my helpmate, our son, the maid, and Bishop (the boy sent to me by the Society) are all bedridden. My dear colleague and I still fare well, as long as it may please the Lord. Starting Sunday, the fever has attacked our community quite suddenly, and not only in our village, for Landfelder, who is working out of Musgrove's cowpen (six English miles from Savannah) has been attacked by it and has returned home. The fever generally starts with much vomiting, and the patients have no chills or only very little but are very hot for one to fifteen hours at a time, and they complain of severe pains in the head and the back. Some of them even hallucinate when the fever strikes.

[NB. NB] A pious woman called me during her fever and requested me to pray with her. After her prayer she confided in me that she bore a heavy burden on her heart, which oppressed her like a millstone and made her fever even worse. She had found something once in Old Ebenezer; and, although she did not know the owner, she knew it was not hers yet kept it, and that caused her much fear. Although she had often wished and resolved to get rid of the object, she had never done so.

Worldly people would not bother much with this; but, since this soul seriously wishes to be saved, she refused to consider this matter as of little importance, and I had much to do to quiet her with reference to the gospels. She recognizes this sin to be a sin and knows what a treasure it is when one is sick with a calm conscience cleansed by the blood of Christ. The healthier the eye, the more painfully quick is our perception of any speck of dust in it. Oh, what lessons God teaches us in dealing with such souls!

Wednesday, the 22nd of June. A Salzburger woman called me in her great pains so that I might give her some medicine. I dispensed it with admonishment to free herself from her bad conscience and the sin governing her heart by a true conversion, and she recognized that she had failed to prepare herself thus for eternity. She had been full of fear during the previous night and promised our dear Lord to think more of her salvation from now on and to seek the company of other pious women. Since I had to spend a brief time in the neighborhood so as to observe the effect of the medicine given to her and to repeat the medication, I took the opportunity to visit another sick Salzburger, a woman pious from the bottom of her heart, so as to edify myself with her. She counts herself among the poor, lame, the halt, and the blind of whom we spoke in a recent Sunday gospel; but she cannot yet bring herself to believe that that our dear Lord will have mercy on her too, since she is too wicked and faithless and because she feels that she is not recognizing and repenting her sins enough. I talked to her according to her condition, making particular reference to the words of our dear Lord Jesus: "Come unto me all ye that, etc.",[109] and I also sang for her the beautiful hymn, "To Thee I come, Lord Jesus",[110] which quite clearly strengthened her confidence in our Lord Jesus, the only savior and friend of repentant souls. Another woman heard my singing and joined us. She also complained that her heart was not as green and gay as her garden, but quite somber and sad. I admonished her to bide her time in good order and things would be better, for God would bring good and pleasant weather in our spiritual domain also.

Last Monday I sent two boats to fetch provisions, one to Savannah and one to a plantation in Carolina, where fifteen bushels of corn had been promised me for our people. The latter brought corn, but the first did not, for Mr. Causton has no provisions, although he would gladly send them if he could. He does expect some stores, though, in the near future. May

God be praised for the corn, which will at least serve the needs of those most in want. Since the planter had sent word that he would let me have another five bushels of corn and ten bushels of beans for cash, the Salzburgers are willing to return tomorrow for these stores. I shall advance the money and hope that Mr. Causton will reimburse me, for I shall distribute both corn and beans among our people as provisions. [I had written him in this regard, but he probably has not had the time to reply.]

Thursday, the 23rd of June. N. N. [Poor Stephan Riedelsperger] has come down from Savannah-Town,[111] accompanied by several Englishmen, in order to fetch provisions in Savannah for the fort up there. Since nothing can be gotten there, he came to our village yesterday on the boat from Savannah; but his only concern is with temporal matters. I have not yet been able to speak to him on the state of his conscience and to admonish him on it, and I fear that there will be little prospect of great achievement there, for he seems ready for God's judgment. His wife, [the Valentin woman], has announced herself ready to come to the Lord's table; but she confided in me today that her husband's laundry and other practical business left her little time for preparation and thus she would rather postpone communion. I warned her of the danger of ignoring the Lord's command and the safety of her soul for the sake of her husband, who only held Holy Communion in contempt. The poor man should be ashamed of his lack of faith; for now God has let him have 30 Florins through the efforts of Senior Urlsperger, whereas he formerly could not believe that God would provide for him as He has done for others if only he would remain in his position and with the gospels and the Holy Sacraments and not let himself get embroiled in outside work.

[NB. NB.] A pious woman has visited my sick helpmate, and I asked her upon leaving whether God had spared her from the fever so far. She told me she had had one attack but that it had quickly passed. She felt the need of being chastised with illness by the Lord; for days of health, while pleasing her flesh, might not be so wholesome for her soul as some suffering in her physical body.[112] She had become more and more convinced that her reason was in constant conflict with the Holy Scriptures and with God's will, which is evident therein. She thought that all her intentions and deeds were wicked throughout. The words were all too true: "My good works shall not count, etc."[113] She felt it a heavy burden to remain in this world, for she kept offending the good and loving Lord (though against her will and intent) and was often chased from the peace of her soul by the matters of this world; this, she added, might cease once she were delivered from this world and its evils by temporal death. She often experienced the sweet love of the Lord and His mercy in her inner being, and then she felt well and in that state she could understand the happy life of paradise which resulted from the union with the Lord in faith.

Last Sunday our Father had so refreshed her with the word of His Son, "Come, everything is prepared, etc.",[114] that she wanted to shout with joy. But upon returning home her lack of faith and constancy had soon deprived her of this feeling. She feels sin so deeply rooted in herself that God will have much trouble tearing her from it. She does not wish to deceive herself, and she often does not know whether the feelings she sometimes experiences are true or hypocritical, etc. This tale cost the poor woman many a tear, but its expression caused me much edification and secretly aroused me to the praise of God. As time permitted, I added words of comfort and sayings from the Scriptures to what she reported of the state of her soul. She much appreciated that; and the saying: "He hath not dealt with us after our sins [nor rewarded us according to our iniquities]",[115] has been impressed on me for several days now. It overcomes in those souls who are aware of their shortcomings the fear that God is angry and will therefore punish them with illness; for truly such souls hate all sins like the very devil, and their greatest sorrow is that they feel so many sins that cling to them and make them sluggish.

Friday, the 24th of June. The Lord Trustees have reported that Senior Urlsperger had written to the Honorable Society to the effect that Mr. von Ploto[116] had obtained a considerable sum for the belongings that the Salzburgers had been forced to leave behind and wished to know whether any of our people still have any claims; and he requested that I make inquiries in this respect and forward him the necessary specifications and powers of attorney. There are some among us here who can submit written proof of their claims in this respect, but some do not have any documents. I shall make inquiries among them next week as to the belongings left behind; since the illness of my family and other matters will not leave me time for such matters this week.

A man called me to his sick wife, who had something to discuss with me. When I arrived, they both told me that they had suffered a misunderstanding since last Sunday. The woman had let her husband know that she wished to be relieved of this vain life and preferred to die, and the man had understood this to mean that she was tired of him and their children and therefore wished to leave this world out of impatience with her lot. She claimed she had tried to convince him that this was only suspicion on his part and that the reason for her wish had not been impatience with her cross but the sweetness of heavenly bliss, where she would be able to serve the Lord without sin. Since the man loves his wife dearly, however, and could not keep house without her, her desire for death seemed to him to be based on the wrong belief; and many unnecessary words were exchanged between them in this respect, and much suffering was caused thereby.

[The man is not worth much], and his conscience may well have told him that it would not be without reason if his wife were weary of him. I told them with great seriousness and love why the Lord had joined them in holy matrimony and had preserved their lives for so many years now, i.e., that the husband should help his wife, and the wife her husband, and the parents their children to find the path to salvation, so that there would not one day be eternal separation between them. Based on Philippians 1:23 and 2 Timothy 4:8, I also admonished them on the true purpose of all righteous Christians. Finally, I warned them of distrust as the source of much evil and told them that their age brought them closer and closer to death and the grave, and that the devil would not hesitate to ensnare their souls in many strange ways. Since their children were present, I also talked to them for their father's instruction about the verse in Psalms 32:9, "Be ye not as the horse, or, etc." and compared it to the parable from next Sunday's gospel for the third Sunday after Trinity, since we find that our dear Savior stays with us poor sinners in love and pity and seeks to glorify Himself by showing them both spiritual and temporal benefactions. However, if this will not help, he shall treat men like horses and mules with bridle and bit, so that they may become aware. Oh, why are men like the beasts, although we are created in God's image? Finally, I prayed with them; and I can only hope that by remonstration and prayer the spirit of distrust and discordance has been exorcised.

Saturday, the 25th of June. [Mrs. Ernst begged me to call for her husband to dissuade him from his plans. He had been persuaded by Rauner and Riedelsperger to join the military at the fort above Savannah-Town so as to make some money there. Meanwhile, he was neglecting his work, the beans had not all been planted, etc., etc. However, I turned her down, for I care little whether her husband stays or leaves. Even while here, he pays little heed to God's word. Those among us with even a little sense in their heads who know how strangely things are being done among the English, particularly among the laborers, cannot but pity those poor souls who have travelled for some months for the sake of a little gain.]

Our people are constantly asking us for medicines at this time, since they know that God has again provided a good store of them. The fever keeps spreading, and young and old suffer much from the paroxysms of fever. God ordained that my dear colleague should learn the art of bleeding through the instruction and example of Mr. Holtzendorf, who bled some people here; and now he can serve our people in case of need in our present circumstances. What will we not do if it is for the glory of the Lord and the best of our fellow man, particularly our beloved flock? If God will only send us a man versed in the art of surgery and medicine, as we have been made to hope, we should gladly desist from such work, busy as we are with the school and our office.

This afternoon, prior to our hearing repentance and confession, I asked several people [Rheinlaender and his wife and a Salzburger and his wife,] who had recently had rough words with each other and a bitter fight, to come to me so as to induce both parties to forgive and forget. I was not content with having talked to each privately but urged them to forgive their brother and desist from carrying grudges; I wanted to make sure and have firm evidence to this effect. God gave me much edification and pleasure in this undertaking, for some of them [the Rheinlaenders] showed such an attitude which I would hardly have hoped for. I believe that God has truly started his work in these people and that, if they remain steadfast, something may yet come of them. Should they again lose faith, now that God has set them on this good path of recognition of their sins and of the absolute necessity of a complete change of heart, there will be little that can be done for them. God's forebearance of sinners is long; but, if they will not let themselves be found and will not repent, He will tame them the more cruelly with the bit and bridle of spiritual and temporal judgment.

Sunday, the 26th of June. [There were _____[117] communicants today.] We held Holy Communion today and, since the last taking of Holy Communion was blessed for many of these souls, as I have learned, we shall hope the same of God's grace for this time. Several of those who had registered were prevented by the fever. A pious woman sent me word of her grief and asked what I would advise her, for she had wished to take Holy Communion but was bedridden from the fever. A pious man approached me with the same question; but I advised them both that I could not suggest the taking of Communion in these circumstances, for their devotion might be upset by the fever, which might become worse should they leave their house. I counseled them to read the 6th chapter of St. John and to enjoy Jesus Christ in faith, seeing that at this time they could not share His essence with the rest of the flock; and God would not consider it a sin. None the less, the woman attempted to join our hour of repentance and confession but had to leave again.

It being required by her condition, another woman was given polychrest pills and rejoiced that these pills made it possible for her to attend church. She said, "Let me come while I am still well enough; for, once I get to be sick like the others, I shall be unable to come." Another good Salzburger woman was prevented by the fever from attending the repentance and confessional; but, since she felt better today, she asked through her husband, and subsequently in person, whether I would admit her to Holy Communion. Seeing that the Lord had restored her health, she greatly desired it. I gladly let her have her wish; [but Ortmann, the schoolmaster, and his wife stayed away. Certainly, their conscience will weigh heavily on them for their malicious deeds; but, since they refuse to repent, they will not come to Communion.

[NB.] I visited B. [Burgsteiner] and his wife, who both suffer grievously from the fever along with their children. Another pious Salzburger was with them to inquire into their condition and to help them with their needs. I learned that he had repeated to them that which had edified his soul from today's comforting lecture for repentant sinners. When I began to talk about the subject of today's sermon, the heart of Jesus that thirsts for the salvation of sinners, the man began to weep, telling me that his conscience accused him of much bad faith and he could not accept the comfort that was offered. I thereupon visited S. [Mrs. Schweighoffer], who also complained of her misery and was like a parched and thirsty soil. It is such souls that our Lord Jesus desires, and He loves them well. Those poor sinners who are aware of their poverty he will make rich. He fills the hungry with goods and leaves the rich (the sinners) empty.

Monday, the 27th of June. In his feverish condition, one of

the Salzburgers came to fetch some powder, having heard that it had benefited another ill Salzburger. He took the occasion to let me know that yesterday's sermon had much refreshed him; he greatly desired that God might show him his misery more clearly, but he felt that he had much need of accepting the Lord's wonderful promises in the gospels and the comfort to be derived therefrom. Last Whitsun, when asked about the condition of his soul, he had said that it was quite miserable, for he failed to recognize his sins fully. Thereupon I, Gronau, answered him that he should not be deterred thereby; for he himself could not deny that the dear Lord has so revealed his sins to him that he was greatly bowed down and humbled by them and that he was worried because he still recognized them so little. Therefore, he should not hesitate, as miserable as he might be, to come to Jesus, who has said, "If any man thirst, let him come unto me, and drink."[118] Even if his thirst were not especially great, let him come, and those who wish to drink should take the water of life as a gift. He should come, simple of heart, and accept what our Lord so kindly offered him in His words. And, if the dear Savior felt it necessary, He would lead him even deeper into the recognition of His sins. I was, therefore, much pleased when he admitted today how our dear Lord urged him so that he could not resist, even if he did not yet dare to accept those wonderful promises fully.

Tuesday and Wednesday, the 28th and 29th of June. Last week Mr. Causton repeatedly requested my presence in Savannah, but urgent business here prevented my going. Monday I travelled early in the morning but found him and his entire family ill of the fever; so it was impossible to do anything about the accounts; and I shall have to return as soon as he improves. The people in Savannah and Purysburg suffer much from heavy attacks of the fever, and some have died, as we have also learned from Charleston. Since there was not much to be achieved at Mr. Causton's place, I returned by night (for the heat of the day is unbearable on the water) after I had settled with Mr. Purry[119] the question of the note drawn on Dr. Gerdes. Mr. Causton was most kind and promises to do all that is possible for our people.

Mr. Wesley is much pleased if I visit him when I come to Savannah, as I did today. He diligently sings German hymns [from the Herrnhut hymnal], and he much praises the advantages of our church over the others in view of this treasure of songs. Since he believes that most of these songs were written in Halle, I said that only a few, but among the most beautiful, were written there; and I gave him two as an example, i.e., "To you, dear Jesus, I shall come." and "Who is like you," etc., both of which are from the pen of Pastor Freylinghausen.[120] He concluded from the latter song, [which he had learned from the Herrnhuters,] that the author must be a man of much grace and force, which I could affirm; and I told him of his experiences in the battles and the paths of the Lord.

[I also mentioned, however, that I was much amazed at the matters which had passed in connection with Mr. Spangenberg's conceited behavior in Halle; for this dear man,[121] who had above all tried to dissuade him from his separatist and damaging principles and return him to the Christian order, had not been successful in this attempt. When I presented these matters to him, Mr. Wesley did not reply; but his ears had heard and his eyes seen that Mr. Freylinghausen was a man like others, etc. Thereupon Mr. Wesley fetched a written octave book (probably his diary) and read to me that Mr. Spangenberg had recounted that he had been called to Halle as professor in the place of the late Abbot Breithaupt. However, since he had displeased the other professors in some matters, he had been expelled from the country *autoritate regia*[122] quite suddenly and without having been heard and given an opportunity to answer his adversaries.

[Because both assertions were shameful lies, I had to express my displeasure at such snaky behavior and tell Mr. Wesley and Mr. Delamotte that he had never been anything but an adjunct, together with the adjunct Baumgarten, in the theological faculty and that originally he had so well concealed his views and acted as an angel of light that in particular Prof. Francke had been much pleased with him and praised God for this worker, who had also been used in the orphanage. After a number of disorderly people, among them (as I knew) hypocritical dissemblers, had formed a group so that he had quite a following around him, he had suddenly come forth with his separatist beliefs and had requested an honest pastor in Glaucha by Halle to offer him (Mr. Spangenberg) and his brothers Holy Communion *exclusis aliis*.[123] From then on he revealed more and more that he had only seemingly but not truly agreed with our Evangelical Lutheran Church. Hereupon Pastor Freylinghausen and other honest teachers and members of the university had tried to work on him in all manners and ways and had asked him to respond in writing to some of their questions. Inasmuch as he could not be brought to reason, particularly as he had conferred with Count Zinzendorff, but persisted in his beliefs and opinions, he was informed that it was necessary to submit this matter to the King,[124] who will not tolerate dissent and disorder at his University. He was warned in advance of the judgment of the King, which could not be changed subsequently, etc.; yet he considered it an honor to be removed from his position and wanted to be put in *extremis,* etc.

[Mr. Wesley at first attempted to excuse his behavior with the argument that some of the teachers might have been unconverted and he might have considered them unworthy of their office, although this was obviously an erroneous opinion. But as I could offer him ample reassurance, based on my own knowledge, of the honesty and probity of Parson Martini and others, his faith in Mr. Spangenberg seemed to falter. I also asked Mr. Wesley whether he was aware that the Herrnhuter brothers were conducting substantial commerce with the heathens and were also received by them, a fact of which there was knowledge in both London and Germany. He replied, however, that that could not refer to these brothers; for it was quite unlikely for them to act that way, others were probably meant, etc. Their commerce probably consisted in trading the Indians rice for game.]

In Purysburg a German man and a woman asked my advice in a confused marital situation. The woman told me that her husband and another man had lost their way in the forest three years ago; and, since nothing had been heard from him, she had married another man after a year had passed. She and the other woman had been married in Savannah by a Mr. Quincey.[125] Now she has learned that her first husband and the other man are living well and in good circumstances on a plantation near Charleston. He had inquired about her circumstances from a Purysburg man; but he had neither requested her to join him nor intimated that he would return. However, she would like to return to him, for she could not get along with her second husband. I admonished her to do penance for her shameful confusion and said I did not consider it advisable for her to go to him, for it was quite clear from what she had told me that he had, under the pretence of being lost, left her quite willingly and would ill receive her if she now returned against his will, particularly since she had meanwhile taken another husband. I also warned her that the secular laws of the English Kingdom would judge her harshly for her deeds, if there were someone to accuse her. She could not grasp the latter, for she and the other woman had sought advice, prior to their new marriage, from the judges in Purysburg and from Mr. Oglethorpe.

The man, who also sought my advice, told me that his wife

had left him last Ascension Day, taking his money and goods and his youngest daughter with her. She now is in Charleston, and he would like to know how to persuade her to return. He was particularly concerned for the child and asked me to write on his behalf. I told him that I knew no other advice but for him and his children to humble themselves before the Lord and to implore Him day and night in the name of Jesus Christ to lift from him the curse that was resting on his entire disorderly household because of his unrepentant and annoying life which he had led with his wife against all counsel; for else things would get much worse for him and his family. If he were to proceed as suggested, God would find a way for him in this matter with his wife who deserted him. The man also wanted to put his two youngest boys in our school if they could be fully supported there, but in such matters I prefer to go as cautiously as possible.

[Thursday, the 30th of June. An Englishman who brought the Honorable Trustees' cattle to Old Ebenezer has fallen ill there; and I was told that the schoolmaster's wife had gone there to attend to him, although there are plenty of people there who could care for this sick man, either those who are building the sawmill or those who are in charge of the cattle. Since this, therefore, is a scandalous matter, my dear colleague and I had the schoolmaster called so as to inquire into his wife's travel and, since he could not well deny the fact of it, to reproach him for the impropriety of such indecent behavior. However, he considered his wife honest, the travel necessary, and us overly suspicious; and he showed his displeasure at our remonstrations with angry and bitter words.

[In view of his conviction that we are only seeking his ruin and destruction, I took the occasion to read him some passages, as I had done recently from Mr. Ziegenhagen's letter, out of the letters from Mr. Butjenter, which I was about to answer and thus had in front of me, as well as from that of Dr. Gerdes, so that he might realize the opposite to be true; i.e., that in the previous period of his poverty and illness, and of the hope which we formerly entertained for the salvation of his soul, we had reported thereon to his benefactors in London, on whose behalf a present of 5£ Sterling had been sent to him. And to further convince him that we held no ill will toward him, we gave him the linen held back for him, with the repeated assurance that we were prepared to assist him as much as possible in material matters, if he and his wife would only desist from the improper company of English people and set a better example for our community. I also read him some lines from a letter by Capt. Coram, who is one of the Trustees, from which he could see that his wife's exceptionable company with licentious Englishmen could only be ill regarded in London. The passage from the letter was as follows:

"I pray, you will make my Complements to all the good people under yr Care, the young as well as the old. Perhaps I may live to see them or some of them. I am sure, they appeared to me, to be much better Christians folks, than the Bulk of the English, which have gone for Georgia. I hope, none are so unchristian as to interfeur with you in your religion affairs, you are Lutherens and doubtless do as you oght to instruct your people to instruct their Children & their Childrens Children, & for them to hand it down to their Posterity in the faith of their Religion for which they were Driven from their native places. And I hope, they will not fall into the Sins, which their English Neighbours are too much addicted to. I pray God, give you health & strength & long life among your flock to their great Edification and Blessing, & to have you & them always in his Protection."

[Mr. Ortmann argued that his wife had good reason to offer the hospitality of their house to Englishmen and to seek their acquaintance, because she received work and wages from them. After all, we had not kept the promise the Trustees made to them, namely, that his wife was to be in charge of the sewing and the instruction of the female children in sewing, for which she was to receive wages. We told him, however, that we were unaware of such instructions by the Trustees; and, even if they wished it, they would not force his wife upon us if she lived a disorderly life. If she were to abide by our order, we would gladly prefer her over others and recompense her for her work. He further argued that they could not now turn the Englishmen away, for they had become accustomed to stay at their house. Would we have him turn them away? We told him that, if they truly converted their hearts to God and lived a truly God-fearing life, they would soon be rid of such guests. He finally admitted that his wife could not do without the company of Englishmen, to which she was already all too accustomed.

[Finally, he could no longer hide his grief at this, and he spoke of either moving away or leaving his wife, if only to get his peace. He also admitted, when his heart had become 'quieter and his anger had abated, that she did not take any advice and intended shortly to travel to Charleston again, and that nothing could be done to dissuade her. We have often mentioned that, in her absence, we can handle the man quite well; but, when she is here, she turns his head and sets him against us, which he was forced to admit. He also stated that she had accomplished so much at her recent travel to Charleston that they would be able to settle there if they could not remain here. However, I could tell him what she had told people of her purpose before her departure; i.e., that Christmas was not well celebrated in Ebenezer, that there was no pleasure here, and that things were merrier in Charleston, where she would go, etc.

[She returned by nightfall and showed herself in our hut too, for we had not believed the husband that she would return the same day. She claims to have gone to Old Ebenezer for the sake of a cow which the sick captain had promised her, but she had not obtained it. Recently she travelled, without our knowledge, to Pallachocolas, of which place we have not yet heard the least bit of good. If both of them feel that one of them should travel, we would much rather give him permission and hold school for him than to permit his wife, as we again told him.]

JULY

Friday, the 1st of July.[126] The people are falling ill frequently, and on good days we try to counter it with bloodletting or with medication. Some of them refuse the latter and hope to get well without it. Some of the Purysburg folk report that those who took medicines had died but that others who had refused them had become well. [*Which I would well believe of the careless preparations and the inexperienced doctors there.*] When I was last in Purysburg, I was told that some had taken black powder, or alum, and had been healed thereby. For some time now the heat has been worse than last year. The crops in the fields do not look good because of the long absence of rain. [We hear thunder toward evening, but nothing comes of it and the gathered clouds disperse without any rain having fallen.]

Saturday, the 2nd of July. Because of the terrible heat, school is held only in the morning. There are only few children in school, and those who are still well are needed for the care of their sick parents or relatives. We have hired a man and his wife to see to those in the village who cannot help themselves, and they are paid some money from the sick and the poor box.

Sunday, the 3rd of July. Since my last trip to and return from Savannah, I have been down with the three-day fever, which comes without chills but causes very high temperatures. Although I had intended to hold the service and was already present among the congregation, the fever would not let me proclaim the Lord's word. Meanwhile, my colleague had prepared a sermon on the gospel Luke 19:36 ff., which he then proceeded to give. I had looked forward to speaking to our people today on the aforementioned text and to call before our eyes, for the well being of myself and the congregation, the heart of the Father and His children. Because of the fever, only a very few can come to church. Whenever the unbearable sun permits it, my dear colleague goes out and visits the sick, of whom there are many; and he would much like to see everyone every day; for the honest souls among us much desire it, and it is of great benefit for their spiritual and temporal wellbeing. Last year the Lord wisely arranged that we would not both fall ill at the same time but that one of us would always be just about well enough to teach our flock both publicly and privately. He shall act out of His Love to us this time also.

Monday, the 4th of July. On my recent return from Savannah, I was told in Purysburg that the shoemaker, A. [Arnsdorff], being quite intoxicated with rum, had caused much annoyance in this condition with talking and shouting. He was together with three other men from our village who had all been sent to fetch provisions from Savannah but returned empty-handed. The shoemaker subsequently went to the Lord's Table; for I had been unaware of his offences and had also hoped better of him, since he has once before been subjected to church discipline for his drunkenness. After having received Communion, he went by way of Purysburg to visit his daughter, whom he would like to redeem from an Englishman from the bonded service into which she had been committed in return for her passage-money. After I heard of his shameful intoxication, in which he had abused the Holy Sacrament as reprehensibly as before the church discipline was imposed on him, I have been waiting for his return; for I fully intended to have serious words with him and exclude him from the congregation until proof of serious and honest repentance.

Today, however, I received the sad and unexpected news that he had fallen into the water and drowned in Purysburg; and thus the Holy and Just Lord, who will not have His children mock Him, has excluded him both from the terrestrial and the eternal church much sooner than we, His unworthy servants, could have done it. God has manifested much of His mercy in the poor man, for he grew up without knowledge of the faith, served as a soldier in Danish service, and came to Carolina as a true heathen, seeking only his fortune. There, he and his large family were indentured for their passage-money. When his master realized that he would not have much use for this old man,   years of age and his children, he released him from his service on the condition that he should repay him in a few years and *leave his oldest daughter* [who is   years old] *in his service for her passage-money.*[127] He thereupon came to Savannah, [where Mr. von Reck had just arrived with the third transport, and addressed himself to the latter, who accepted him and brought him along] and on to Ebenezer; although the shoemaker and his family had requested Mr. Causton to send them to the new town of Frederica.

His wife took God's word to herself for her salvation and has thanked the Lord with her children for having brought her and her husband away from the disorderly life and to the rich and pure recognition of His word, and she assured me that her husband had started on the path of reflection and might well be won over. But old sinners must repent, and it has become clear by this example that God, when His mercy and proof of bounty to man is not returned in the form of His glory and His praise, will act toward such souls with stern justice, as shown by His acts toward the Egyptions and the Israelites. The shoemaker had intended to return with the boat which Rauner and Riedelsperger had helped to row up to the new fort above Savannah-Town; and late last Friday night, when he was about to board the boat, he fell into the water (see journal for 11 July). The owner of the boat and Rauner and an English rower assured me that it should have been humanly impossible to lose one's life in such bright moonlight; but I impressed on them that God's justice might very well render it possible and I did not fail to make *the necessary remonstrations* [*to poor Rauner, which he should pass on to the miserable Riedelsperger.*

[When this terrible news had become known in the village, Mrs. Spielbiegler came to see me, an old woman who is close to her grave because of her age, and close to hell because of her unrepentant and arrogant manners. She inquired after her son, who left here four weeks ago to seek work; and she told me of her fear that some disaster might have befallen him, too, as he had stayed away beyond the agreed time. I told her that both she and her son would do well to look at themselves in the mirror of this example and to repent seriously; or else God might well come over her, too, with His judgment; and she could not ascend to bliss without true conversion, which she was still lacking. These words fell harshly upon the ears of the miserable woman and they brought her into a rage, so that she uttered rude words and left, shouting and cursing.

[She returned after a little while and insisted on being given greater comfort, also inquiring earnestly and intensely what it was that I knew to the disadvantage and shame of herself and her son. She told me to *inquire in Memmingen, for there I would be told that there was nothing against him or her.* She had left Austria for the sake of the Lord's word many years ago, had worked industriously in *Memmingen,* had remained an honest woman, and was neither a *whore nor thief,* etc. Here, too, her life was work and prayer; and she would come to church whenever possible. What was it that I held against her and her son? She was incapable of pretence, I might prefer that and be satisfied with her if she pretended. I could well have given her specifics of the lack of conversion in her heart, i.e. her present and recent behavior; for I know only too well how people will react to evidence of their sins, which in their blindness they consider but trivial, and how they will strengthen their obstinacy by referring to the faults which they have observed in pious people, (but with other eyes.)

[I therefore pointed out to her the true essence of conversion, and how our Lord Jesus, particularly as shown in John 3, insisted upon it; and I asked whether she had ever truly experienced such conversion and revivication. She affirmed that she had, in Holy Baptism; and, when I argued that this was not sufficient for obtaining eternal bliss, seeing that she herself had admitted breaking the pact of baptism, and that she and her son would have to convert to the Lord fully and honestly or there would not be much hope for her salvation, she was besides herself with anger and, while praising my sermons, strongly objected to my treatment of her. She ran out, but came back several moments later, still full of argument; and, when she found me adamant in my previous belief, she left a third time, crying and yelling and with tears of malice streaming down her face.] Today's example again convinced me that, sadly! only a very, very few are converted by such judgments as long as they refuse to become obedient to the gospels of our dear Lord Jesus. The fear and awe of sin impresses itself more upon the senses and is a fleeting shock, over too quickly to permit a true humiliation of the heart before the horror of recognized sin.

Tuesday, 5th July. I had R. [Rothenberger] here who, like the shoemaker A. [Arnsdorff], has been said to have drunk too much rum. However, he assured me with tears in his eyes that, as he would take it upon himself to swear on the day of judgment, his mind knew of no such sin, for his inability to row, which might have led others to believe him inebriated, was in fact due to great physical weakness which had already struck him in Purysburg. Nevertheless, he had known of A's [Arnsdorff's] drunkenness and had thus been witness of the fact that the latter had abused the Holy Sacrament; yet he had failed to notify us so that we could restrain him, for the salvation of his soul, from committing this heinous transgression. Therefore I told both him and H. [Hesler], who also was aware of the matter, that both had ample reason to repent from the bottom of their heart; otherwise the sins of A. [Arnsdorff], of which they had become guilty by their silence, might well be held against them. I read them James 5: 19-20, and admonished them therein.

Since yesterday, [Rauner, Stephen Riedelsperger, and] some Englishmen have stayed in our village on their way to bring some provisions by boat to the new fort above Savannah-Town. They have done everything in their power to persuade some of our people to travel there also; but, since I could not give my agreement to this request, their efforts were in vain, although some of the men were quite willing in view of the high wages promised to them against all natural and Christian equity, i.e., 30 £ in paper currency or 4 £ sterling per month. God has enforced a twofold judgment against this boat: first in regard to the shoemaker A. [Arnsdorff], and the other this morning against one of the Englishmen on the boat, who went into the water to bathe, only to be attacked by a large crocodile and seriously injured, so that he came crying and hollering to our hut to ask for some remedy. This is the fellow in whose presence Arnsdorff had drowned.

Today my fever abated early so that I could hold the prayer meeting, to which I was driven by the grief caused me today by the behavior of some people who wished to leave us for three or four weeks for the sake of some pounds. I announced to my listeners from the letter of the court chaplain Butjenter that the latter is attempting to obtain some bedding and old clothing for our people, and is assuring us kindly and definitely of the shipment of these goods. [Secondly, I read them a passage from the letter of Prof. Francke to the court chaplain Ziegenhagen, which praises the spiritual and professional qualities of our future medical man,[128] and that this man, for the love of God and our poor Salzburgers, was willing to travel here in true self-denial and without intention of furthering his own interests]. I also told them of the friendly offer of Dr. Gerdes to be of future service to our community, etc.

I thereupon proceeded to show them the reason for these quotations from our correspondence, i.e., to demonstrate to them the loving providence of the Lord for our congregation. For He had up to this day given us so many clear examples of His care in deed and spirit, and there was clear hope of future beneficial acts. Therefore, it was an ill sign that there were some among us who would escape their trials and their need by leaving our village for some time and follow their human beliefs and paths. It was impossible to assume of such persons that they had left their country only for the sake of the gospel; for, if this were true, they would stick with the gospels to the utmost. I knew of some, who have now entered the Lord's rest, who told me how they had met in caves and in the mountains in Salzburg for the chance of joint prayer, song, and reading, whenever they had an opportunity. But, since many among us do not show this serious and eager spirit, they must be lacking in this honest desire and will.

I was forced to let them know, I continued, that those who willingly excluded themselves from our community by their own will and travel would in the future also have to be excluded from the distribution of whatever material benefits we would receive. This procedure, of which I hope our benefactors will approve, had recently been followed in regard to the gift of linen. And I asked my listeners to repeat this point faithfully to those who were absent because of bodily weakness. It is a cardinal fault among us and most Christians that in times of need and privation, we will not remember the help and providence of the Lord as experienced in previous times as well as His certain promises. As Moses and other servants of the Lord had to remind their listeners not to forget the Lord's munificence, so we have had to do so here (Sirach 2: 10 ff.). "Consider the ancient generations and see."[129] [When Stephan Riedelsperger's wife asked him not to leave the village for such a long time, he used as an excuse the example of merchants back in Germany, who travelled much by water and on land and had to remain far from home for long periods on end, etc. Thus reason speaks against faith.]

[NB.] Wednesday, the 6th of July. A woman came to me and asked me, in her own and a sick person's name, to convey her thanks, especially for the gift of linen we have received, when

I write to our benefactors in Germany. She told me she had discussed the contents of yesterday's prayer meeting with the sick woman, [and it was to be considered a true blessing that we would have such a skilled man of medicine among us; everyone would be gladly prepared to give him some of the fruits of our harvests, which might prove to be of help and a welcome contribution. I was much impressed by her simplicity!] We have recently heard thunder daily, but the clouds have always passed without rain. This afternoon God finally sent a long and penetrating rain which, if it would last, should prove of much benefit to our parched lands. The corn is in bloom, and it is said that lack of rain during this period will cause the ears to remain small.

Thursday, the 7th of July. I have set pen to paper several times in order to write to our benefactors in England and Germany; but each time I have been disturbed, for all of our many sick want this or that and there is much extraordinary business. Some letters have been written meanwhile, but I shall postpone the most important ones until we have learned how Mr. Causton executes the recently received orders. Our dear God is beginning to restore me to health, and the first violence of the fever has much abated.

[NB.NB.] A pious Salzburger visited me after the paroxysms of his fever, which had struck him quite badly, to ask for advice. He told me how, when his headaches had been severe, he would remember the so far greater pain of Jesus Christ for all of mankind's sins; and tears welled to his eyes for his failure to recognize and feel proper gratitude for His suffering and His love. His salvation was of a great concern to him, and he was eager to save his soul. During the attacks of severe headaches he had believed that he might not remain constant, and harsh times might befall him if he ceased to resist, etc.; but God had again helped him. I spoke to him of the faithfulness of our Savior, who was more than a friend. A friend who turns away in our hour of need is no friend. Therefore, would our dear Savior, who paid so dearly for our friendship, turn away from him in his hour of final need and leave him alone? Upon leaving, the man complained of his ignorance, the wickedness of his heart, etc.; but, when, apart from His faithfulness, I praised the tenderness and the patience of our dear shepherd, he said: "Well, then everything will be all right."

Friday, the 8th of July. The recent rains did not last long; and, although we hear thunderstorms daily, no new rain has fallen.

We have not received any provisions yet; and, the longer they fail us, the more scarcity is suffered by our people. [There is little corn, flour, beans, and meat; and not even money can buy any in the surrounding country.] The small amount of flour which we recently bought from the ship from London serves us well, and we give as much of it to the sick as is within our circumstances. Next Monday I shall again send the boat to the plantation at Pallachocolas, where we recently bought several bushels of corn and beans, to see whether we cannot get some more food. Mr. Causton has given the money therefor and has agreed to this expense, if only we can find something to buy. Captain Diamond has been sent to New York and Pennsylvania with his ship to fetch butter and flour, and perhaps some meat.

Saturday, the 9th of July. G. [Griening], who is well known to Mr. Ziegenhagen and who came to us with the third transport, served as a soldier in Frederica all of last year and will probably remain there; for he has not only sent for his belongings but intends to get married in that town. Some people in Savannah are much annoyed that he should leave our village, a good opportunity for edification, and the good example set here and seek his domicile at a place where nothing but wickedness and ostentation reign. If he would only stay in Savannah, he would at least have some opportunity to live a good life. He spent some time in N. [Herrnhut]; and from the very beginning he has not really been in harmony with us, although he showed his pleasure with the Lord's word as taught here. He will probably now be deprived of any good that may have been in him.

A good Salzburger woman brought my dear colleague the gift of a melon (which is the kind of present our flock is eager to give us). When she passed my house, I told her that we should hear tomorrow from the gospel for the Fifth Sunday after Trinity, from Luke 5: 1 ff., i.e., "Where the Lord Jesus is, there is blessing",[130] to which I added a few observations for her family, which is ill at home and cannot attend the service. She accepted my encouragement with such words and expressions that I was greatly edified and impressed. There are many among us who seek nothing but the Lord Jesus and the mercy he has earned us, and they speak the truth from Psalm 73: "Whom have I in heaven, but thee," etc.[131]

Sunday, the 10th of July. Today, praised be the Lord, I have felt as well as if I had never been struck by the fever. Thus, I have been able, without impediment, to read the lovely gospel of Jesus which contains an abundance of salvation and grace;

and I have also been able to visit some among the sick. Toward evening, however, I felt a relapse into the fever and, in order to save my strength, I cancelled the repetition hour. I plan to repeat today's sermon tomorrow night during prayer. It is most edifying to observe how even those whom the fever has kept in bed are quite keen to return to the Lord's word, and this is clear proof of their strong and pure desire for the gospel. Some cannot stay for the whole service, but even so they have received some food for their souls and will learn the rest either from us or from others. A woman told me that she and her husband had been so impressed with the sermon that immediately afterwards they had both fallen to their knees and begged the Lord to preserve this treasure in their souls. Of another woman I learned that she would have liked to preserve the content of the sermon on "Where the Lord Jesus is, there is blessing" for her memory and recollection and had asked her daughter to write it on the margin of her Bible close to the text, but there had not been enough room.

Monday, the 11th of July. Our pious Salzburgers feel much strengthened in their hearts by our visits to the ill and the healthy; and those whom we visit first tell us at once how this and that one have been waiting for us with great eagerness. On such occasions we need not look afar for subjects of discourse, for they offer so much matter for talk that an hour will pass as nothing. And if we should leave without prayer, they would be only half sated. The lack of food is greater than ever before, and the poor souls are much in need of our comfort and encouragement. A widow confided in me how much the tragic death of the shoemaker had impressed her heart. A terrible judgment had come over him, she said, for his mother-in-law, who had formerly lived in Halle and in the service of Prof. Francke, had been drawn to the Lord, had much labored with this her son-in-law during her lifetime, and had reproached him for his soldierly vulgarities and meanness.[132] He, however, had kicked her and treated her harshly, which she had borne patiently for the patience of the Lord Jesus, not without warning him, however, that such behavior would do him harm, etc. And the widow, who told me this story in the presence of her children, remembered the saying of Solomon, Proverbs 30:17. "The eye that despiseth to obey his mother . . . the ravens of the valley shall pick it out," and truly, when they found him, one of his eyes was missing from his head.

[The lack of food being quite serious], my dear colleague is travelling to a plantation in Carolina with a few of the Salzburgers to see whether he can buy some provisions. We accompanied him with our prayers. May the Lord be with him and soften the minds of those who, for reasons of this world, refuse to sell what they can well spare. In our prayer meetings we have reached the 15th and 16th chapters of Exodus, which show us that God has travelled the same paths with His people; and this gives us confidence that, if we but believe firmly in His promises, He will not let us linger in this want, any more than did His people, even though they had sinned by murmuring.

Tuesday, the 12th of July. Yesterday we had thunderstorms and a strong shower that penetrated the ground and blessed the parched land. The strong winds, which lashed the rains down, bent down much of the Salzburgers' corn in the fields. However, since it did not break, but was merely bent with the root, it is being straightened and reinforced with new soil. Only a few of our children can come to school and attend catechisation, for most of them are ill with the fever. In the meantime, we teach the few who can come. N. [Ernst's smallest child] died last night from fever and diarrhea; and it was buried this noon. His wife is in bed with the same illness; [but, as in other matters, she is most careless in her use of medication.] Before the funeral I went to her and tried to persuade her, in serious words, to prepare for eternity by a true conversion; for in her present condition she can not die a happy death. She did not contradict me and did not try to offer arguments, as is her want; but the word cannot take root among such people; they are full of wordly thought and false comfort and do not pray sincerely for the recognition of their sins.

Wednesday, the 13th of July. This morning during school hours my dear colleague returned home without having found any food for sale. The man who ordinarily sells us corn had been [in drunken company] at Fort Pallachocolas. My colleague had waited for him for a long time, only to be told that the corn had been fed to the horses and the voyage was therefore in vain. Because the dearth of food is so serious, I had to resolve to travel to Savannah this very afternoon so as to be able to return by Sunday. I must speak to Mr. Causton about the accounts anyhow, and I shall take the opportunity to present him personally with our [extreme] want.

Thursday, the 14th of July. My dear colleague, Mr. Boltzius, having left yesterday for Savannah, and finding myself alone, I have used this afternoon to visit the ill. I would have continued school; but few children are well, and I feel that it is good to visit those who are sick. For, when they are well, they are rarely home; but, when they are ill, they can be found in their houses and they accept our words in their heart. When I visited one of the people [a young Salzburger], who normally is quite impudent, he expressed his wonderment that man could thus refuse God's mercy. I replied that this should show him the truth of our song: "Adam's fall has quite corrupted man's nature and being."[133] And, if only a man believed the truth of this song, he could be helped. The fever also gives us a good opportunity to speak to the heart of the children. One of the mothers told me that her child wished to die, for she was sure to go to heaven. I was much astonished at that and asked the child where she gained this knowledge; for our Lord Jesus had said, "He that is of God heareth God's words."[134] She knew full well, I continued, that both at school and in church she was among those children who caused me much grief; she would not listen and, even if she did listen here and there, she did not listen well. Thus, she was not of God and neither His child nor an heir of eternal life. She could not reply to this and started to cry.[135] [I was much pleased at having remembered this very saying, for the parents are also not among our good hearers; yet they are convinced they are good Christians; particularly the mother refused to let go of her opinions, regardless of our words.]

Friday, the 15th of July. I again visited the sick today and took the opportunity to speak to them according to their circumstances. May the Lord bless everything for the good of their souls. One of the children who are still healthy, and of whom many complaints were made, promised earnestly to change and do well. May God make this promise come true.

[NB.] Saturday, the 16th of July. Yesterday and the day before in our prayer meeting, we discussed the 16th chapter of Exodus, from which we learned that God had made bread rain from the heavens. So that our audience might realize that even today God still thinks of the physical care of his people, it has been so ordained that this very day our boat returned from Savannah with twenty bushels of corn. Having been forced to stay behind for the settlement of the accounts, my dear colleague sent a note that this corn had come from New England, that is to say, a place whence we have never received any such food. The Salzburgers told us that the captain of the ship had not wanted to come here, instead he had intended to travel to the Spanish fort at St. Augustine but had not been able to reach it and thus had turned

his ship to Georgia instead.[136] Since Mr. Causton had believed
that we should get corn in Carolina, I am convinced that he
would not have set any aside for us, had it not been for the fact
that the dear Lord inspired my dear colleague, when I returned
with empty hands, to travel to Savannah so that we might obtain
some provisions. This is clear proof of the Lord's concern for
us and of the nearness of His help when the need is greatest.
He is also testing us, whether we shall now follow His law and
shall place greater trust in Him than previously. May God grant
that His final will be done with us.

Sunday, the 17th of July. [Since it is quite clear that matters
with most of our listeners are not as they should be], I took
occasion today to show them from the gospel that there was
more to salvation than they imagined. I am well aware that many
are displeased if we deny their salvation and consider it harsh
preaching if we show them publicly and specifically how they
should put a firm foundation under their Christian belief by
means of a true conversion, if they wish to be truly saved, and
that they remain confident of their safety just as they are and
say in their hearts: "Nothing shall come of it, we shall stay as
we are";[137] and therefore I read them the example of the Jewish
People in Jeremiah 18:11–12. At the very beginning I impressed
on them that they should not fall back into their old ways but
for once should believe the word of their Lord Jesus Christ and
become obedient. For in this manner they would surely enjoy
the fruits of the Kingdom of mercy and of glory.

Immediately after the sermon I felt quite ill; and upon reaching home I came down with a severe attack of cold chills. I took
to bed, but towards three o'clock in the afternoon God had so
strengthened me that I managed to hold a short catechisation
on the 6th petition. May the Lord be praised! Toward evening
I was called to a widow, who confided in me that she felt so weak
that she believed she was coming closer and closer to her death.
I asked her at this opportunity whether she hoped to be saved;
and, when she affirmed it, I told her of the Lord's demands, in
today's Scriptures and elsewhere in the Bible, of those who
wished surely to be saved. If she was not yet aware of these
demands, things were not well with her. But if she knew of true
conversion and rebirth and of better righteousness, and knew
that she would pass from death to life, then she should not
doubt her salvation but be sure of it as she was sure she was lying
on her bed. She thereupon replied there was nobody in
Ebenezer as sure of her salvation as she. Since I could tell her

truthfully, however, that there were such people among us, and since I could tell her what the Holy Scriptures said of them, she believed me. I then advised her to choose the path of simplicity, for the Lord Jesus so loved her soul that He would not refuse her if she came. And when I told her how some in our flock ill received advice as to their defects, she answered that she did not mind that, but much liked our words of criticism. May God convince them all of their damnation, so that they may be helped.

Monday, the 18th of July. Today has been spent in work, that is, I have given medication to the ill and helped them with their needs; and subsequently I distributed the corn which arrived last Saturday. I hope that the large boat which was sent to fetch Mr. Boltzius will bring more provisions.

Toward evening, the surveyor, who had been here before to allot the gardening plots, arrived from Purysburg. He intends to mark a line around the entire land, so that we might know how much good earth is here in all and can report on it to our benefactors in England and Germany.

Tuesday, the 19th of July. Late at night, I (Boltzius) returned home under divine protection, accompanied by the Salzburgers and with some provisions in the form of corn and a little flour. Praise the name of the Lord, who has protected my health and has seen to it that my departure and return should not have been quite in vain. Mr. Causton has again done everything in his power and shown me much love and also communicated to me the contents of the letter the Honorable Trustees wrote him on behalf of our flock, the contents of which are quite in accord with those of the letter I received. When he insisted that the corn that the Salzburgers had planted in Old Ebenezer prior to their moving and had harvested with such difficulties should be considered part of the provisions allocated to them, I impressed on him the difficulties and sad consequences which were bound to follow from this demand; and he was moved to waive the demand and to inform the Honorable Trustees accordingly. [He is quite variable in his resolutions, promises and permissions; and this has caused me much trouble with regard to our congregation so I shall not speak of it in detail.]

We have examined both our private accounts and those relating to the provisions for the community, but not in such detail as to establish clearly where we stand in regard to our salary on the one hand and the provisions received from the store-house on the other, nor with regard to the Salzburgers and the provisions received by them. [Everything there is done in its own good time. On this occasion I learned of a number of details which cause me much grief and for whose outcome I shall have to wait.] Upon my departure Mr. Causton promised me to visit and observe the Salzburgers' work; and, since the preacher there, Mr. Wesley, also wished to come, I asked him to accompany Mr. Causton. This might well serve to persuade him to come sooner, which I consider to be most desirable.

[I have become quite familiar with Mr. Wesley during this somewhat longer stay in Savannah, and we have joined our hearts in the Lord. He performs the work of the Lord; and, since he takes his Savior and the souls of his congregation seriously, our faithful Shepherd will provide him with an even larger measure of the true evangelical spirit. He takes the duties of Christianity quite seriously and he diligently visits his parishioners, some of whom receive him well. He is a great enthusiast for good German songs, of which he has learned quite a number with their melodies; and he has translated some of these into English and had them printed in Charleston, together with some psalms that had been done into English verse. He intends to print some more of these songs. He revealed a matter to me which he carried in his mind against me, my dear colleague, and other teachers of our church and which he feared might divide our minds. But, as far as I could learn, and of which I shall report privately at the proper place, these matters seem to be of no consequence and an unnecessary scruple on his part.]

Wednesday, the 20th of July. The fever still persists among us, but not quite as violently as last year. Many being ill and the others busy with their own work, some of the fields cannot be tended as properly as they should. The recent heavy winds have bent much corn to the ground which has not yet been raised up and supported by firm earth. The people work as hard as they can and leave the rest to the Lord, who will arrange everything for the best. The surveyor has started today to establish the land which is to serve for the Salzburgers' plantations and to make the first demarcation lines, in which he is accompanied by Salzburger men knowledgeable in such matters. He has instructions to heed my advice and wishes; and I have informed him of the intent of our dear benefactors, who truly wish the best for the Salzburgers and have asked him to survey the land in accordance with their wishes. He will closely follow Mr. Oglethorpe's orders to survey all plantations in a square of sixteen English miles,[138] [for which reason some of the land will turn out to be poor ground.] If only each family would receive some good land, we should be content.

Thursday, the 21st of July. This morning before school I visited some of my flock, and God has given me much edification and joy in seeing that the strength of the death and resurrection of Christ is so beautifully evident in them. I found a woman reading her prayer book and sighing deeply for the lack of clear comfort. A few days ago, while she was lying on her sick-bed, she had felt that the blood of our Lord had flowed on her clear and red, and her heart had taken great joy at this. [To be sure, it had occurred to her that this might be but a dream, phantasy, or deception; but it had been too clear for her not to accept it as the truth.] Thereupon I read her the last lines from the song: "A little lamb goes and bears the guilt,"[139] etc., which shows how a faithful soul uses to good avail the blood of reconciliation shed by the Lord. Because of her present anxiety I comforted her further with God's word and with the words of an edifying song: "I know Thou canst not reject me. How couldest Thou be unmerciful to him whom Thy blood has redeemed from guilt and pain, since it flowed so abundantly,"[140] etc.

Another woman, who had been greatly weakened by fever, said that it seemed to her as if the Lord Jesus were calling to her: "Jump right in, it won't be so deep."[141] And when, to strengthen her faith and that of others persons present, I said something from yesterday's prayer-hour about the exceedingly great father-love and goodness of God toward His children and showed how the children of God should imagine their Father in heaven such as He himself has pictured it in His words, the woman turned in her bed and said, with a special look on her face: "I must remember that." I and the others received much blessing from the verse in Luke 6: "He is kind unto the unthankful" (and how much more for His children, Psalm 23:10), likewise Isaiah 43: "Thou hast wearied me with thine iniquities" (but do not think that I shall be angry because of that, but) "I am he that blotteth out thy transgressions for mine own sake"[142] (because I am so kind, even though you might not merit it with your piety, repentance, and penance.)

Toward evening we received a slaughtered ox from Old Ebenezer, where the Honorable Trustees have recently begun to have cattle kept on their behalf. Due to the difficulties in bringing it here, however, the carcass had almost spoiled and we were much pressed to distribute it. We also received about 600 lbs of salted beef from there, which shall relieve our needs for a brief time.

Friday, the 22nd of July. The preacher in Savannah and Mr. Causton and his wife have done their best to persuade me to use *China de China* with our people to combat the fever and have assured me, giving themselves and others as examples, that there was no fear of the least ill effect from this cure, if only the method is followed of giving the patient some vomiting powder prior to use. The medication from the aforesaid bark is prepared as follows: Take two ounces *China de China*, a handfull of wormwood and as much snakeroot, mix it with four quarts of water and boil it down to two quarts. Then the water is poured off, the mixture is cooled and filled into bottles. The ingredients are again boiled with four quarts of water until only two quarts are left, and again filled into bottles. When the patient has a good day, he must take a vomiting agent, and about seven hours later he must take a wine glass full of the concoction every half hour, until nothing is left. It is said that there will be no more cramps after that. I took along two ounces of *China de China* from the store-house in Savannah, so as to give it a try. We do not trust it much, for in Germany such cures are considered quite dangerous. One of our women has agreed to give it a try, although we would hardly encourage her. The large number of patients causes us much work with their bodily needs, and I have been kept from writing letters to England and Germany.[143]

Saturday, the 23rd of July. This afternoon I met with those in our village who are still well, to reflect on a few matters. May God bless all our undertakings, to His glory and our salvation! The present sad circumstances require some disbursement for the sake of the poor and the sick, and it is clearly the providence of the Lord that the last ship should have brought such a welcome gift. May the name of the Lord be praised for His mercy, now and forever!

Sunday, the 24th of July. I announced to the congregation that we shall go to the Lord's Table in a fortnight's time and that those who wish to participate should start timely preparation for this holy and important act by serious prayer. I could not but mention the terrible judgment which our Lord has recently executed on the shoemaker, A. [Arnsdorff], which we should take as a warning. I recounted that, after being disciplined for a previous offence, and after having promised true improvement, he had again become completely intoxicated and immediately thereafter had gone to the Lord's Table and had now experienced the word: "Be not deceived; God is not mocked."[144] Those among us who had known of this matter and failed to advise us accordingly would have to bear his sin until they confessed from the bottom of their hearts and cleansed themselves with the blood of reconciliation shed by Jesus Christ. They could have saved the unfortunate man; but they had failed to do so, which was a terrible matter. I therefore earnestly requested from everyone not to conceal, because of human fear, the disorderly behavior they might notice in their brethren, since their own salvation and that of the sinner would depend on it.

A few days ago my dear colleague suffered his share of fever and diarrhea; and, since he has lost much strength, I counseled him to protect his strength on this day and to let me do the work which is normally his share. If God should strengthen him, he will all the better be able to take care of the school and the congregation during the coming week, for I would like to remain at home so as to write letters. This afternoon, instead of catechisation, I related to our listeners for their benefit the life of the blessed Schaitberger, whose memory is highly regarded by our Salzburgers. I felt this to be the lightest task in view of the terrible heat and my still failing strength.

Monday, the 25th of July. An Englishman from a Carolina plantation has sold some butter here; and, when we asked him for the sale of some corn, he told us of the terrible scarcity of foodstuffs further up the river. It had not rained there either for a long period, and the worms were doing terrible damage to the green corn, so that increased dearth had to be expected. Even the butter is scarce and costly, for many cattle have drowned in the recent inundations of the Savannah river. Salt beef and pork are so scarce that not even money will let you see a bite, let alone buy it. This morning we sent the boat to Savannah in order to fetch at least some salt, if there is nothing else in the store house. It is a most unusual sign of God's providence that I should unexpectedly have been able to purchase corn on my recent trip to Savannah and had forty-four bushels either sent or carried on my boat. Our people here have the same complaint, that the worms are eating up the green corn and there is no remedy against it.

Tuesday, the 26th of July. For the last few days I have dwelled during the prayer meeting on the fact that the wicked Israelites, Exodus 16:3, had accused Moses in a shameful and lying manner that they had previously lived better sitting by the flesh pots and having ample bread to eat, whereas in truth it can hardly be believed that the harsh and cruel Egyptians would have slaughtered, and given them for food, the oxen and sheep which they

worshipped as Gods. Besides, the Israelites had suffered grievously in their bodies at their hard labor. I explained this unfounded praise and wicked thinking by the behavior of many of
our contemporaries who praise previous days and conditions,
however modest they may have been, for the sole reason of
denying and negating the present providence and munificence
of the Lord. They acted like soldiers on their march who compare the present quarters with previous ones, praising the latter
and despising the present one to the anger of their host, and
going on in this manner at the next stop. I told them, however,
that this constituted a grievous sin if man, to whom God shows
his love in body and soul every day, should hold his present state
for little and long in a material way for his old condition, which
was surely covered with much sin and abuse.

I warned my listeners not to do like the rest of the world, as
some of those among us whose material state may previously
have been better than now are tempted to do. This warning so
touched one of the men among us that he came to me afterward
and confessed that he had on occasion harbored such feelings
and thus sinned. Although he had not knowingly and with bad
intent praised past times during which he had been somewhat
better off, he realized that it was not good for anything and
could not edify his neighbor. For the comfort and insight of our
sufferers, I showed that those among the Israelites who would
have stayed with, or returned to, those flesh pots of Egypt, if
they had ever had them, would have failed to receive mannah
and bread from heaven; for God would bestow the latter only
on those who previously had eaten the bread of misery (unleavened tasteless bread) while He was guiding them through the
wilderness. For these have always been the ways of the Lord with
his people, to lead them away from the pleasures and ease of
the world and to feed them with the bread of tears and misery
so that they might recognize the sins commited in their spiritual
Egypt. However, if they remained faithful, He would send mannah and our Lord Jesus would comfort their suffering with Himself and all His mercy. Hallelujah!

Wednesday, the 27th of July. The heat is so great that we can
hold school only in the morning with the few children who are
still well. We much regret having to spare our strength as much
as possible, whereas the needs and the wishes of our flock would
require us to visit them throughout the entire day and to speak
to them from God's word, which is of much benefit. To be sure,
thunderstorms will gather towards evening; but they bring nei-

ther rain nor coolness. This afternoon we had an unexpected shower, which somewhat refreshed our land.

This morning I visited a hut where I met two women in useful conversation: one of them told me with great joy that she had suffered much discomfort and physical need; but she had prayed to her heavenly Father as a child would to his father, and at that very moment the Lord had clearly come to her help. Since both women were kept from last night's prayer meeting by their feeble state, I told them what the Lord has communicated to us from His word in Exodus 17, which describes how the Lord, having saved the children of Israel from one danger, had led them into another, that is, the lack of water. In this condition they should have encouraged each other with knowledge of God's previous help and said thus: "Do not murmur, but think of the danger in which we have found ourselves and from which the Lord has so miraculously saved us! Has He not promised us many a time to be our Lord of the covenant and to have mercy and provide for us? Let us hold onto His promises, He shall and will neither leave nor abandon us, however long the trial may last."[145]

But the contrary is true, and we see many Christians who cease being Christians in time of need or rather show clearly that they had never been true believers. Such as those would have to learn their lesson in the school of the Lord Jesus, the lesson learned by St. Paul and all believers (Hebrews 11:35, Romans 8:35,38), which we find in Philippians 4:11–13: "For I have learned, in whatsoever state I am, therewith to be content. I know both to be abased, and I know how to abound: everywhere and in all things I am instructed both to be full and to be hungry, both to abound and to suffer need. I can do all things through Christ which strengtheneth me." The Lord Jesus is a patient schoolmaster, even if we cannot learn this lesson right away. And the lack of this necessary state of mind causes much unrest, injustice, and evil among man, whereas a truly contented person is quiet and accepts everything as God's gift and blessing, be it poverty or wealth, luck or misfortune, illness or health.

The other story I told them concerned the stone upon which Moses struck at the Lord's command and in the presence of the elders of Israel, causing water to flow for the thirsty Israelites, in which water other peoples and generations have shared as a sign of God's encompassing grace in Jesus Christ. For our spiritual and eternal salvation, our dear Savior had been struck and his side had been pierced with a lance, and blood and water had flowed therefrom for our purification and sanctification. We have thus received the full bounty of grace, and He invites the sinners kindly to slake their thirst, as had the Samaritan woman in John 4:13-14. However, many are lacking in true spiritual thirst; and thus they honor Christ as little as the rich regard water, since they have much else to drink and fail to thank the Lord. We were all much pleased by this story and discussion.

N.[Paul Lemmenhofer] has also been ill for some time; and, since he has been arrogant and recalcitrant in his days of health, God has now started to soften him. I have told him much, during my recent two visits, of the absolute need of a complete change of heart and prayed with him to this effect. May God give him a chance for repentance. I feared that he had a secret curse of injustice, theft, fraud, etc., on himself, of which he should free himself; but he feels that his conscience is free of such transgressions.

Thursday, the 28th of July. A pious man told me that his corn, that had grown so well, was so badly blighted by the worms that he had little hope of a good harvest, if God were not to avert further damage. He was quite composed, however; and he quite trusted in the Lord that He would provide for him if he should only keep the faith. This new trial imposed by the Lord left him with a number of meritorious thoughts: God can grant us a blessing but then take it away. One should see that His blessings are everything and man is nothing. Last year the worms had also caused damage, which had been attributed to the late planting. This year, on the other hand, he and the others had planted early enough; yet the blight had still recurred. The man continued, however, that he had proof of the Lord's providence, of which he cited a simple example that had happened yesterday and which had much strengthened his faith. The fever had so weakened him and his wife that he had not known how to get the water needed for boiling beer. But soon thereafter God had sent a heavy rain which filled a whole barrel close to his hut, so that there had been enough water for boiling beer. Because the letters I had just written to our benefactors were lying right before me, I told him to his joy and new edification what was strengthening my belief and gladdening me, i.e., that our dear friends and benefactors never tired of hearing our complaints and the descriptions of our trials and used them in praying, caring, and providing for us as if our want were theirs. I had also informed them of the blight caused by the worms, etc. I had advised both Mr. Vernon and, through the letter to Mr. Verelst, the Honorable Trustees how well and industriously our people had planted their corn and how well it had grown, until the worm blight had ravaged everything. Perhaps God will bless this report in due time.

A pious woman told me how her son had been attacked by the heat of the fever, and how she kept reminding him of God's purpose in this. In days of health he was much too frivolous and forgot his promise to walk in the ways of the Lord and to pray industriously: God would not free him until he seriously resolved to convert to His grace and to present his misery to Him seriously in prayer. She had observed, she added, that he now followed her remonstrations more closely, etc.

I had sent the boat down for salt, but it returned with six sacks of flour. Two sloops have anchored at Savannah that are carrying flour and I do not know what else, of which Mr. Causton has made provisions for the third transport. Since there are many sick people among us who cannot very well make do with Indian corn, the boat returned to Savannah today to buy a few more kegs of flour, and we intend to contribute from the poor box for the sake of those among us who cannot afford it.

Friday, the 29th of July. About two years ago an old German schoolmaster named Uselt,[146] who may still be known to Court Preacher Ziegenhagen, came to Purysburg with his wife and four daughers. He died not long thereafter, before we had an occasion to meet him. His widow and two of her daughters went into service at a place near Savannah; and shortly thereafter she travelled with her youngest daughter to Charleston, where she recently died. The third daughter, also young and uneducated, lasted another year at the aforementioned plantation; but her master and mistress left the country, leaving her behind without any means of support or payment. She has now come here and would like to be prepared for Holy Communion; and, since she is utterly ignorant, we cannot but accept her, provide her with the bare necessities for her support, and instruct her in our school. Her oldest sister is married here but is not in a position to support her.[147]

Saturday, the 30th of July. N.N. [Paul Lemmenhofer] was very fatigued for a long time and could find no rest day or night, although he suffered neither pains nor fever as others do. Yesterday, his condition changed to a severe diarrhea; and, although his condition seemed to have improved by this morning, he died suddenly and against all expectations. Not being able to leave the house today because of the medication I have taken,

I had him reminded, by his cousin, of my recent advice, i.e., that he should above all implore the Lord for the recognition of his sins so that he might be truly saved; and this message was delivered. In his lifetime, he [was one of the most improper young men who] refused to accept the word of the Lord; and because of his material concerns he could not bring himself to accept the trials of the Lord, so that he had made up his mind to leave our village if matters did not improve. In the end, he felt oppressed on his sickbed and prayed. This may well have been accepted, but whether he had been truly reborn, of the absolute necessity for which I had tried to convince him, he is the only one who knows. May God grant that this example will make a proper impression, particularly among his young fellow men who are of the same spirit. I shall not fail to use this lesson to good avail.

Our letters to England and Germany have been written, and we only await opportunity for sending them by a safe carrier, which may God provide. The package, which also contains the diaries, is quite heavy; and this gives us all the more reason to wish it in safe hands. Mr. Wesley, the preacher in Savannah, and others have complained that their letters are often lost; but, praised be the Lord, to the best of our knowledge none of our mail, whether written by us or to us, has been lost so far [148], with the exception of the four guineas which Mr. Ziegenhagen sent the congregation and which were not delivered, of which we sent advice. May God continue to protect us and our letters, so that they may not only reach their destination but have some effect and good influence. We have written four English letters to London this time, one to Capt. Coram, two to the Honorable Trustees, and one to the Honorable Society; and we have reported the contents of the last three to Mr. Ziegenhagen, for his information.

My most important letters to Germany were addressed to Senior Urlsperger, Prof. Francke, and also to my dear family, such as my cousin, Wachsmann in Berlin, our dear benefactress Mrs. von H. [Heslin], and Mr. Schauer and, in London, to Dr. Gerdes, Court Chaplain Butjenter, and Mr. Mathiessen, who has much love for us and our dear flock. Some of the pious people here have also been encouraged, by the many signs of love and good will, to write to their benefactors in London and Germany, as well as to their friends. I have tried to persuade the schoolmaster, Ortmann, to write to the Honorable Society so as to gratefully report receipt of the gift of 5 £ sterling, which he has promised to do. We have been asked to report at the end of the diary the number of the deceased and living members of the congregation who have been with us from the beginning. Thirty-one of the adults have died here and in Old Ebenezer and twenty-four children; among the living are eighty-nine adults, and forty-three children. If we should add the names of both the living and dead, we request orders to this effect.

Sunday, the 31st of July. Today I tried to warn our listeners, on the basis of this Sunday's texts from Matthew 7: 15 ff. and through the Lord's word, of seduction and self-deceit. I also warned them that the seducers are not only found among the teachers, but also among the listeners, in particular where God has appointed honest teachers, etc. There was no doubt that in Germany young men, although well raised in their parents' house, were often seduced and led astray by other young men; but here, too, the young in our congregation were party to such sins, for with their unruly behavior they attempted to tear down what the teachers had spent much effort to erect, thus causing much grief. On this occasion I remembered N.N.[Paul Lemmenhofer], buried before the morning service, in that he too had schemed with others of his kind and led some of the young men astray and had been led astray by others, so that the word of truth could not take hold in him. I told his companions publicly that he would ill thank them in eternity for their efforts to talk him out of God's word and to support him in his unconverted state. However, what joy and praise of God there would be in heaven if they had strengthened him in his salvation with their encouragement and had prepared with him for eternity. We had seen little proof in him on his sickbed which would have indicated with certainty that he had accepted, for his true conversion, the advice we gave him on the occasion of our last visit.

After the afternoon service one of the Salzburgers came to me and admitted with tears his sorrow at having let the young man die without having remonstrated with him for his serious sin against my person and office, of which I had been unaware, nor had announced this matter to me in time. Now he had died with this terrible blasphemy on his heart, almost in the condition of excommunication. This caused the man much anxiety, and he begged me to come to his house this week so that I might assist him with prayer and advice. He complained much about sloth and human fear and assured me that these would never again cause him to remain silent about sins and other evil deeds, no matter what might happen to him.

Prior to and during this Salzburger's visit I was much bothered by the fever; but God so strengthened me that I could go out to speak to N. [Pichler] and his wife, as I had promised yesterday. N. [Mrs. Pichler] recently sinned greatly in wrath and offended the congregation by uttering offensive language and evil expressions; and her husband has seriously tried to bring her to repentance, recognition, and serious confession of such improper conduct, for else I should and would have to exclude her from Holy Communion. However, he had not even been able to persuade her to come with him to see me, [even though she lives right across from me.] He twice complained yesterday of these and other matters which he suffered from her every day.

When I entered their hut in the name of the Lord, I found them both ill and much weakened by the fever, which had prevented them from coming to church. Therefore I took the occasion to repeat the contents of my sermon and to warn them seriously and with much emotion of self-deceit and seduction. Much to my surprise, she was much pleased at my coming; and her husband told me that the death of the late N.N. [Paul Lemmenhofer] had been constantly on his mind while he was suffering from the fever and that it seemed too terrible to him that the man may have fared badly. This gave me an opportunity to mention to them both that I had only now learned of his terrible transgressions against me and my office and that he had now departed without confession and repentance, but in the wickedness of his heart, which was a terrible matter. This moved them both to tears, and the husband admonished his wife with sighs to contemplate and reflect on this example.

I added only that I did not feel anger at her, but pitied her deeply for her miserable condition; but I also said that I could not speak well of her chances of salvation as long as she remained in this state of unrepentance. She thereupon came close to me, offered me her hand, and confessed with many tears and sighs, while her husband almost dissolved in tears. I showed my joy at her testimony and told her how I forgave her from the bottom of my heart; since, however, she knew of the resentment against her behavior among the congregation, I could not let her take Communion unless I publicly announced her repentance and apology. Did she wish this to be done? To my and her husband's utter surprise, she willingly consented; for he confided that she had formerly always refused this, even if she might never again take Communion and if the gallows were erected in front of her door. How wonderful the Lord guides His house;

I was despaired of winning this [spiteful, wilful, and arrogant] woman, and her husband, too, had despaired; but God knew the right way!

AUGUST[149]

The 1st of August. M. has been working for Mr. C.[150] [Causton] for the last three months, and he returned at this time to take Holy Communion. I have been told, however, that he has behaved improperly and has caused much annoyance, so that he shall not be admitted until we have proof of a change of heart. Although I have no knowledge of his actual misbehavior, I cannot in good conscience admit such people who have been away from us and our spiritual care and supervision for long periods to Communion until they have been with us for some time and have prepared themselves in a Christian manner in accordance with our instructions.

I sent for two people this morning in order to show them, with God's word, that the state of their souls was still most unsatisfactory and that, therefore, they would have to spend this week in earnest effort if they were to benefit from their intended use of the Holy Sacrament. Since their arrival here they have had to be kept away from the Lord's Table; but now they make a better impression, at least outwardly; and they promise much good. I warn them, as much as is in my power, of sins against the body and blood of our Lord; and I shall repeat this warning, which is customary in our prayer meetings, several times this week.

The 2nd of August. A certain person has told me of the island of St. Thomas,[151] where he has spent some time. The air there is said to be quite unhealthy, the white people there live most wickedly and treat the Negroes or Moorish slaves in a most tyrannical fashion, but that many of those slaves had opened their hearts to the belief in our Lord Jesus and now had begun to remind the whites of their duties, causing the latter to persecute them. The slaves' ardor and eagerness for good is said to be considerable. Both the Lutherans and the Reformed there are now without preachers, because two have died in succession. This afternoon, my dear colleague left for Savannah, partly to post our letters and partly to discharge our debts to Mr. Causton, who has sent us our private invoices for the provisions and other necessities advanced on our salary.

The 4th of August. NN has called me to visit him and talk with him in regard to the condition of his soul. On his sickbed he praised the Lord for having brought him into this wilderness and there shown him His word; he wishes he had never been brought into the Empire,[152] because other young people and pretended Christians there had caused him to become entangled in the tentacles of sin. Since God had brought him here, He had opened his eyes to the nature of true Christianity. However, he had to admit that he had not yet experienced a true rebirth, and I admonished him about this from the bottom of my heart and prayed with him. Since he has been confined without any care and attention, a married Salzburger has now taken him into his house.

The terrible heat and an internal fever have so weakened me today that I have been confined at home for most of the day despite the need to visit our flock, particularly those who are preparing to go to the Lord's Table. Toward evening we had some more thunderstorms and some rain, which, however, has not penetrated deeply.

The 5th of August. This morning I visited some of those who are planning to go to Holy Communion, and it caused me much joy and pleasure to hear how God is leading them both to the recognition of their misery and to the living awareness of Christ and His merited grace and what a struggle they are having in this respect with their body and flesh and with that archtraitor, Satan.

The 6th of August. I had two people come to me yesterday afternoon so as to reunite them in a Christian manner and to remove and clear away the source of their animosity. However, the fire smoldering in both of them erupted with such passion that I was much taken aback at the horrors they said to each other's face. In consequence of this, N. had to be kept from the Lord's Table, which he himself recognized as warranted. It also became evident on this occasion how these two offensive people have sinned against me with lies, insults, and evil talk whenever I have to perform the duties of my office toward them and approach them with matters of discipline relating both to the law and the church. May God let them recognize and repent such sins, as N. has done, and let them find forgiveness in the blood of Christ. I am not so much upset by their lack of gratitude and wickedness as I am sad for the blindness of their souls.

I have been much disturbed, both in the morning and the afternoon, by a fever racking my stomach, but I could not help but hold a necessary conference with the community and conduct the preparation which is customary on Saturdays, in which, upon her and her husband's request, I dealt with Mrs. N.'s offences before she could be admitted to Holy Communion. Therefore, in the course of the preparation, I showed the assembled flock that most people err grievously in their judgment if they confine their Christian ways to outward exercises, to the use of the means of redemption or the discharge of certain duties. Instead, for everyone who wishes to be a true Christian, it is important to learn in truth 1) the nature of sin and 2) what true rebirth means, and 3) what God's grace is.[153] Those who obtained such knowledge would also know what Christianity implied and what treasures are to be found in it.

The 7th of August. NN testified how his sins oppressed him and how in his fear he was anxious for God's mercy and thus desired to participate in Holy Communion. I let him go, for I hope that the good Lord may again work on his soul and he may well experience repentance for his recent sin. In all, twenty-nine attended the Lord's Table, many among them having appeared with a heart full of hunger for grace.

The 8th of August. Since both corn and rice are in short supply in the country and Mr. Causton has received some stores of flour, he is letting the first and second transports have some more of the latter, although it is not, properly speaking, part of their provisions. In view of the weak physical state of these people, we may well consider this another sign of God's paternal care.

The nights are now beginning to cool off again, but the heat during the day is still scorching and is debilitating the bodies that are still suffering attacks of fever. Since two persons have used *china de china,* prepared according to the recently described prescription, to good effect, several are demanding it from our little pharmacy, which we cannot refuse, recommending their use to the grace of the Lord.

The 9th of August. Our poor people are about to lose most of their fowl and other small livestock. They cannot give them much feed at home and therefore let both chickens and hogs run free so that they may find food in the swamps and bushes, where they are preyed upon by bears, crocodiles, and a certain type of large wild cat, which do much damage in this manner. Mrs. Holzer has suffered a consuming disease for some time now and is approaching her end rapidly. My dear colleague was called to her after our prayer meeting; and he spoke to her according to the condition of her soul and also gave her some of the *essentia dulci* to strengthen her. She seems to be suffering from a slow consuming fever but we cannot see our way to provide medicine for it. The store of medications recently sent from Halle has been much reduced by the many illnesses, and we must keep the rest for our own use.

The 10th of August. Ruprecht Steiner told me he wished I had enough time to go out into the fields of the Salzburgers to inspect the damage the worms have done to the corn. He had planted four acres and put much work in them but is now ready to give it all up if he could only get four bushels from it. Others have said the same thing. The worms have done most damage to those fields where the land is best and the corn the most beautiful. With all this, the man was quite calm and believed that the Lord will provide in some manner, even if the fields do not bear fruit. He and others have learned from this experience that it is not good land alone that provides a good harvest, but that the Lord's blessing provides the biggest part, in fact everything. May God grant that all come to believe this.

Mueller's oldest son[154] is seriously ill. When I visited them this morning, I found both parents and children in tears, and I was much pleased that the parents should be concerned that their son had not yet been converted to the Lord and thus could not be saved. This he himself recognized, as I noticed, with much repentance and sorrow, and he complained that his physical weakness would not let him repent and pray strongly enough. I talked to him from God's word and prayed with him and also took some steps to provide him better with care and medicines.

The 11th of August. A young Salzburger man who in his healthy days led a mediocre kind of Christian life (as the world will call it) has reached the recognition and awareness of his sins now that he is on his sickbed; he told me of this in the strongest manner. I reminded him of some sayings from the Scriptures from which he could learn that God did not reject him, as he might think, but would accept him gladly for the sake of Christ if only his repentance were to be truly felt. A woman complained of the damage to her soul that her illness caused her in preventing her from attending our prayer meetings. Seeing that God had returned some of her strength, she had wanted to come to us tonight if one of us had not come to her, for she urgently needed God's help. I recounted some of the words from last night's prayer meeting, which edified her and the others present. Mrs. Holtzer wept for the amount and severity of her sins and testified that it was her greatest concern to prepare for eternity. The earthly matters of which some of her visitors talk are as nothing to her and she could and would not think of them anymore.

The 12th of August. Yesterday afternoon we had a heavy rain, which has lasted today. The previous drought has been severe and has kept the people from planting their beets. May God grant that the beets and other roots will turn out better than the corn. The blighted corn offers a sad sight to those who go into the fields, as both my colleague and I did yesterday. As soon as I go to Savannah, I shall ask Mr. Causton to report the present sad state of affairs to the Honorable Trustees, and to let me enclose a letter to them at the same time. NN[155] has taken along our large bag of letters for delivery; and, since ships are sailing for London constantly, we need not worry about their proper arrival in that city. Mr. Eveleigh, who has until now taken care of our mail in Charleston, is fatally ill and there is doubt of his recovery.

The 13th of August. This morning I received word that the watchmaker's oldest son died early today. The father assured me that he had well prepared himself for death by serious prayer and struggle before God, and both parents and brothers and sisters had constantly spoken to him of God's word and prayed with him, which he had always been willing to do, notwithstanding his extreme weakness. This example has left a great impression on his many brothers and sisters, urging them to prepare in time for a blessed death. He had heavy diarrhea accompanied by strong internal heat, and there was nothing that could help him. At the same time, his limbs were cold and bloodless and could not be restored to a normal warmth by hot compresses.

This diarrhea is again very prevalent, which may be due to the fact that the heat is very severe, both day and night (with some exceptions) and almost intolerable. Therefore, against all caution, everyone is eager to obtain some relief by whatever refreshment he can get. They undress while in a sweat, wash, bathe, and lie down in cool places; and all this is bound to have some ill consequences. Yesterday and last night the rain brought so much cold with it that the drop in temperature can hardly be believed; and those who do not look out for themselves may well fall ill.

The 14th of August. While most in our community suffer from weakness caused by the fever, we do not see this prevent them from listening to the Lord's word. They attend the sermon; and, when the fever strikes them, they simply leave, which is otherwise rare in our meetings. For we insist, and our listeners themselves see to it, that everybody commences the public worship with prayers at the same time and everybody leaves as one group after we are finished, unless there is some emergency. This is also the case with Holy Communion in that even those who do not go to the Lord's Table will stay in church and join in the singing and praying.

The 15th of August. The crop failure, with some of our people not having any harvest from their fields, will cause some noticeable changes in those who have failed in their faith. However, the Lord will provide for those who are His children and will guard them from temptation. The illnesses this year are not confined to the fever, but there are many strange incidents and symptoms to be observed in a number of people which we cannot explain; therefore we urgently request a proper doctor. The hut purchased for him is now being fitted more conveniently and will be provided with a fireplace and chimney so that, should he come this winter, he may not be inconvenienced by the cold. My fever causes so much pain in my bowels both day and night that I am quite incapable of discharging my duties; and yesterday, I barely managed to hold the morning sermon. The only relief is to be obtained from exterior remedies, such as applying olive oil and hot compresses.

The 16th of August. I had planned to prepare some of the older children more closely for Holy Communion. However, their and my bodily weakness have forced postponement of this preparation until conditions have improved with God's help. Two persons have lived in hate and enmity toward each other and could not be reconciled when I talked to them in my rooms. Therefore I addressed the one mainly to be blamed for this state of affairs with harsh words and expressed my displeasure at her behavior. She has now been so touched by my remonstrations that she went on her own to the other's house to seek reconciliation; and now they are friends again, at least on the surface. Both women could be of much use in the community and this would also be to their own benefit, if only they had not acquired a bad reputation with the Salzburgers through their offensive conduct.

The 17th of August. Some of the people who had used *china de china* lost their fever, to be sure, but have suffered recurrences and now are not prepared to resume this medication, nor do we advise them to do so, although this is the generally used remedy against the fever in this country. Some are beset by abcesses and swollen hands, and this affects both small children and adults. I have been so strengthened by the Lord that I could hold the evening prayer meeting, wherein I and the listeners sought to gain joy from the beautiful promises made in Exodus, 19:5-6. Oh, how we would love to work and use our strength for the physical and spiritual benefit of our dear Salzburgers, if God would only provide and maintain such strength! He knows and is aware of our desires, and in His time He will give us what He considers right for us.

The 18th of August. To be sure, Mr. Causton had promised me and the preacher in Savannah to come to inspect the work of our people; but his arrival has been so much delayed that perhaps nothing will come of it. Nonetheless, I shall take the next opportunity to renew my request that he undergo this inconvenience so that he himself may observe the terrible damage that the worms have caused the corn and be moved to pity. The people are busy picking and bringing in the corn; but they cannot obtain a full bushel from each acre and are forced to feed the hogs with those ears that have been quite destroyed. The damage is considerable, and this is another great trial for our poor Salzburgers; and they will need comfort which our dear Lord will doubtless have prepared for them.

The 19th of August. Our boat brought some rice, flour, and cheese for the third transport from Savannah, which provisions I immediately distributed this afternoon. This evening I was called to a patient whose end appeared near. I administered some of our medicine to her, which has shown good effect. I sincerely pray that God will extend the life of this person so that we shall more time to work on her conversion.[156]

The 20th of August. I found Mrs. Holtzer very weak, and she expects nothing but her temporal death. This does not frighten her, for she has come to Christ as a poor and suffering sinner and believes that He has forgiven her. I told her of the example of old Simeon, much to her profit, and then prayed with her. Her daughter having fallen ill as well and thus being incapable of caring for her, they will both be taken in by a pious Salzburger family near by.

I had a most edifying conversation with N. and his wife. He told me how God had worked wonders during his heavy attack of the fever, when he had been prostrate and had lost all reason; and she added that, in these circumstances, she had prayed from her heart and been heard by the Lord. The woman can read with greater ease than her husband, and this makes her most useful to him, and he esteems her highly. We had a most fruitful rain this afternoon; but it and the accompanying thunderstorms stopped in a couple of hours.

The 21st of August. Mrs. Kornberger was delivered of two girls last night; I baptized the youngest one immediately because of her weakness, and the other one received the sacrament of holy baptism this morning in a public ceremony before the morning worship. After their recent communion, N. and his wife are well reconciled, not only in their work but also in their prayers and application of the Lord's word, and they have come to observe the Lord's blessing of their ways. He told me this afternoon that the Lord had shown him and his wife great mercy in the course of the last week and that they had to praise Him for His clear acceptance of their prayers. They had been quite ill with the fever early in the week; and, since for want of a doctor they did not know what medications to take, they had encouraged each other to present their physical suffering and domestic needs to the merciful Lord in their prayers. They had persevered for several days in this, whereupon the Lord had relieved them of their fever so that they regained their strength and noticed its effects only occasionally.

Last week my dear colleague had to travel on business, and therefore I was alone today with our flock. For the past few days and today, our dear heavenly Father has strengthened me quite noticeably so that I have been able to conduct the repetition hour in addition to the morning sermon and the afternoon catechism. In the latter meeting I took up the important and necessary message of the Office of the Keys,[157] to the great comfort of the faithful among us and to the terror and fear of the unrepentant and Godless. They will learn from this that the enactment of church discipline is not a new exercise invented by us but an old office instituted by Christ Himself. In the repetition, I confirmed and strengthened the morning sermon on the regular gospel by reading an edifying example with several comments.

The 22nd of August. N. is using the little strength remaining her to dig deeply into the recognition of her sinfulness so as to be quite reassured of the forgiveness of her sins. The sins of her previous life, for which which she has not yet done penance, have cost her many tears and cause her such fear that she needs the help of the good N., who has taken her into his hut, with prayer and encouragement from the Lord's word. By his experience and knowledge of the word, he is well suited to help her. We have often seen that many of our flock want to be considered good Christians but have never truly repented. Therefore we take every opportunity to remind our listeners not to overlook the basis of all Christian faith, that is the rebirth and thorough conversion and change of their hearts, in which task the examples which we occasionally read give us good guidance and make a great impression on our listeners.[158]

H. S.[159] has travelled by boat despite a strong diarrhea and has thereby so aggravated his condition that he is now suffering from severe disentery and other serious conditions causing him much pain. God, however, has given him a large measure of Christ's patience. He is an honorable and just man, who can be of good use in the community and is much loved and appreciated by everyone. His early departure from this life would be all the more to be regretted. Both his wife and child are also ill with diarrhea.

The 23rd of August. I had another meeting with the congregation, and the people asked me to travel to Mr. Causton and persuade him, by my own entreaties, to undertake a trip to our village so as to inspect in person both the work done by our Salzburgers and the heavy damage inflicted by the worm pest. They hope that he might thus be moved to intercede on their behalf with the Honorable Trustees so that their provisions will not be suddenly discontinued despite the bad harvest and their great losses. I am planning to embark this afternoon in God's name and to insist on this visit, if not by Mr. Causton himself, then by the preacher, Mr. Wesley. May God bless this project.

The 24th and 25th of August. Mr. Causton will not be able to come and inspect the fields of the Salzburgers; for a complicated matter is taking place in the townhall in Savannah.[160] He well believes the claims of the damage caused by the worm pest, for the entire country and Carolina too have been so affected. He agrees that I should write the Honorable Trustees in this matter, and he says he will do so himself too. I took care of my other business as quickly as possible so as to return home with the briefest delay. Upon my return, I learned that the oldest Kornberger child, which had seemed the strongest, had died and had to be buried this afternoon. The children in our community are all suffering from the fever and other illnesses.

The 27th of August. A young Salzburger, whom the dear Lord has guided to the recognition and repentance of his sins in the course of his recent illness, now esteems it more highly than all the treasures of the world to have a good conscience and a gracious God, whereas the sins of the world are of such evil nature that they afford Satan much and terrible power over man. He now seeks God's mercy earnestly and through Christ, and I instructed him in his hut as to how to continue on the path on which the Lord has guided him with strength and eagerness; I also pointed out to him an experienced Christian whose company he should seek often, while keeping himself from other suspicious or hypocritical company.

In the hut of NN. I had to preach serious repentance to a certain person and her family because both the father and the children, despite all better knowlege and ready talk, were well advanced on the wide road to hell. They know full well that things are not as well with them as they should be, and there is this one person among them who knows how to speak so thoroughly and impressively of spiritual matters, of heaven and hell, and of the order and the treasures of salvation, that one would believe him to be converted or on the point of conversion to the Lord. However, I have known him in this condition for several years. There is much danger in the case of old and hardened sinners, and among the many very few will be saved. The woman has been sick for a long time, and as she is preparing for blissful eternity and longs to see her dear ones in heaven, this situation causes her much grief.

The 28th of August. Susanna Holtzer, a widow from Austria, has passed away in a state of grace this afternoon at one o'clock. Until her end, she has kept her faith in the fight against sin and Satan, as difficult as this has been for her in the last days. She could still speak a little yesterday; but today, when I visited her after the morning sermon, she had lost the power of speech almost entirely, and I could not hear anything from her except a weak "yes," when I asked her whether she recognized me. I called several Bible verses and prayers out to her and fell on my knees, jointly with the others present, so as to bring her to Jesus in prayer, as was said of the deaf mute in today's gospels. In the last four weeks we have had three deaths (not counting the Kornberger infant), and these have occurred partly in the period of the new moon and partly at full moon.

Mrs. Holtzer leaves behind a single daughter aged 14 years whom we will take in as an orphan for special care and supervision. The mother was quite placid as concerns the provisions made for her daughter, as she has in general refused to be distracted from her preparation for eternity by temporal matters. She was a good and industrious woman in matters of housekeeping and was faithful in attending all services with her daughter, as well as in seeking to serve her neighbors as much as was in her ability and power. But, in the course of her long period of confinement and at her death, she has learned well that these matters are not enough for salvation and that for all good appearances and conviction of one's own worth, the heart may still remain unconverted. May God be praised for having taken mercy on her.

The 29th of August. Today the Lord has again let me know that His Word as pronounced yesterday has not been without good effect. He also continues to dispense His blessing on the evening repetition, which is always well attended by young and old.

The fever and other circumstances have so reduced Mrs. Mueller in body and spirit that on occasion her behavior is like that of a simple child. Today, when I visited her, she was somewhat better, and it appeared to me as if her spiritual circumstances were such as to leave room for the grace of the Lord to prepare her heart for blessed eternity. Both parents and children encourage each other to attend the services and to pray and constitute a good example in this and other Christian traits. The oldest daughter is sick as well, which protects her from the debauchery and frivolous behavior so easily engaged in by young people and confirms her in the treasure of grace which she attained at her recent first communion and the preparation preceding it.

The 30th of August. Last night, in the course of the prayer meeting, I received an unexpected letter from Petersburg by the neophyte preacher there, Mr. Plaschnig, which pleased and edified me much.

We have not had any rain for a long time and the severe heat persists during the day; this may be one of the reasons why the fever is still so violent among us.

The 31st of August. Late last night a thunderstorm accompanied by heavy cloudbursts passed over us, and today the heavy rains continued almost throughout the day. It looks as if they might continue through the night. Our people are still sowing beets and radishes, because the recent seedlings were largely spoiled by the heavy heat or did not come up at all. As the corn crop has failed, they hope at least to harvest a good amount of beans, provided that God may not withdraw His apparent blessing from this crop, as from the corn. Two years ago heavy fall rains caused much damage to the beans.

Schmidt's infant died last night and was buried this morning.

Schmidt's health is still very poor and his recovery does not proceed well at all, inasmuch as the medication failed to have the expected effects, and we also are lacking in many of the things that are necessary to cure such a disease. On my way from the funeral, I visited some ill Salzburgers in their hut and enjoyed an edifying discussion with them out of God's word. On my leaving, a Salzburger woman asked me to call on her too but I was too tired and promised my visit for another day.

SEPTEMBER

The first of September. I recently learned by chance in Savannah that, in addition to the regular provisions, the Honorable Trustees had ordered the issue of half a quart of strong ale per day to each man who has faithfully fulfilled his daily work assigned to him. Since our people have never had the enjoyment of this provision, I recently wrote to Mr. Causton and requested him to send some ale to us, especially because this would be of much benefit to our people here who are much debilitated by diarrhea and other diseases. I also asked him to let me know if I could dispense some of this ale to the men of the first and second transport, who had never received such rations from the store-house, and who could use it as well and with as much benefit as those of the third transport. He did not reply, but instead sent along four barrels of ale with today's boat, which had fetched salt and corn. As soon as possible, I shall dispense some pints of this to the third transport, hoping to receive firm instructions regarding the others. The instructions and intentions of the Honorable Trustees are much to be praised, but their execution is bound to be delayed in their absence. Neither tools nor cattle can be furnished to the third transport until all the accounts have been examined, a process which will be delayed even further because one of Mr. Causton's clerks is sick and the other has been dismissed from his office.

Kalcher is a reliable and serious Christian and he and his wife do much violence to the Kingdom of Heaven, attempting to force it into their hearts with much prayer, tears, vigil, and struggle, which causes him no little travail. In other matters also I find him of good service, and he works faithfully and without ulterior motive. Whenever this is at all possible we try to reward such people who are faithful in both material and spiritual matters and serve as a good example to others.

The 2nd of September. Last Tuesday's rains have persisted

until now both night and day. This has brought down the temperature; and it is so cold now that to prevent untoward accidents, we have to wear heavy clothing such as is customary in the middle of winter in Germany. It may be well imagined that such extended rainfall causes us much inconvenience in our huts, which we gladly support, however, until such time as the Lord shall Himself bring about a change. I recently reminded Mr. Causton of the order of the Honorable Trustees to have a house constructed for us; I asked him for his advice, as the sum of 16 £ sterling, which has not even been entirely allotted to this purpose, is not sufficient to begin construction. He replied that our Salzburgers should proceed to build and see how long the money will last; afterwards, we will again have to address our petition to London. This proposal is not sufficient, in our mind; for we cannot start the house knowing well that insufficient payment for the men will only cause us unrest and embarassments.

The 3rd of September. The surveyor has again broken his word. He promised to be back toward the end of the last month in order to continue the survey of the plantations for the Salzburgers, but nothing has been seen or heard of him.

NN, who was dangerously ill recently, has improved somewhat; but it is clear that she has not truly accepted the words of repentance preached to her on her sick bed, and is not inclined to full conversion. As soon as she is quite recovered, I shall have her come to me several times weekly so as to instruct her in the truths of the catechism, of which she is still ignorant and inexperienced, as is true with regard to other matters of her salvation. Also, I shall discuss with the leaders of our community how to improve her material circumstances and conditions.

The 4th of September. Last night we had an unusual cloudburst and strong winds, but during the day the strong heat returned. We suffer much inconvenience from both rain and sun in the hut that now serves as a church, and our dear benefactors would do a praiseworthy and Christian deed if they were to help us toward the erection of a well-built and proper church with their kind munificence. Our Salzburgers are much too poor to undertake such a building on their own. God holds the hearts of all men in His hands and will in His time arrange matters so that we may praise Him and pray to Him in a proper church.

The 5th of September. A woman, whom the Lord with His strong word has recently awakened from the slumber of complacency of the flesh, complained to me that her prayer was so weak that she could not know whether God had heard her or not, although she cried out to Him both day and night that she so much desired to persist and be assured of the state of grace before she should fall ill. She has started to rise a few hours before daylight, while the others are still asleep, so as to talk to the Lord alone in her garden, praying on her knees to Him Whom she so much desired to know and appeal to as Her father in Christ. I furnished her with the comfort that God has so richly provided in His word for poor suffering sinners and admonished her to persist in her struggle and prayers, for God would finally bring about the day when she would praise Him with a joyous tongue.

On Sunday afternoon, in addition to the five main parts of the catechism, we now have the children publicly recite the instructions concerning the Office of the Keys and the questions of the blessed Luther, for this is of great benefit to both the children and the adults. Old Mrs. Schweighoffer must have found great pleasure in the questions recited by the children yesterday, for today she sent her daughter to ask for a catechism with the intention of acquainting herself well with the aforesaid portions and questions prior to taking Holy Communion.

The 6th of September. An Englishman who trades with the Indians in Savannah-Town called on me yesterday and told me among other things that the Swiss who recently began building a town in that area are mostly ill, and some are dying. Their preacher is not yet with them, and they are thus ill provided for both spiritually and materially.

Mueller the watchmaker and all his family are quite ill and suffering, and his oldest daughter is in the most critical condition. Both parents bear this cross and their extreme poverty well, and this assures me more and more that their Christian faith is not only lodged in their words but above all in their hearts. Whatever God has provided us with in the manner of material blessings we pass on to such and other people in our community, as warranted by individual circumstances.

The 7th of September. Mrs. Schweighoffer is aware of the clear decline in her strength and is therefore beginning to believe that her final day is not far. She is well prepared to die if only God will give her a clear indication of His grace before her end. She has many temptations,[161] yet she shows particular faith both in her prayers and in her struggles. Her main distress is that she cannot feel the grace of the Lord, for she perceives herself as quite lost and wicked and thus fears that God may have avoided and abandoned her, for she has previously tasted the presence of His grace, but does so no more. This she confided to me with many tears. I instructed her from God's word what the people are like in whom God shows His pleasure through Christ and with whom He has promised to dwell; these are the suffering, those of broken spirit, the miserable, the hungry and thirsty, and the poor in spirit. She erred in trusting more in her emotions than in the clear word of the Lord and the promises contained therein: "Be more confident in His Word; and, if your heart says only 'Nay,' let not terror seize you."[162] I referred her to the words of the 23rd Psalm, which says: "Though I walk through the valley of the shadow of death, I shall fear no evil, for Thou art with me." Likewise: "Zion said, The Lord hath forsaken me and my Lord hath forgotten me," etc. Isaiah 49.

I told her she would have to distinguish among the day's normal food and drink and that which God bequeathes to His children only now and then as He considers it fruitful. Our daily ordinary food is to do the Lord's will and suffer by His command in the succession of Christ; but sometimes He so ordains to let His children taste from the fountain of joy that is His grace. This, however, they should not take for granted and as a matter of daily occurrence. She also complained that her oldest daughter, who is still with her, increases her sadness; and she therefore much desires a change of circumstances. This shall be effected for her and the children, upon completion of the large hut which now is progressing through the work of nine Salzburgers, who are building it in Christian unity and good spirits. The widow was paralyzed by a stroke and is therefore incapable of providing the necessary ministrations for the welfare of her body; it is only fair that she should be provided for in the aforesaid hut in some manner.[163]

The woman NN is in serious physical condition and is much aggrieved that she has heretofore served the Lord more in a strictly formal rather than evangelical spirit.[164] She believes that the Lord has visited her circumstances on her for her spiritual best and wishes for nothing more in her prayers but that He might reach His goal with her without any obstacles. An example that I had discussed in a recent repetition and subsequent prayer meeting had given her the opportunity to become aware of several matters in herself. She is an honest woman who is serious about her salvation. She is also one of the quiet in the land[165] and edifies me by her humble and quiet behaviour. In Germany she had been in the service of a pious but separatist

Gichtelian man,[166] who had done her much good, but God has protected her from his deviations and teachings.

The 8th of September. After the recent rains, which persisted night and day, God has again blessed us with sunshine. This much delights our people, for otherwise they would have been deprived of the bean harvest, which cannot stand any prolonged wetness.[167] My dear colleague returned this afternoon from his voyage to Charleston, which he had to undertake for a number of good reasons. He is well and has discharged his business there with success, for which the Lord be praised. Kieffer from Purysburg had also traveled there with his sons on his own boat, which provided a useful opportunity for him. However, it had not been foreseen that Kieffer would be detained in Charleston by the authorities for more than a fortnight, which fact has delayed his return. In Charleston, he was contacted by some Germans, whom he was able to benefit by the pronouncement of the Lord's word, both in private and in public. He also found occasion to write to Mr. Ziegenhagen, the court chaplain, to advise him of several matters, among them the mailing of our recent letters and the diary.

He has now brought complete news of the barrel of linen which has been mentioned in the diaries on several occasions. It was sent by a merchant from NN[168] so that we might sell it here to the Salzburgers in return for rice, turpentine oil, or silk. He seems to believe that the Salzburgers are already in circumstances allowing such a trade and thus might benefit from it in that he is prepared to offer the linen for a good price. He also had intended some time ago a gift of 24 £ sterling for our poor Salzburgers, of which he has now sent approximately 13 or 14 £ sterling worth of linen, and he asks that each of them be given five yards as far as the supply will last. The remainder will be sent in the same manner. The name of the Lord be praised for this act of munificence; may He crown the benefactor with His grace as with a shield! The consignment of linen meant for the aforementioned barter trade will be kept by Mr. Seaman, a merchant, until I shall inform him of my views in this matter. Inasmuch as trade is not possible here, I shall consider with Christian friends what steps we should take so that the good man might not incur a loss. The value of the consignment is about 71 £ sterling.

In tonight's prayer meeting I told our listeners of the material blessing that our dear Father has bestowed on them from afar, and which should give them renewed occasion to thank Him, to pray for this and other benefactors, and to fortify themselves in the trust of the living Lord, who had promised food and clothing and has now provided it in His time. I also told them how our benefactor had stipulated the distribution of this gift and that it obviously would not suffice for everyone to share in it. I asked them to pray to the Lord to lend wisdom to my dear colleague and myself in the just distribution of this treasure and to give them peace of mind and satisfaction so that they might not sin against Him by suspicion and complaints, etc. If some among them should be empty-handed on this occasion, they would be the first to benefit from any future gift that God might provide. For complaints, suspicion, dissatisfaction, and envy would insult the Lord and thus repel any further grace that He might bestow on us.

At the same time, I received a letter from Mr. Zwiffler, who is still in Pennsylvania and had delivered our letters for forwarding to Mr. Ingam (Mr. Wesley's colleague) as early as the 22nd of May.[169] He regrets the confused situation obtaining there in matters of religion and remembers well the advantages we enjoy here in our village with regard to the undiluted gospel.

The 9th of September. The deceased Mrs. Uselt's youngest daughter had been brought to Charleston by her mother, where she fell into a certain woman's hands after her mother's death. Said woman had taken her to Pennsylvania, where she would by all accounts have been brought up in wild and improper circumstances. God, however, has so arranged it that she will now be returned to our care and supervision. She is a gay and intelligent child, who, if she accepts the Lord's teachings, may well grow up to work for the honor of the Lord and in the service of her fellow man. The large hut which is being built for the rearing of our poor children and orphans is not yet ready. They are now nine in all, and we shall place these orphans in the hut built for the expected doctor until such time as the other house shall be finished.

The 10th of September. The gift of linen has been distributed, both yesterday and today, among those Salzburgers of whose urgent needs we were aware. We accompanied this gift with admonitions for the praise of the Lord and sincere prayers on behalf of this and other esteemed benefactors, and we do not doubt that it will prove of great spiritual value for many. As the linen did not go as far as I had thought after my first rough calculations, I was forced to add the 32-yard piece of linen that I had recently bought for the sum of 28 shillings sterling for our orphaned children, so as to provide for those in greatest need. If our dear benefactors and other Christian friends of the Salzburgers only realized the extent of the good that their generosity causes in our community, they would join in our praise of the Lord, Who has made them rich and willing to share of their abundance. Most among us are in quite poor material circumstances and they would be forced to leave us and the Lord's word, at least temporarily, and go into service with strangers, if there were not some relief for them in their dire poverty.

The honest[170] souls among us are so fortified in their faith by such unexpected generosity that they confide their trust in the all powerful Lord without hesitation and learn to expect His help without fail in the most dire circumstances, since He has given so much proof already, even in the face of our lack of faith. If the marvellous Lord should continue to awaken the hearts of other benefactors, as He has done before, and move them to show their munificence in contributing across the oceans for sheltering and educating the German orphans who are in dire need in this country, there could hardly be a better use for their generosity and charity, which would doubtless be richly repaid to them in eternity for the sake of Christ the Lord, Who also was poor and Who bears a tender love toward all children. The misery caused by the lack of care for orphaned and other German children here should doubtless cause those to weep bitterly who bear any love whatever for Jesus and immortal souls.

Inasmuch, however, as food and clothing are very expensive in this country compared to Germany and Pennsylvania, we are incapable of accepting any children beyond those who are now with us. Also, the gifts received by us for this purpose would not last long if some of the children whom we have accepted for special supervision and maintenance were not being given some provisions from the store-house. Kalcher and his wife have been chosen to care for these children, both materially and spiritually; and both during the day and at night, in the place of their parents. This couple is well equipped for this task above many others inasmuch as they not only possess a true and sincere fear of the Lord but also much of the physical and other skills that are necessary for such an important undertaking.

The 11th of September. I visited a mother with her children and tried especially to convince the mother of the horrible plague of sin with which she is dangerously ill. She is so blind, however, that she will neither recognize herself nor understand that she is lacking even in the prerequisites of conversion, that is, the recognition of her entirely wicked heart. Instead, she has much pride in her pretended piousness, her love of God, and her Christian faith, which are quite invisible to others, however. I therefore read some passages to her from the story of a life that demonstrates how easily man can deceive himself with his repentance, faith, and Christian beliefs and how such people can show signs of many qualities which, not being based on true faith and a reborn mind, cannot be considered with favor by the Lord.[171] There is little hope of progress with such people who are convinced of their long-standing Christian faith, and there is little else we can do but pray for them and with them so that God may open their eyes for them to see the truth.

The 12th of September. We have learned that the prayer books translated from English into German and acquired in London for the German people in Purysburg have been delivered to the preacher there, who had distributed them among some of the families. They had not reached the just mentioned preacher by the time of our last letter, and court chaplain Ziegenhagen had been informed accordingly.

For a number of reasons, NN[172] had recently been kept away from the Lord's Table. In view of his conduct since his return from the service of NN, and his recent promises, he has now been admitted. He now realizes with sorrow the plague that is caused by the society of wicked and perfidious men or those who lack the foundation of the true Christian faith, and how, as long as one tolerates their company, one forfeits all the mercy that God bestows on the heart from the gospels and thus renders true conversion impossible.

The 13th of September. The Salzburgers are now bringing home the poor corn harvest that the worms have left them, but all those to whom I have spoken show much satisfaction and /contentment with what the Lord has granted them. They will have a larger crop of beans provided that the deer do not eat them, a frequent occurrence in other parts of this country.

A poor widow spoke with me and requested that we accept some of her children into our institutions for their maintenance and education. She is very poor and has many children whom she cannot support on the limited provisions allotted to her. For this reason we could not simply refuse her request but instead advised her to wait patiently until the new hut should be finished. For only a few can find accommodation in the doctor's hut; and, since the carpenters and other workers must now harvest their corn and beans, they cannot work on the new house without interruption. We are also glad to be patient, for there is no true damage to be expected from this delay. True, we have but little provision for this important task; but, because God continues to provide, contrary to our thoughts and expectations, and has thus given us a hint to commence this undertaking in faith in Him, we hope that He will open His generous hands for us again, for God's well carries abundant water.[173]

The 14th of September. This summer our Salzburgers have lost almost all their hogs and poultry, and more are lost almost every day, causing much damage to these poor people. As mentioned previously, they are not in the position to feed the animals in their houses; and therefore the latter forage for food in the swamps and the brush, where they are devoured by either bears or wild cats. Those living in the first row of houses have had particularly severe losses, for toward the river there are several large lots which the surveyor, on Mr. Oglethorpe's orders, has set aside for wealthy future settlers.[174] Inasmuch as the trees and underbrush have not been cleared on these lots, many harmful vermin live there and they even come into the stables and kitchens during the night and decimate both livestock and poultry. We therefore propose that, for the preservation of the cattle and poultry and for our better health, the whole waterfront should be cleared of trees and underbrush. If the Salzburgers are given liberty to fence this land in with one large enclosure and to work the land for one or two years, they might be all the more ready to undertake such a hard and arduous task. I shall consider this matter jointly with the congregation.

I am again forced to place N.[175] under supervision in another locality because he cannot live in peace with his present host, he being the guilty party in this respect. He desires to be without constraint and as free as other residents here, whereas he is much too young and not capable of directing himself. The same is true for NN who has insisted with all seriousness upon living by herself, a condition, however, which would provide her and other disorderly people with an occasion for committing manifold sins. Since she neither can nor will stay with N, she will have to ask other good people for shelter.

The 15th of September. I am dividing those who wish to go to the Lord's Table next Sunday into four groups, as indicated by the state of their Christian faith, and each group comes to my house at an appointed time to pray, sing, and listen to the Lord's word in preparation for their task. This also gives me an occasion to pray and talk to them every day in consideration of their circumstances; they are much pleased by this arrangement, which is of great benefit. Two certain persons[176] are also going to take Communion on this occasion, for it appears that they are quite serious this time about their preparation. They found a cause of disagreement with N. and N. on some material matters, and I will take the occasion tomorrow to reconcile them in my presence and in a Christian manner.

The 16th of September. Last night Mrs. A.[177] gave birth to a young daughter who had to be baptized immediately after birth, being of a weak constitution. The poor woman, recently widowed by her husband's sudden and sad departure, now has five children on her hands who will justly have to be considered in our plans for the orphanage, once that institution is arranged in a more orderly fashion. She is an honest woman and sees to it that her children attend school and behave in a proper fashion. It so occurred that, without my knowledge, N, his wife, and NN had been asked to serve as godparents; and they came at night to be present at the baptism. Since their reconciliation had not been effected, I told them that I could not admit them to this holy act unless they would assure me of their mutual forgiveness. However, I shall have occasion today to enter into this matter in more detail. Mrs. A's daughter died this morning. From the hour of her birth, the child had sighed, moaned and whimpered just as her mother had done when she learned of her husband's drowning in the river at Purysburg. The reconciliation among the persons just referred to has been so well effected in my presence that I am much pleased by it. N. and his wife have so proven themselves on this occasion that I believe in their serious desire to rid themselves of their sins and to prepare themselves for the Lord's Table in the manner of true Christians.

The 17th of September. The fever still persists with some of the members of our community, and many untoward incidents occur that we cannot control for lack of requisite knowledge. True, in Charleston my dear colleague purchased some items such as are prescribed in Dr. Richter's medical treatise for the preparation of medicines against the fever; and these are given to the sick in view of the insufficiency of our present remedies. However, such medications cannot work as expected and desired, since we do not really know the conditions afflicting them and their severity, nor have we sufficient experience for using the medications in a proper manner. An Englishman in Old Ebenezer returned six head of cattle that had strayed from our herd, and the people were obliged to give him one shilling for each head. Our neighbors in this country demand much love from our people, but are little prepared to show such love themselves.

The 18th of September. Today's communicants numbered forty-four. During the entire week, and in particular during the last three days, we have had occasion to work on their souls with the Lord's word, so as to well prepare them for this holy undertaking. We hope the dear Lord may accompany these labors with His blessing.

The 19th to the 22nd of September. I have been forced to make a voyage to Savannah. Our private accounts are now completed and I was made to sign them in testimony that all items named were in fact turned over to us from the store-house on account of our semiannual salary. I have again had occasion to see proof of Mr. Causton's true affection, as he is also well inclined to our congregation and serves them well with many favors. He let me hope that the few provisions assigned to the Salzburgers for their trips to Savannah for the purpose of fetching food stores, but which amount to much in view of the frequency of such travels, shall be donated; and Mr. Causton instructed me to adjust the accounts accordingly. The good Lord has so arranged it that this or that order or instruction often works to our benefit and proper recognition at a later date, which again gives rise to much praise of the Lord. The Lutherans in Purysburg request that one of us provide Holy Communion there. As soon as we have more detailed information of this request for our services, one of us shall travel there for a few days.

The 23rd of September. The surveyor Ross has finally returned to survey the plantations of the Salzburgers. In Charleston, he bought[178] two young Swiss men from Canton Bern who are both afflicted by the fever but must nonetheless continue working in surveying the ground. Once these two are incapable of work, he shall have to use some of our people and pay them for it, and he has already requested the assistance of an able-bodied man. I very much doubt, however, that he shall find such a one, for most of our people are quite weak from the fever and would soon suffer a relapse were they to work in swampy areas all day and in the still-continuing heat and then camp out at night and be sustained by nothing but the cold food they carry as provisions. This is this man's manner of living. He carries prepared provisions for several days or even a week and takes out no time for cooking for himself or for those accompanying him, and the work goes on from early dawn until well into the night, with only short breaks for breakfast and dinner. We consider it a great blessing that Mr. Oglethorpe ordered this man to use none of our people unless he pays for their labor.

The 24th of September. During several prayer meetings we have heard with great edification from Exodus 25 and 35 how the children of Israel gladly brought their levy for the erection of the hall of the covenant, and how both men and women showed their eagerness to such an extent that Moses had to restrain them in accordance with the recommendation of the workers. In this connection I recalled two letters from the continuation of the reports from East India,[179] which I had read last night for the pleasure and edification of myself and the others. One letter dealt with a person of noble birth who gave her pearls and other jewels to the Lord for the erection of his temple among the heathen in East India; the other letter was by an honest inspector in Lautereck who was so moved by this example that he presented his poor congregation with the needs of the Christians of Malabar with such blessed effectiveness that innocent children, widows, orphans, and other poor but honest people brought their modest mite for this purpose—and for the great strengthening of his faith.

The circumstances of and the appended reflections on this event are so moving that everyone who reads or hears of them must be deeply affected. I had learned even last night how well the congregation loved this lecture and received more detail today of the edifying effect it had had on several among our listeners, which pleased me much. I could not let the opportunity pass to stress again that the dear Lord has already moved the hearts of some benefactors to show their love and charity to our congregation, and that these had lightened our misery partly by gifts of money and partly by gifts of linen and other items of necessity, for which we are fairly obliged to thank the Lord and to beg Him eagerly and warmly to reward such works of love by His grace. The all-knowing Lord knows full well that we urgently need a good and solid house to serve as church and as a school. He also knows that, in view of their poverty and their weak health, the members of the community are unable to undertake such a construction, however necessary and beneficial it may be.

We thus trust in Him that He shall awaken some pious Christians, wherever they may be, to whom He has entrusted some temporal wealth, so that they may contribute to the building of a temple for the Lord. Since many benefactors in Germany were gladly prepared to help the Lutheran people in Pennsylvania with true acts of generosity in the building of several churches and schools, we do not doubt that the Lord shall make them equally willing with regard to us and our needs, particularly as our Salzburgers in this desert are far from enjoying the benefits that those colonists enjoy in their fertile, well-planted, and easily acquired land, but are nonetheless and despite all their poverty honest believers in the Lord and His word. We shall therefore ask our father in heaven and await His help.[180]

The 25th of September. A pious woman told me in tears of the messages that her husband had carried home from the sermon, inasmuch as she was detained at home with her sick child. God had again made her realize how much meanness, wrong beliefs, and addiction to the things of this earth were still hidden in her heart, and how badly her Christian faith still fared. True, she cried to the Lord both day and night with many tears of repentance and fear; but it appeared to her that her prayer was far from being as serious as it should be and she did not know whether she would still be admitted. She urged me to speak to her often, etc. Another man praised the Lord that among all his brothers he had been chosen to be in such circumstances as permitted him to recognize the true road to heaven and had found so much opportunity for the salvation of his soul among us. On this very day he had again been encouraged to seek his salvation with all seriousness, so that he too might reach that blessed place to which his father had preceded him when, just prior to their departure from Salzburg, he had died the death of a true Protestant, for which he had been refused burial in the Catholic churchyard but had been placed to rest in his own garden. He suffered much sadness on account of his mother, who had remained blind and a Catholic, etc.

The 26th of September. A house visit yesterday gave me the occasion to read, during our repetition, a most edifying story which is well suited for that part of the gospels with which we have just dealt. Several in the congregation have been much impressed by this example of a man whom God has led to the recognition of His sins, to a true conversion, and to eagerness in holy matters, and who in addition has caused much blessing for others by the example of his word and conduct. An honest man came to me and asked me to lend him this vita so that he might read it to a friend who was prevented from attending church by his ill health. He also mentioned that his wife had been much moved and awakened to a good resolution by my lecture. For I had made a certain comment that had clearly demonstrated to her her previous conduct toward him, her husband. When they returned home together, he had reminded her of this point, which had previously caused him much suffering at her hand; and she admitted under tears that she knew full well that she had been wrong and had sinned, and begged him to be silent. The man is now full of hope that his wife will finally improve her temper and desist from her fits of rage. Mr. Wesley has offered to carry some letters to London for us, for he would soon have an opportunity for a safe transmittal. We should like to write and send our diary; but we shall have to wait for another month or so, inasmuch as the surveyor is just now in the process of surveying the land of the Salzburgers, so long awaited and hoped for. Once each family has received its share, we shall write and describe the condition and other circumstances of said land.

The 27th of September. It has turned quite cold all of a sudden and we even feared a frost, which, however, the good Lord has averted, for it would have spoiled both beans and potatoes, which are still in full growth.

A poor man from Purysburg asked whether we could accept his son, who is almost 12 years of age, for instruction and care. He could not earn enough in Purysburg to support himself and his family; therefore his wife had been forced to go into service. He is working in Old Ebenezer, and his daughter has also been given away for several years. Now he has only his son, whom he would like to send to school. I am much saddened by this case; but I cannot grant his request, for we have so many poor children in our village that we cannot accept all into the charitable care that we have begun to provide. Last Sunday, on the occasion of reading the gospels, I was much impressed by the two verses from Isaiah 25:4 and Psalm 10:14. I do not doubt that Jesus shall prove Himself with us as He has been portrayed, loving and gentle, in these and other verses. May He with his allpowerful strength awaken charitable hearts to take pity on the poor and straying German children in this country. How we would rejoice if we were to assemble a group of them around us so as to work on their souls. With God's blessing, this might even be a way of working fruitful results among the heathen here.

The 28th of September. There is much talk here that Mr. Oglethorpe is already en route to Georgia, and this special news has been carried by some sloops that have arrived in Savannah. May God incline his heart to us and our community, since many are in poor circumstances because of this year's failed harvest, a situation which is made even worse by some of the physical weaknesses that are still among us and which hinder our dear people in their work. May God direct everything according to His will, His glory, and our welfare.

The 29th of September. N. and his wife[181] are faring quite well after their last Holy Communion. Both attend sermons and prayer meetings with great industry and their conduct is quiet and orderly, and he shows his willingness and his faith with the little children whose instruction is entrusted to his care. In some instances he still holds to his old methods, which are not really harmful, so that we are willingly patient. If only both of them would experience a true conversion! For self-deceit is a dangerous snare.

The 30th of September. The carpenter, Sanftleben, intends to return to Germany after the three years that every colonist must remain here. At first, I did not wish to credit this rumor, since I had never observed such intentions in him, but quite the contrary; and God has given Him much blessing for the salvation of his soul. Therefore I summoned him so as to learn the true circumstances and to give him my opinion in this respect. When I heard from his own mouth that this was truly his desire,[182] I clearly told him of the evil consequences that his return was bound to cause and seriously admonished him to examine his plans before the countenance of the Lord and not to take another step until he was certain of the Lord's desire. I am of the opinion that none in our community may leave without special permission by the Honorable Trustees and the Society for, in view of the great costs incurred for them and of other circumstances, their condition is different from that of others in this country. I state this view to all those who seek a change in their conditions.

OCTOBER

The 1st of October. This afternoon I assembled the men of the congregation to discuss some matters that need to be well arranged and at the same time to cast lots for the plantations that are now being surveyed. To be sure, according to Mr. Oglethorpe's orders the first transport was to have preference over the second and third and to draw the first lots. However, they all agreed to be treated equally and to let the matter depend upon divine dispensation in order to avoid murmuring and objections. The surveyor gave me suggestions about the distribution of the land that pleased me very well; and I hope, provided everything is carried out honestly, that everyone will receive a good piece of land with which he can be satisfied.

The 2nd of October. Because the surveyor is going back to his work tomorrow morning and had some things he had to ask me before then, he prevented me from visiting the members of our congregation. And the same thing happened to me last week when I had to bring my accounts to order for the provisions that have been provided so far and which are to be concluded as of the end of last month and also to calculate what each person has received during the entire time and what he is still to receive. Otherwise house visitation is a very pleasant duty for us; and those people in the congregation who are really honest find great pleasure in it. May our dear Lord not hold the omission of such an important and useful service against me, because I am kept from it so often by so many external things that do not pertain to my spiritual office.

I was informed that our dear Lord has again blessed today's repetition; and this has raised me up again somewhat in the distress I feel in my present circumstances. My time might well be short, and I would like very much to accomplish something meritorious in my major task so that I will not have been sent into the New World in vain.[183]

The 3rd of October. Our people are being compelled to harvest their rice green and unripe because an uncommon multitude of birds, like sparrows but smaller, settle on it and strip off the grains while still green and immature.[184] This year the mice here, as well as in Purysburg and perhaps in other places, have done much harm to the sweet potatoes. Most of the beans that lie at some distance from the town have been eaten by the deer. And if one plants sweet potatoes on land where one cannot be present, the wild animals not only eat the leaves but also dig up the roots entirely. Under such conditions the Salzburgers will be unable to be in Ebenezer much when, in the future, they plant their rather remote plantations and wish to protect their crops, especially since most of them are unmarried. May the dear Lord Himself direct us as to what ways we should go in order to perform our office for our dear congregation.

The 4th of October. Among other things our worthy Court Preacher Ziegenhagen has done us a most pleasant favor by requesting a pair of very fine millstones from the Lord Trustees, which are better than those that can be bought here in this country. To be sure, we had requested them for ourselves, but they were sent for the congregation, so we will have just as much use of them as if they were our own. Among us we have a skillful carpenter who will build a compendious rice and corn mill with them that is to be driven by two men. At present I am having a hut built for me in the vicinity of the orphanage, in which we keep the iron mills that have just recently been repaired at great expense. And thus such a mill will be to the benefit of the orphans' home also. A spacious bake oven is being constructed in this same hut. Communal things must be under someone's supervision, otherwise they are soon ruined.

Through my intercession the third transport has recently received two stones, and with them they have built a mill in the fashion of this country. The upper stone, which is fastened to an iron capstan and to an attached capstan-bar, is turned by a vertical shaft that is secured at the top in a hole bored in a beam and fits in a small hole in the stone with a spur. Beneath the lower stone, directly across the hollowed out board in which the stones are set, there lies a transverse bar of wood, upon which the capstan lies in a somewhat recessed piece of iron. In order to grind either fine or coarse one can raise or lower the diagonal piece of wood by means of two wedges placed under it that are tapered to a point.[185]

For some time Mrs. N. has been very miserable and sick of body; and in her distressing and suffering condition God is clearly letting her recognize what she formerly refused to recognize, namely, that from youth on she had greatly sinned against God and had not yet felt penitent. She is very contented with this suffering, because in it she well observes the finger of God, who is thereby furthering her eternal salvation.[186] With many tears she told me how she now recognized herself and what she so greatly desired, namely, that, before she died, she might achieve conversion and a certainty that her sins are forgiven. Since her last participation in Holy Communion (since she had previously been freed in a Christian manner of the calumny she had uttered against me) we have been able to see a change in her, and from this time on she has left more space for the spirit of God than formerly. Since then her husband has led a contented and peaceful life with her, whereas he had previously had to bear much contradiction and vexation. Oh how happy I am that, through the grace of my gentle savior, I can feel no trace of vengeance toward this woman. If, as an example for other people, I had acted severely toward her, as she deserved, she would probably not come to such a wholesome penitence but would have embittered her spirit against us even more. Oh, may the Lord teach us to act according to His pleasure in all things, and may His good spirit lead us on an even path!

The 5th of October. The warm and dry weather is continuing and is very good for the ripening and harvesting of the beans. The sweet potatoes, which are in their best growth, are suffering somewhat from it, as are the turnips also. We harvested hardly any squash at all at our place; the great heat of the sun and the long drought of summer spoiled them in their growth and ripening. I have again kindly admonished N. and his wife to penitence and advised them to invoke God again seriously for right recognition of their many sins they have committed from their youth. As long as they remain blind to such a right recognition of their sins, we cannot hope for any remorse or whatever else is necessary for a fundamental conversion. Outwardly they listened to the admonition calmly and devoutly and prayed with me; and he assured me that he will now attend all the prayer hours and tell his wife about them, since she cannot get away because of the baby.

The 6th of October. Mrs. Schweighofer is still sickly and miserable of body, and her physical weakness may have an influence on her spirit, for she is very depressed and worried. For three days after she last participated in Holy Communion her heart was in harmony with her Savior and she tasted his goodness and love after much previous seeking and knocking. But afterwards she has become so miserable and parched that she cannot pray, and this causes her a thousand worries. I comforted her from God's word, especially with some verses and promises that concern souls in precisely her condition, such as Psalm 51:19 and Psalm 133:13–14. I also told her that she had many fellow prayers and intercessors, namely, our merciful high priest Jesus at the right hand of the Father and so many thousands of pious Christians who are praying for her, even if they do not know her by sight. In particular I named for her several righteous ministers and servants of Christ, by whose letters we have often been assured of their constant and hardy intercession for the comfort of our congregation. At the same time I advised her to continue with sighs and moans before the Lord, even if she cannot pray formally. I also commended to her several pious women, with whom she should bring her prayers before the throne of God, etc. She is a sick woman who has been afflicted by a stroke and is also very poor with three young children (of whom the middle one is already enjoying the care of our orphanage); and she is also full of fear of the Lord. Therefore, if she can be accepted into our orphanage, as she greatly hopes, she will profit from it more than others would and will be well applied in her case.

The 7th of October. Recently I spoke again with the congregation about the hut that is to be bought for the doctor whom we are hoping for; but now I learn that it is not considered comfortable and large enough. Therefore the Salzburgers would prefer to build a spacious and well constructed hut along with a good kitchen just next to me on the other corner of the middle street; and for this they are willing to contribute as much money as they can afford. I prefer this suggestion, even though I wish I had known about it beforehand; for then I would not have laid the attic floor in it. Nevertheless, the orphan children who are now living in it are enjoying it very much, and I shall come to terms with the carpenter Sanftleben, who is meanwhile living in another hut.

The four men[187] who took service for five months with a captain above Savannah-Town have now returned and cannot complain enough about the bad treatment they received there and about the behavior of the English workers towards them. Because they had only smelly half-spoiled corn to eat they became sick, and one of them has arrived here sick. Everything there is said to be very expensive because food and other necessities must be brought up there from Charleston and Savannah on boats, and it is a very arduous journey. Anyone who is afraid of discomfort here is not suited to new settlements where people lack many things and have great difficulties.

The 8th of October. This year not only corn, rice, and flour but also beef and pork are very expensive; indeed, the last mentioned food is hardly to be found. Our boat brought salted fish from Savannah, but the people who had to eat it in place of meat suffered much harm from it. The cause of the dearth of meat is that in New York and Pennsylvania as well as in Carolina, from where the salted meat is usually brought, many cattle perished in floods this spring.

The 9th of October. Afternoons we are now catechizing the questions in Luther's catechism, and in this we find more opportunity for edification. I recently used them as a basis in preparing some children for Holy Communion; and, since they are now hearing them publicly, I plan to go through the passion story of our dear Savior with those who are now being prepared. I shall make a start this week, if nothing intervenes again. Necessity may require me to journey to Savannah and hear Mr. Causton's opinion about a certain piece of land that the surveyor did not dare survey.

The 10th of October. Cornberger's youngest daughter died last night and was buried this afternoon. She was sick and miserable the entire time of her short life. Those children who have been plagued with fever up to now are mostly well again and attend school regularly. In this harvest time, since the bean gathering demands much effort, those whose parents request it are permitted to miss school once or twice for the sake of field work. Although we have had a crop failure in corn and a few other things this year, the honest members of our congregation are content with their small supply and thank God for it just as well as if they had much more. We trust our loving Father in heaven to look upon our plight and lack with the eyes of His mercy and to let no one perish who trusts in Him. There are some widows, very poor children, and impecunious people among us who cannot earn as much as they need to sustain their lives, so we shall give something from the poor-box to them in their need.

The 11th to the 13th of October. I was compelled to travel to Savannah both by the matter of the land which is to be surveyed and by some other circumstances concerning the congregation. However, I did not find Mr. Causton at home; and, because the time of his return was uncertain, I could not wait for him more than one day. Our carpenters, who built my dear colleague's house in Old Ebenezer and have not yet received any pay, journeyed with me in the large boat to receive some things from the store-house instead of money because of the present lack of provisions. But, because Mr. Causton was not there and I did not wish the people to return home in vain and with an empty boat, I took some provisions from the store-house for them on my own account, and I shall speak with Mr. Causton about it shortly. I also left a letter for him in which I petitioned him for the payment of our carpenters and other workers and also presented him with the surveyor's request for him to express his opinion about the matter to him and me as soon as possible. I did not find Mr. Wesley at home because Tuesday morning he had come here to Ebenezer, mostly by land, in order to ask us about several matters.[188] He intends to journey to London. Through him we have a good opportunity to forward our diary and some letters to London and Germany. Because, as I learned in Savannah, the day of his departure is very near, I hurried all the more from Savannah to Ebenezer in order to write some necessary letters.

The 14th of October. Last night we had very cold weather, and the first frost fell this fall; but it did not harm the sweet potatoes and beans as much as frost usually does.

The 15th of October. We have now written several letters to London and Germany, which Mr. Wesley will forward. Because of lack of time we have been unable to write to the Lord Trustees and the praiseworthy Society,[189] but this should be done soon. Ships are expected in Savannah that will probably bring us letters, which we hope to answer then with reports on the Salzburgers' plantations, which have now been surveyed. The letters that have been sent are to Court Preacher Ziegenhagen, Senior Urlsperger, and Professor Francke, and also to two merchants, one in London and the other in St. Gall, Mr. Schlotter, to whom we wish to report the reception of the linen he has sent and to tell him that it will be accepted by Mr. Causton for the stipulated price.

The 17th of October. Mrs. Schweighofer called for me yesterday late in the evening. She had been taken sick suddenly and forsaw her demise, for which she has long been sighing. I found some pious people in her hut, with whom I prayed to our righteous Helper, the Lord Jesus; and I spoke with her briefly in accordance with her circumstances. She is prepared to suffer everything and accept it from the hand of God, no matter how painful it is for her body, if only God will not reject her but assure her of His grace before her death. In her heart and her physical condition she is like the man sick of the palsy in yesterday's gospel, Matthew 9:1 ff.; and therefore I could bestow upon her the same comfort from the mouth of our dear Savior that the palsied man received. Her seriousness in prayer and struggle makes a great impression on me and on others who consort with her. She penetrates with force through the narrow gates, and she will seize that treasure through the power of Jesus Christ, for which alone she yearns.[190]

Yesterday in the repetition hour I read an edifying example to confirm the delightful matter that had been presented; and, through the grace of God, this was again of blessed benefit for me and, as I learned today, for the others. Our dear Lord gives His grace so that our people struggle seriously to be right certain of how they stand with God and to learn for themselves the blessed article of reconciliation with the Lord. God be praised for all His goodness!

Again today the children seemed to be spiritually awakened when, as usual, they were with us at our house after catechisation. May God control their frivolity, which hinders them in seriously receiving the good and is the cause of all their excesses and misbehavior. Early this morning my dear colleague journeyed to Savannah to transmit the letters that were written at the end of last week to London and Germany to Mr. Wesley, who is speedily departing from Savannah. Mr. Wesley intends to journey to Germany too.[191]

The 18th of October. A Salzburger whom I asked about his progress in Christianity complained of the many frailties and shortcomings of which he was becoming more and more aware both in himself and in his wife; and as a result he had to realize that he was not faring as well as he saw in the example of other honest children of God. Both he and his wife still lack a knowledge of the truths of the catechism; and therefore he has begun to learn the catechism and also its interpretation better and he is now in the three chief articles of the Christian faith. He must recite them to his wife, who cannot read. He and his wife are both honest souls, who live in great poverty of spirit. The grace which God has granted them and of which they are little or not at all aware is recognized very well by others, and they are a good scent to me and to other pious people among us.

My dear colleague came back again from Savannah already after our noonday meal, because his business there was not extensive. Moreover, the people who had taken him down in the boat were also in a hurry to get back home and to their work. He gave our letters and diary to Mr. Wesley, who, however, will not go to London himself now that he has received pleasant and favorable letters from the Lord Trustees. One of his friends will be travelling to England in six days, and he will give him our packet for proper delivery. My dear colleague brought back the joyful news that the Lord Trustees had written to Mr. Causton and given him orders to give the Salzburgers of the third transport not only swine and poultry but also a cow per each five people. May God be praised for this benefaction too! May he strengthen us in our faith, and we will not lack his support.

The 19th of October. The surveyor intends to leave us again, even though he has not surveyed the land entirely according to Mr. Oglethorpe's order; but I cannot give him my permission for this. The people who carry his chain and go along with him to show him the boundaries of the plantations complain greatly, so I can find almost no one willing to work for him. However, because he wishes to use this as a pretext for going away, our people must make an even greater effort and go with him each in turn so that the land will finally be completely surveyed. I am planning to give the people necessary instructions for this after the evening prayer hour.

The dwelling for our expected doctor has been so fixed up with the kitchen and also the cow shed pertaining to it that he will, we hope, be able to enjoy all the comfort that is to be had here in the desert. We only wish that we could have him here with us soon, because we need him very much for the various physical ailments that many of us are again suffering. Fever, diarrhea, and dysentery are very common now that the nights are so cold and the days so hot.

The 20th of October. Last night Ruprecht Steiner's wife bore a young son, who was baptized this morning after my morning class. Our dear people do not fail to baptize their little children soon, even if they are sound and healthy, because they themselves are so regular and serious in their use of the means of salvation and because they well know what grace God has promised both young and old through the correct use of the means which He himself has ordained. So far our Salzburgers have had fine dry weather for harvesting their beans, and they have gathered quite a quantity on those spots where the deer have not eaten them. Picking the beans and carrying them home is a hard job and will be even more difficult on the plantations, which mostly lie inland away from the river, because at present we have no hope of horses and wagons. Because of the lack of rice and corn they have almost nothing to eat but beans; and therefore they get diarrhea, which is caused by beans. If they had not been able to earn some money here at home in order to buy some pounds of flour and lard, then they would have fared even worse with such food.

N. has recently used abusive language towards N., his wife, and towards his son and has blamed them for things of which he has no proof. Therefore Mrs. N. brought her complaint to Mr. Causton, but he has relegated the matter to our judgment and disposition. Therefore I sentenced the man to chopping wood for our school for three days as a punishment, since his punishment can thus be a charitable and useful work as well. He was quite agreeable to this.

The 21st of October. Instead of money, our people who have

claims on Mr. Causton for their work will receive provisions and other things found in the store-house, but some of them are not satisfied with that. It is the same case with the Englishmen, who are sinning with blasphemy and evil judgments about it. There is a lack of money in Savannah. When sloops arrive there with provisions, they would have to leave again without having sold their cargo; and therefore Mr. Causton must buy everything. Otherwise the provision sloops would go to Charleston and elsewhere and no foodstuffs would come to Savannah. And, because the whole city and country profit from that, and because Mr. Causton is buying many supplies for their sake, they should not insist so obstinately on payment in cash money.

The surveyor would have liked to be able to show our people their surveyed plantations and to leave us tomorrow or next Monday; but, before they can receive their surveyed lands, he must first measure off all the plantations that belong to the entire city so that I may know in which region the best pieces of land lie together. This is so that our Salzburgers, who have suffered so much until now, may enjoy some advantage over the new-comers, which Mr. Oglethorpe himself does not begrudge them. If it were possible for them all to receive their land on the Savannah River or Ebenezer Creek, it would be very profitable for them in bringing home their crops, since they are lacking horses and oxen. He has orders to survey all land belonging to the plantations in a square of sixteen English miles.[192] It remains to be seen whether he will survey everything properly according to the wishes of Mr. Oglethorpe. It is easiest for him in the forests where there are only pines and firs, but there the land is of no use.

The 22nd of October. The boy Franck, who was accepted with our orphans, is not turning out well; and Kalcher must complain about him. He himself does not accept the word of God for a change of heart and seems to be harmful for the other children too. Therefore, if he does not improve after so much admonition, we will have to send him home to his mother. Externally he has improved rather well and has become better behaved. Also, in school he has learned the catechism, Biblical verses, and reading and has begun to write, whereas he was previously entirely ignorant and has committed much mischief in Purysburg. We have around us many poor children who deserve the benefaction of being accepted into the orphanage and will, we hope, be better able to achieve the desired purpose.

We have seen no Indians at our place for a long time, and we do not know why that is. The Salzburgers show them every kindness and pay them well with rice, beans, or other things whenever they bring meat. We endeavor to give them and everyone who comes to us a good example and to show them as much love as possible, for which purpose our parishioners are earnestly admonished from time to time. Recently, while I was waiting in Purysburg to go to Savannah on our little boat that had been detained at Kieffer's place, some Moors[193] on the shore saw our Salzburgers coming in our big boat and said to one another, "Those are the people from Ebenezer." I asked them whether they knew them and what kind of people they were. One of them answered that they were very good people, better than those at Purysburg. They have been at our place once or twice,[194] and one would hardly expect them to be able to make the distinction.

The 23rd of October. A man from Purysburg has sojourned here for several weeks to help our surveyor with his work. In him God so blessed today's sermon about the gospel, Matthew 22:1 ff., that he shed tears of joy at my house and made the good resolution to convert himself sincerely to God together with his wife and children, whom he will tell about the good he has enjoyed here. The expressions he used about the power of the divine word that he felt in his heart and the superiority of our parishioners over others were most moving and entirely in accordance with truth. At his request I gave him a testament and hymnal. If there were a righteous preacher in N.,[195] a few more souls could be saved from confusion, in which they are straying around like sheep without a shepherd.

The 24th of October. Yesterday we lovingly invited our congregation to call upon us diligently in our huts, because at the time we do not always find them at home when we visit them and wish to edify ourselves with them in good conversations and prayers. I set the time from twelve to four o'clock for them, because I am busy in the morning, partly in the school and partly in preparing some children for Holy Communion and other regular duties. Today after the midday meal some of them did me the pleasure of letting me pray with them in my hut and speak with them according to their spiritual situation, which is truly a right blessed and profitable undertaking. I prefer it when they call on me rather than make me take the initiative. In this way we are better able to learn about their desire for edification and their spiritual hunger and thirst; and, since they tell the reason for their visit, they give us good material for our conversation, instruction and comfort; and we also learn whether they have comprehended the sermon correctly and what part of it has especially touched their hearts.

It became clear to me already yesterday, but even more this morning and this afternoon, how much our true Savior has blessed His gospel and particularly an amazing example which I read aloud again in the repetition hour to confirm the matter that I had presented. If the gospel resounds in the consciences of the congregation, as it now seems to do in the case of some of them, we have good hopes that the devil will be more and more driven out and that the kingdom of Jesus will spread into their souls. After the prayer two conscience-stricken women, who are suffering for their sins, found two little sayings in the *Treasure Chest*,[196] of which one stands in no. 84 and the other in no. 288. The joy and refreshment they got from it was most impressive, because their thoughts and yearnings and God's love for them were expressed in it so emphatically and according to their wish.

In the case of simple souls who become like little children in their conversion, one can and must use all means for edification, awakening, and comforting. Two of the women, one of whom was married already a year ago, are entirely ignorant in the catechism; or, what they know according to the letter they do not understand correctly but in garbled form, therefore they have had to come to me three times a week for some time; and I am endeavoring to teach them the words of the catechism as long as my limited time permits. Mrs. N. has comprehended a bit, but it is difficult with the other one. Yet I am glad that they are not tiring of the matter but come at the appointed time, even if they sometimes come in vain or have to wait because impediments occur.

The 25th of October. A pious woman told me that her daughter had become sick and had unexpectedly said to her, "Mother, the Pastor may well think that I am a pious child because I am externally so pious, but my heart is very wicked, so please admonish me all the time to become different." Thereupon she turned to her two brothers and said, "If you see anything wicked in me, please tell me about it. I will not hold it against you; I will also tell you when I am aware of anything like that in you." And because this mother had also noticed some good in the two afore-mentioned boys, she asked us to speak to these three children often so that they would soon become heartily pious children. I was told that another girl used to play with her hands during the prayers; and, when she was lovingly reprimanded for it after the prayer, she shed bitter tears, expressed her remorse for such sinful behavior with clear words, and proved much more devout from that time on.

A woman complained to me in the presence of her husband that she had served the devil in committing her youthful sins; and, since she had sinned against God so gravely and had loved and practiced so many works of the devil and of the body, her heart must without doubt be trapped in his snares and entirely in his company. She had not yet noticed that she had freed herself from his snares and his wicked company, and what did I think about it? I well saw that she meant a deep felt and clearly recognizable liberation from Satan and his snares and that she wishes to feel, grasp, and observe how one snare after the other is cut off. Therefore I explained to her the nature of God's Kingdom, the beginning, progress, and the entire work of our new creation; and I illustrated the matter with a few verses, such as John 3:8 and Mark 4:26–29. I also gave her a few criteria by which she can distinguish her present penitent condition from her previous unrepentant one.

This same woman was deeply troubled that she was recently wearing a shirt at Holy Communion that she did not rightfully own. To be sure, she was chastised and disquieted in her conscience but had given herself a false peace and comfort from the fact that she had no other one to wear and that she wished to get rid of it as soon as she could get another one from elsewhere. But now she no longer wishes to keep it but rather to give it to a poor person, since she can no longer give it to its rightful owner. She and her husband also had a guilty conscience about a prayer book that they had found on the ship and that the commissary had given to them because no one claimed it after much asking around. Another man complained that he had a pair of scissors wrongfully; and at my advice he wishes to give them to a poor widow. On the occasion of such confession and voluntary returning of goods we show the people that such confession and giving back do not of themselves make things all right; but that it requires the Lord Jesus and his reconciliation, which must be seized by hearts laden with remorse and contrition.[197] However, returning belongings is required for good order, and no one can do proper penance and feel disgust at all sin if he still wishes to keep wrongly acquired goods among his possessions.

The 26th of October. A girl in the congregation has noticed

that another girl, with whom she recently went to Holy Communion for the first time, has become very lazy in her pursuit of the good; and, because she had obligated herself with her in the preparation hour to serve the Lord Jesus in truth and because they had obliged themselves to advance each other in Christianity, she had gone to her and reminded her of her laziness in a friendly way, and she hoped that his had done some good. She herself stands in a serious state of Christianity.

Late in the evening a man came to me because he had not been able to come by day because of much work, and he discussed with me the circumstances of his soul. He well recognizes that he is one of those who, when God calls them, go either to their fields or to their other work and, while neglecting the offered grace, maintain themselves with good resolutions for future improvement. But now, with God's help, he will be serious. For this purpose he would like to bring his wife too, and therefore he asked me to take her on as much as I could, for which purpose he will send her to me diligently. He was very happy to be able to attend evening prayers with me and my family, and then he went home greatly moved.

The 27th of October. We now have very gentle and warm weather both day and night, which is very helpful for the sweet potatoes, turnips, and radishes, and also for the beans that were planted late. Last Sunday our surveyor received a letter ordering him to go to Purysburg with a boat sent expressly for him. He requested my consent for this trip, whose purpose he did not know, and he promised to return in a few days and to continue with his work of surveying. Today I learned that he has gone to Port Royal, no doubt to survey a piece of land there; and I have been advised that he will be here again in a few days. If he does not come soon I shall inform Mr. Causton about it, as I told him clearly before his departure.

N. did me a very pleasant service in my present frame of mind by coming into my hut at just the right time and helping me pray and sing the song "Continue, Zion, etc."[198] He caused me great pleasure by telling me of the situation of his soul; and we cannot help but be greatly refreshed when we realize how this and that parishioner is gradually losing all thought for his body and how Christ is taking new shape. He is truly a very dear soul that the Lord Jesus has picked as his chosen bride, although in the poverty of his spirit he thinks himself still far from this honor. He is unusually pleased that he has learned of Christ and his office of intercessor in the images of the Levitic divine services during our daily prayer hours. He cannot help but marvel that some people among us are discontented and cannot accept our conditions, which are quite bearable, for he on his part heartily praises God, who has led him out of so much misery and such grievous circumstances, indeed out of Germany into this desert, where he is provided for both spiritually and physically.

The 28th of October. N. has much need of private instruction. He is very simple and incapable because of his weak understanding. Yet he has an honest heart and walks in the way of truth. The lesson of human misery and redemption from it through Christ, the son of God and man, is well enough known to him for him to be able to answer questions about it, only he cannot recite any Bible verses. He could recite the verses: "The Lord has so loved the world," etc., "That is surely true," etc., "Come unto me all ye who,"[199] etc. more with understanding than with words. I said a few short verses for him and will continue with it in the future, as often as he visits me. His wife can read well; and, because she too wishes to be saved in truth, she does as much for this her simple husband as she can by reading out loud, praying, and warning; and I admonished her to this duty when I visited her yesterday on her sickbed.

N.'s oldest daughter is also very incapable and of childish understanding, and I now have her together with other children in the preparation for Holy Communion. She knows the catechism and important Biblical passages by heart, she likes to read, sing, and pray; and she is often moved by God's word. Yet, when we examine her privately, her answers come out very imperfectly so that we can observe that she in unable to grasp anything in an orderly way or critically but merely retains this or that in her memory though constant hearing or reading. She has been taking the preparation for a long time; yet I find it necessary to have her here with me often so I can talk with her according to her understanding and teach her the basic truths of the Christian religion. She is very shy, bashful, and timid; and we have quite a job before we can calm her spirit and bring her to any composure.

The 29th of October. Our people greatly need provisions but do not dare go to Savannah through fear that they will have to take fish instead of meat, which they do not know how to use. They are expecting Captain Diamond, who was sent to Pennsylvania and New York for all kinds of provisions, so it is hoped that everything will be more plentiful. During this week some of us have made a beginning in clearing out the large areas in front of our huts towards the river that are overgrown with trees and bushes, which until now not only furnished shelter for many destructive varmints such as wild cats, bear, wolves, etc. but also prevented the winds from reaching our place. Many experienced people have given this as a reason that we have had longlasting sicknesses here. The work in this is very great; and, in order to repay them for it, they plan to plant such places as long as they can, the way they did last year with the lots in the middle of the city. Because the lots are near the huts, the women and children have a useful work once the men have chopped down the trees and burned the branches, bushes, and stumps and have thus done the heaviest and roughest work.

The 30th of October. N. N. and his wife came to my hut to undertake something useful for their edification. The wife is still very young and uninformed,[200] and he greatly wishes she could become a little more knowledgeable in her Christianity and her house-keeping. He means well in this, but he does not use the right method to accomplish anything towards her improvement. Therefore, I again found it necessary to tell them both what they should do if they wish to lead a God-pleasing Christian life and to have blessings on their household. In the case of the man, it is all a drive to obey the law and an anxious compulsion toward the good, and he complains how weak he still stands in regard to his denial of himself and of the world. Therefore I held out to him the living recognition of Christ as the only pure basis for all denial and for all practice of Christianity.[201]

The man told me how edifying and impressive it had been for him when, a short time ago, he had happened upon some girls in a solitary and hidden spot praying together so earnestly that they did not notice him and did not become confused; and he said that these children are still persisting in their seriousness. A couple of pious women and also two of the children who are now being prepared for Holy Communion dropped in today on N. N. and prayed with her so seriously that their gathering was crowned this time with much blessing of edification. She told me that the children deeply feel their sins and are greatly concerned with them. This person is a loyal steward of the grace she has received.

The 31st of October. A deeply honest Salzburger asked for advice as to what he should do. He has been invited by another Salzburger to act as Godfather for his child when God has helped his wife bear her child. He and his wife are, he said, very simple sinful people and entirely unworthy of such a holy and important matter as baptism. I directed him briefly to prayer, in which he should present the child and his unworthiness to the dear Lord, since all worthiness comes from Him and He gladly gives it to those who are unworthy, awkward, poor, and miserable in their own eyes.

Another man, to whom I read something about righteous earnestness in Christianity, told me while I read to him that previously he had misunderstood many Bible verses and had wrongly used them for worldly security and laziness. Among these was the beautiful verse 2 Corinthians 6:17: "Come out from among them, and be ye separate, etc." which words he had understood only as physical departure from the Papist church and its errors in dogma. Because he had obeyed this command of God, he had given himself much comfort and hope for eternal life. To be sure, he had seen more seriousness in his brother, but he thought he was going too far. Because this man's wife cannot read and also misses church often because of her physical ailments, I admonished him to act like the nobleman in yesterday's gospel, who repeated at home, for the advancement of his family's conversion and to make them believe, all that he had heard and experienced about Jesus.

I had shown in the repetition hour yesterday what a great spiritual profit this produced for the nobleman and other young and old people in Capernaum.[202] If those who had heard the teachings and miracles of the Lord Jesus at the festival in Jerusalem had told their families and others about it after their return, that would have been more profitable than if they had brought back and told vain and useless and even annoying stories. On this occasion I warned our people not to bring the filth that they often had to see in other places on their trips to this place to the scandal of other people. Rather, if they wished to bring and tell something new, then it should be something good and serving for edification. How necessary this admonition was I learned today from this same man, who told me that recently when fetching provisions with three other Salzburgers he had landed one evening at a place where he had found some Indians and white people of both sexes jumping around in the hut in a shameful manner as if they were entirely mad.[203] He had been moved by such unheard of disgrace to return to his boat. He had said nothing about this at our place, but he had learned that others had done so.

NOVEMBER

The 1st of November. The N. girl, who is one of our orphans, is receiving good marks for her diligence, obedience, and Christian behavior, so we have good hopes that she will become a sincerely pious child. Oh, what a joy it is for us and for those who love the Lord when the children turn out well! How gladly one makes all possible effort to advance their spiritual and physical well-being! N.,[204] who was also received into the orphanage after the death of her mother, is likewise serious in prayer and in contemplating God's word and at the same time docile and orderly in all things, although previously she had shown the opposite, to the distress of her mother. She is among the children who are being prepared for Holy Communion.

The 2nd of November. N. had wished to go to Holy Communion too next Sunday; but I advise him not to be too hasty but to prepare himself ahead of time very carefully, for which he now has an opportunity again in the regular prayer hours, which he has had to miss for over five months because he went away to take outside work. N. and N. had to agree to the same thing. They had withdrawn from our spiritual care and supervision for a rather long time, and therefore we must first get to know their spiritual condition better if we are to let them partake of Holy Communion. N. is becoming more and more worldly and returning to the old ways that he had gone both in Germany and also on the journey to America with the first transport. That is the result of absence from our place. During his activities in Savannah he became acquainted with Mrs. N., to whom he has indentured his daughter as a baby-nurse for seven years, without telling me a thing about it; and I had to show him my displeasure at this. Not only will the poor child be treated very harshly, but she will also forget all she has learned and will, through bad examples, be strengthened all the more in the wickedness in which she is now mired.

Our dear parishioners have called on us diligently this afternoon, and we have prayed with them and given them good advice for the serious conduct of their Christianity. Being together, we can practice recognizing the idolatry that lies in our hearts and our manifold deviations from God, the one true Good and Savior, through the grace of the Holy Spirit; for which purpose we are given sufficient opportunity in the present prayer hours in the lesson of the terrible story in Exodus 32. God mercifully grants that our congregation visit the evening prayer hours with especial zeal and accuracy, and the blessings therefrom reveal themselves abundantly to the praise of the Lord.

N. had hired himself out as a laborer in N. for several months and learned many kinds of misbehavior there, which I called to his attention today. He well recognized the harm and told me something of the horror of the crass desecration of the Sabbath there, and he said he was entirely fed up with such people. And others who have had to live among the English laborers for a while because of their work no longer yearn to leave us. One person, whom I had held back with my arguments, thanked me heartily for such love, because he now hears and sees through other people's experience the harm he too would have suffered by going away.

The 3rd of November. Shortly before the prayer hour last night I received two very pleasant letters, one from Professor Francke and one from Councilor Walbaum. The first was from the 13th and 23rd of July and the second from the 14th of June of this year. Their content is so enjoyable that I must let the members of our dear community share it for the praise of God and the strengthening of their faith, as soon as we have completed the story of Genesis 32, which serves as a preparation for Holy Communion. May the Lord repay the two worthy benefactors with more than thousandfold blessings for what they have done for our dear congregation through their communications, intercessions, and loving care. The afore-mentioned letter from Professor Francke says nothing about a doctor, whose early arrival we have until now so greatly desired and requested. We wish all the more to call upon our dear Lord to incline our dear benefactors to this important matter and to make them willing to provide something for the maintenance of a trained doctor or surgeon. The dwelling is now entirely ready for him; and a large and well made kitchen has been constructed, for distilling and other uses, at the side of the dwelling, which has a heated living room and a bedroom. So we hope he will be well satisifed with it. The preacher in Savannah sent me a letter that the Baron von Reck had sent me on 28 July of this year from Germany from a place named Windhausen.[205]

The 4th of November. Last night we had a very cold wind, which has continued raw and unpleasant all day. Winter is now really beginning; and, since a few poor people among us are not supplied with clothing and blankets, we are praying for them to be provided for. With the expected arrival of Mr. Oglethorpe we hope to receive a supply of blankets and old clothes through the loving efforts of our dear Court Preacher Butjenter. However, since a letter from Mr. Vat to Kalcher advises me that several months may pass, we must buy the most necessary things with the money God has put into our hands. Praise be to God, who still lets the fountains of His mercy and fatherly love flow out to us and who, through our worthy Professor Francke in the afore-mentioned letter, also lets us hope for other generous gifts of money and other things. In the orphanage, which we have begun with God's help, this has become our motto: "God's fountains have an abundance of water."[206] Today, while I, together with the two Kalchers, was pouring out before His throne my prayers concerning our and other people's needs, our dear Father in heaven filled my heart with comfort and sweet hopes that He will neither leave us nor abandon us and that He will advance the glory of His name through these institutions, however small they may appear.

The 5th of November. Last night the freeze was very severe; and now our people are very busy in digging up their sweet potatoes, which cannot stand any freezing. As long as it is warm, they are accustomed to let the tubers remain, because they continue to grow and get thicker. However, as soon as the night frosts begin, the leaves begin to shrivel and the tubers do not last in the ground but must be taken to a warm and dry place. Someone told me that after our prayer hour yesterday he had a very restless night, in which his sins and their judgment appeared to him dreadfully in his sleep. In his dream he received some hope of escaping his deserved judgment from the saying: "I have no pleasure in the death."[207] He also told me how he had made the serious resolution to convert himself with all his heart to the Lord Jesus, who had brought upon himself the execution of the judgment earned by mankind.

This man's wife, who is heartily sincere in her Christianity, recently complained to me that two things made the sincerity of her conversion dubious: 1, because she was still too timid to chastise people who do evil; 2, because she could not yet love her enemies and do good to them as she should. I explained this Christian duty of chastising one's neighbor and showed her that, if God gives joy and wisdom for it, it can and must be done with words, but also with gestures. For that, one needs the spirit of gentleness, love, and humility so that the neighbor will see that it is all for the Glory of God and the salvation of the neighbor. In the case of angry or sarcastic resistance it is better to

remain quiet and to sigh and to see that you are not brought
out of your own tranquility. The more she learned to taste the
friendly love of our Savior, the more she would learn to practice
the commandment of loving her enemy. If she felt her failures
in this and other things, she should penetrate all the more
deeply into Him with prayer and He would make good her
shortcomings. But she must take care not to seek and find her
salvation in the practice of this or other virtues but only in the
wounds of Jesus, as a poor and often failing sinner.[208]

This week we have prayed diligently with our parishioners
both in my hut and in that of my dear colleague. Our loving
Father in heaven, who heareth all prayers, will accept this holy
exercise for Christ's sake and give us everything we have petitioned for ourselves and other people. It is very profitable when
our parishioners come to us of their own accord to pray with
us or to be instructed. We immediately drop all scheduled business that can possibly be postponed, because we consider what
God drops into our hands to be more important.

The 6th of November. This Sunday forty-two people participated in Holy Communion, among them many souls hunger-
ing and thirsting for grace, whom God without doubt hath abundantly refreshed at this His table of grace and love. Yesterday
in the Holy Communion preparation our dear Lord granted us
a fine awakening from Isaiah 4:4; afterwards several souls joined
us and our families in the doctor's newly constructed kitchen
for singing and praying, and this provided a great blessing for
us and others. Because this kitchen is spacious and right comfortable for Christian assemblies, we met there again this evening. The people, both young and old, had gathered there
before our arrival and sung the beautiful song "Be Joyful in the
Lord, you Holy Soul."[209] This edifying behavior on the part of
the assembled people impressed me greatly.

Among the people present I knew some who have a heart-felt
yearning to become righteous Christians or who have already
become so and wish to become even more so. Therefore, after
singing the song "I will love Thee, my Strength."[210] I began to
acquaint myself and them with the short but very important
rules that the late Collin gave in his book *The forceful Entry into
the Kingdom of God,*[211] and I confirmed them with other emphatic
scriptural passages and also with examples. During the address
I remembered three examples of honest souls with whose serious Christianity I became acquainted in Halle; and this memory
was very pleasant and impressive for me and the others with

regard to the purpose for which I cited them. It is very loyal of God on occasions when we are edifying others to let us recall what we have heard or seen some years earlier without having taken it to heart as we should have at the time.

A poor widow told me that God had inclined the heart of a Salzburger woman to give her a couple of shirts for her naked children, which had stood her in good stead in her need during this sudden cold weather. By this her faith in the living and all satisfying God has been so strengthened that she no longer doubted that He would provide for her and her children this winter too. This news pleased me because I could recognize this charitable work as the fruit of the divine word that had been proclaimed and had penetrated into our hearts. For the woman had possessed the linen without right and preferred to get rid of it, although she herself is poor and needy.

The 7th of November. This morning one of the Swiss who were travelling on a boat from their newly founded city[212] to Purysburg called on me; and I would gladly have had something warm cooked for his refreshment, if only the skipper had been willing to wait. He was sick and miserable, and it is the same with all the rest. Dreadfully many (as his expression was) have died in the new city (which scarcely has the appearance of a city). They are people without food, sheep without a shepherd, and therefore in miserable circumstances. For some time we have had with us four daughters of the schoolmaster Unselt, who died in Purysburg and who was perhaps known to Court Preacher Ziegenhagen; and they have given good hope of a thorough conversion to God. The oldest has been married for some time to a Salzburger,[213] the second was in my service a short time ago and is letting the good that she heard and saw in my house shine forth in her heart now even more than then, and she is proving very serious in earning her salvation. The two youngest girls have been accepted among the number of orphans, and the older of the two is being prepared for Holy Communion. Today I heard someone say how these children look upon the good that they are now receiving in soul and body as a blessing for which their pious father had prayed on his death-bed. He had been very concerned about his children, since there is no school in Purysburg and their mother, who died a few months ago in Charleston, did not know how to manage them.

The 8th of November. I read the Passion story piecemeal to those who are being prepared for Holy Communion and work it into the prayers we pray together; and, in addition, I find it necessary to impress upon them the Order of Salvation which

Pastor Freylinghausen has composed,[214] especially since two children are among them, also my English boy Bishop, who are still somewhat lacking in a true recognition of the basic truths of the Christian religion. May God be pleased, for Christ's sake, with these and all work that is done among us with both children and adults; and may He accompany them with his divine Blessing. The surveyor arrived here again at the end of last week and is beginning again in earnest to finish surveying our lands. I had advised him to hire people in Purysburg whom he could better use than ours so that I might at last be relieved of his complaints and annoyance; but he brought nobody with him, presumably because no one wishes to serve him for such poor pay as he has offered our people for such hardships.

Several poor members of the community suffer both day and night now that winter has begun; and therefore my dear colleague has undertaken a trip to Savannah to buy some inexpensive winter clothing and blankets. Praise be to God, who still provides us with food and clothing or blankets; He shall surely continue to provide for us, as His unfailing word assures us. May he grant spiritual and physical blessings to our dear benefactors, whose charitable gifts have refreshened our poor and sick so far, with praise to God and prayers for the benefactors.

The 9th of November. Last night we had a thunder storm with lightning and rain, which, however, did not last long and was not so violent as in summer. At this time, it serves as a foreboding of a severe winter and much rainy weather. An Indian borrowed a lancet from us to bleed a sick old Indian, who has been here for several days. Because this Indian knew some English, I asked him about his age; but he could not tell me anything certain, he could only say that he had lived for a long time and that he was already living when this or that happened in the country. Since he can no longer make his living in the forest, he is supported by his son-in-law, who is with him in our place. In the old man I found such a great natural honesty and a patient and quiet resignation in his sickness and poverty that I had to marvel. Without a doubt such a heathen would put to shame many Christians, who, despite the light of the gospel, have not come so far as this old man and probably others like him have come by natural strength. The other, who bled him, admitted he had learned to curse and swear as long as he was among white people, otherwise he had never found such improper things among the Indians. I gave them both something to eat and drink.

The 10th of November. Our boat, that I had sent to Savannah

for provisions, returned empty, because Mr. Causton is of the opinion that our people have already taken what was coming to them, Nevertheless, my accounts show that all three transports are still due a considerable amount of meat, rice, corn, and other things. With God's help, I shall go there next week, since Mr. Causton has asked me to put the accounts in order. My dear colleague brought with him the blankets he had bought and cloth for some of the Salzburgers' clothes.

The 12th of November. This evening my dear colleague was fetched to Purysburg to preach the gospel of Christ there tomorrow, as the people there had recently requested him to. The Lutherans there are no longer so close together as previously, but are scattered here and there on their plantations or in other occupations; and therefore we preach God's word and hold Holy Communion seldomer than formerly. At that time I got back the letter I had written already in May of last year to Messrs. Siron and Weissiger in Philadelphia. Schonmansgruber had taken it with him for forwarding but had died under way; and his wife, who is still in Charlestown, must have forgotten it. We are again having dry and very gentle weather, which is very comfortable for the people in harvesting their sweet potatoes. The weather must not be the chief cause of the fever; because some of the people have it now just as much as in mid summer, and others are getting it again. Our dear Lord is keeping both of us in health and strength, although, according to God's will, one of the other member of our families must suffer some physical weakness.

The 13th of November. A Salzburger woman complained to another one that her husband was so very concerned with providing food that he was sometimes needlessly upset and that he wished to worry about the future. By this he made his struggle difficult and could never overcome it. When he recently wished to go to Holy Communion, he prayed earnestly and sincerely in his garden alone and with her; and she thought that he would now break through and achieve spiritual freedom. However, she finds that that is not yet the case. Otherwise, this is an honest man, who is very much bowed by his sins and seriously wishes to be saved. What I have now learned was previously unknown to me; and I am pleased to discover that the woman can see what is causing her husband to be held back from the real essence of Christianity. And since I have discovered this and can assume that other impoverished parishioners are suffering from this sickness, I can all the better see such harm and recommend and apply the correct means against it in my preaching of the divine word and in my intercourse with the people.

In this evening's prayer hour, in which many worthy souls again presented themselves for singing and praying, I also spoke about this obstacle to the right penetration into the Kingdom of God; and, as I hear, this had its blessing. Our familiar intercourse with our parishioners is very profitable for edifying their souls and averting the pitfalls to which one is accustomed to be tempted both right and left on his Christian pilgrimage. We can well experience their shortcomings, and in presenting the holy gospel we can apply ourselves accordingly, if our loyal God grants us a blessed revival of our hearts from reading good books, then at the same time we have an opportunity to present it, just as warm as it is in our hearts, to our dear congregation according to their circumstances and to pray with them about it. God lets this occur with His blessing.

The 14th of November. Because the catechism has been completed in the afternoon catechism class and we still have two Sundays after Trinity left in this year before the new church year begins, my dear colleague has undertaken to take the two beautiful gospels for the 26th and 27th Sundays after Trinity from Matthew 25 as the basis of the catechisation; and during his absence yesterday I catechisized the gospel for the 26th Sunday after Trinity. The construction of the orphanage should be begun early this morning. One of the carpenters fetched me from the orphans' prayer hour because I had promised him on Sunday, through God's word and prayer, to sanctify the construction of this house, which is being built solely for the glory of God. (I Timothy 4:5). There are sixteen workers in all who stepped before the countenance of God with me in awe and humility at the place where the building is to be constructed.

First I read to them the words of the verses 34, 35, and 36 out of gospel text Matthew 25, which we had treated yesterday afternoon; and I showed them what pleasure the Lord Jesus has whenever any arrangements are made for the support, care, and refreshment of his hungry, thirsty, exiled, naked, and sick persons. He will so highly esteem this charitable work, which will be accorded even to the least of his children with upright hearts, that He will remember it in the presence of all angels and all assembled nations. Our dear Savior would like to see that needy people whom he would like to refreshen, both adults and straying and abandoned children, in our place and in this land and in this neighborhood were brought up in the fear and admonition of the Lord. For this reason he awakened a benefactor, totally unknown to me, who has given a considerable sum of money through the hands of our worthy Senior Urlsperger for the erection of such a blessed and useful institution. Since this money has already been largely expended for the preparation of timber and other building material, he has already given us a fond hope for another considerable gift; for our dear Professor N.,[215] in his recently received letter of 13 July of this year, has given us the news that he shall soon send us 200 Reichsthaler for our disposition through the hands of our dear Court Preacher Ziegenhagen. All this shows, I said, that God in His love earnestly wishes that such an institution will be established so that His praiseworthy name will be glorified and many miserable souls will be helped; and I told them that God had especially selected them (the sixteen workers standing before me) to build a house for Jesus, in which he will be refreshed in his children. This should incite them to perform their work in faith, honesty, loyalty, unity, and good order. I recommended to them the verse I Corinthians 15:58, "Your labor is not in vain in the Lord." I compared this with Colossians 3:22–24, in which is clearly written how the Lord looks upon even simple labor that is done in faith. Hereupon we prayed together heartily to God and invoked Him in the name of His son to give his blessing to this structure, mercifully to keep these workers from harm and danger, and to crown with rich physical and spiritual blessings the dear benefactors who have contributed something for this or who will do so through divine ordinance. It is also a benefit for our people that such construction gives them an opportunity to earn something during their present poverty resulting from the bad harvest and that they do not find it necessary to separate themselves from God's word and the supervision of their ministers in order to find work. At the end of last week two Purysburg men came from Old Ebenezer and wished to return to Purysburg; but, because there was no opportunity and they were lacking food in the meanwhile, we assigned them some work from which they earned some food and a little pay. They were very pleased by this and performed their work honestly.

Continuation of the Diary[216]

Tuesday, the 15th of November 1737. Today my dear colleague, Mr. Boltzius, travelled to Savannah in order to go over the accounts with Mr. Causton. May God let us see the day when all this travelling will no longer be necessary. He also took letters and the diary in order to post them with the first available safe carrier.

Wednesday, the 16th of November. Last night, during the prayer meeting, I informed our flock of the letter by Mr. Walbaum. It is a most edifying epistle; and what strikes the reader in particular is the true humility and Christian simplicity of this dear benefactor's faith, with which he attempts to walk before the Lord. May the Lord strengthen him on his path by His spirit and may He bestow all those things on him that he so kindly and generously wishes for us. Only last night, my dear colleague had also read the letter of the honorable Prof. Francke to our flock. Oh! for the heart-felt concern shown by this good father, who shares in all the joy that the Lord sends us as well as in all the tribulations that He may place on us as if we were his own children. May the Lord Jesus reward him for this richly, both here and eternally before His face.

Thursday, the 17th of November. I was fetched to Purysburg last Saturday to preach to the Gospel there. I was much pleased to have the occasion to declare the goodness of Jesus Christ at that location also. I conducted two services there on Sunday, in the place where services are usually held for the Germans and some French Swiss. For the latter, the preacher there[217] usually conducts one service with a proper sermon every other Sunday; on alternate Sundays he only conducts a prayer meeting for the former based on the English prayer book, which has been translated into German, and thus he changes every Sunday. He never preaches in German, except, as I have been told, on High Holidays, when he will read a sermon; but he is said not to be good at it, since he has never learned the language well. The place where the service is conducted is at the preacher's house, which was finished only a short while ago. He does not yet live there; for the house is being used for a church and destined for that purpose until such time as the church, the construction of which has been started, shall be finished. The Germans there would be much pleased to hear a sermon every Sunday; and, as I had occasion to notice, this would be of great benefit to them. They are very happy whenever they learn that one of us will come to their place to give a sermon or to hold a prayer meeting.

Only few of them are of the Evangelical Lutheran faith;[218] but the others come in equal numbers, if not more, when they know of the service in advance and do not live too far away on one of the plantations. Kieffer, one of our people there, had fetched me with the intention of keeping me there, not only that Sunday, but for the entire week, so that I might hold a prayer meeting every day and offer them Holy Communion on the following Sunday. However, I had not understood him well in Ebenezer; and thus I had failed to bring the necessary utensils for this purpose. As soon as I had realized his true intention, I told him that I could not stay this time, particularly since my dear colleague, Mr. Boltzius, had to travel to Savannah. He therefore brought me back to Ebenezer this Monday and took the opportunity to inspect his land, which is almost directly opposite our village. He intended to work on his land until this Thursday, when he would return to fetch me again. This he did, and I thereupon returned with him to Purysburg, particularly as my dear colleague had agreed to this course of action and had promised to hurry back from Savannah as soon as possible so that our flock should not be left quite without a spiritual helper.

When I arrived in Purysburg, preparations for a prayer meeting were started forthwith and a number of the people there assembled immediately, since they had been given hope of such a meeting at the occasion of my last sojourn there. I based the meeting on the words: Christ "was delivered for our offences, and was raised again for our justification."[219] After the meeting, they desired to know at what hour they should return tomorrow, and they were told that a sign would be given to them. However, in the evening, when our boat returned from Savannah to Purysburg, I learned that my colleague had been forced to stay over in Savannah, for else he would have had to repeat his journey on the coming Monday. I thus was obliged to return to Ebenezer, which much grieved the dear people here, for it hindered them in their plans.

Friday, the 18th of November. Kieffer brought me back to Ebenezer today. I found our flock in good spirits; and we jointly edified ourselves in the evening prayer meeting, as is our habit, and particularly at this time of the year, when the approach of Christmas demands that we keep in mind the fact that God's Son became incarnate. The Bible story gave us a good example for this, when the occasion of the pitching of a tabernacle for the congregation demonstrated the human nature of Christ, which is the tabernacle that He has erected among us.

In Purysburg I learned that twenty of the recently arrived Swiss had died there and another nineteen further up near Savannah-Town. Among those who had died in Purysburg had been a smith by trade, who, believing that he was well accustomed to the heat, had continued working despite the hot sun. While he may have felt that that would not hurt him, he must have experienced the contrary.

Saturday, the 19th of November. Our two boats were sent to Savannah today, and my dear colleague intends to hold a service there tomorrow for those manning the boats, God willing. This week, two sloops have arrived there; and, therefore, it is hoped that Mr. Causton will have received provisions and thus should let our people have the remaining portion of their allotment.

Sunday, the 20th of November. Until now the weather has been quite warm, but this morning it turned very cold. Nevertheless, our dear listeners did not fail to come to the preaching of the Gospels both in the morning and the afternoon; and we sought to use this last Sunday of the Church year to good purpose and our salvation. And our good Lord has richly given us blessing and edification, both from the ordinary lessons for this Sunday and from the story of the ten virgins.[220] Particularly the latter text has encouraged us to become prudent through the Lord's grace and to run forward to welcome the Bridegroom in this period of grace, so that we might be found worthy at the end of our life to go with him to the wedding and to enjoy eternal peace and joy before His face after all the struggle and fighting shall be over. May the Lord Jesus remind us of this through His spirit.

Monday, the 21st of November. This noon I visited our people who are constructing the orphanage, and I found them well advanced with the Lord's help. May the Lord continue to assist them and make everything redound to His praise, for Christ's sake. In particular, I spoke to a carpenter to whom I had recently given a small book, *The Beginning of Christian Life*,[221] for I knew that he is eager to learn how to conduct himself in his Christian faith. I asked him how he liked the book, and he assured me that it served him well to this end and that with the Lord's mercy he would seek to apply the lessons contained therein. True, he said, his faith had not yet advanced to the point that he well recognized it in others; but he took much comfort from Mr. Boltzius' recent words to him to the effect that this was a good beginning, provided that he earnestly desired faith.

Tuesday, the 22nd of November. Some among our listeners attempt to penetrate ever deeper into God's mercy and to impart that which they seek to others around them; some among those are well prepared to receive such a message. In the evening prayer hour we spoke of the High Priest of the Old Testament who, when ministering before the Lord, had always carried with him the children of Israel, in that the names of the twelve tribes of Israel were engraved on the breastplate he carried on his chest. We used this to our own profit by recognizing that we ourselves were the believers; for our Lord Jesus, as the true High Priest of the New Testament who is sitting to the right of the Father, is forever carrying them, in a manner of speaking, on His breast and, what is more, in His heart. He loves them tenderly; and thus it is impossible that He should forget them. Oh! that the Lord Jesus might grant to His children to recognize such bliss more and more clearly so that they may be well comforted in all spiritual and physical circumstances and that others might be awakened by their example and cease to serve sin but make a timely dedication of their entire heart to our Lord Jesus and deny all and every other thing for His sake!

Wednesday, the 23rd of November. This afternoon I returned to Ebenezer with God's help. I found enough reason to praise the Lord for the good that He has done to my dear colleague and our flock. [Mr. Causton kept me in Savannah for a long time in the hope that he would be able to completely satisfy me, on behalf of our people, in the matter of provisions. My own accounts on the provisions are so well kept that it should not have taken more than a few hours to settle them, and they should have clearly shown him how much our people have received in the manner of provisions and how much remains open in their favor if the amounts allotted by the Honorable Trustees are to be fully delivered. However, he has his own method and placed the entire matter in the hands of a young boy who made many errors so that in the end everything was wrong and unacceptable.

[As a result, I do not yet know where I stand with him in the matter of provisions. He refused to consider whether the provisions sent to me arrived in good shape or half spoiled and whether they had the proper weight or not; and he insists on entering all provisions in exactly the same manner as recorded by his employees in the store-house. He even wishes the accounts on behalf of our people to show some live oxen, whereas these had run away. Also, Mr. Vat had permitted some provisions to spoil, and others arrived in insufficient quantities and of incorrect weight; and now these people should make up for it. The third transport is to receive the short rations for no more than half a year, and therefore they will owe the store-house for the provisions received from the 12th of August of this year until now. Since he well knows that they cannot subsist on what they have managed to harvest this year, he is prepared to let them have their provisions on credit; if the Honorable Trustees are subsequently willing to forgive them this debt, he would be well satisfied. There were other difficulties; but, thanks to the Lord's help, these were well taken care of, for the good of our flock.

[As far as the unpleasant matters just-mentioned are concerned, I shall refrain from making further serious objections in this respect until I have received his final statement of what is still due to us in the way of provisions; and Mr. Causton has promised to forward this statement at the next opportunity. I am much hurt by the fact that our dear Mr. Causton tends to be all too ready to go back on his promises, orders, and his word. This has caused me much confusion and also harm; because our people, to whom I now and then make promises and announcements in his name, feel misled by these, a situation which I have had again to bear on this and other occasions. Thus, I have had to pay in cash for some things which he had previously promised as gifts, and some goods which had been given as gifts to the sick are now not to be considered as such, according to his recent words.]

I have, nevertheless, been able to settle a number of matters with God's blessing, above all, that our people have been paid in full for the work they have done in the service for the Honorable Trustees, after having had to wait for such payment for over a year. Also, he has now paid a shilling in silver for each bushel of corn and beans we harvested in 1736. Mr. Oglethorpe had given orders to this effect even before his departure so as to spur our people's industry and willingness to produce crops. I fully trust our Father in heaven that He shall arrange the remaining matters in such a way that we shall praise His name.

Those of our affairs that are beset by difficulties and trials reward us all the more if finally they are arranged in accordance with our wishes. Thus, with much praise of the Lord and joy, our people are now receiving the flour which has been allocated to them instead of money for their additional harvest of beans and corn, whereas they had ceased hoping for any recompense in view of the long delay. Others around here, particularly the poor people in Purysburg, whether German or French,[222] fare far worse than our people here; some of them are suffering much want, and others are forced to work elsewhere for wages, a fate our flock need not share, for they do have occasion to earn some money here in our village, seeing that they must not leave the place of God's word. Our dear Father will surely reward our benefactors who until now have so often given us welcome gifts, which have benefited the material wellbeing of our flock. For example, I have just received and brought home with me more blue cloth and lining material for winter clothes for our poor and naked.

Mr. Causton has also assured me that the Honorable Trustees will contribute something to the support of our orphans and widows. However, since he has previously held different views and has not yet given me any written confirmation to this effect, I shall be forced to await Mr. Oglethorpe's arrival to be fully assured of this matter. He has again expressed his pleasure at our provisions for the orphans and the appointments of the orphanage. Should the Honorable Trustees allocate something for the support of the orphans, we would shortly be able to accept some poor children from Purysburg; but we shall not wait for this, rather we shall observe the indications and the will of the Lord only, as He can and will arrange everything. During our prayer hour I and the Salzburgers who came to fetch me in Savannah on Saturday were edified by the fourteenth Psalm, which, considering our circumstances, came as a balm on our heads for me and the others. The Lord is God, the Lord is God, let us give praise to the Lord. All the miserable, the oppressed, the hungry, the imprisoned, the blind, the dejected, strangers, and orphans have their certain assurance from the Lord, who keeps his faith eternally, the time of their help and salvation shall certainly come. Hallelujah! I have addressed our letters and diaries to Mr. Eveleigh in Charleston, who will surely forward them safely. I have also written to Mr. Schlatter, the merchant in St. Gall, as well as to his correspondents in London, Mr. Norris and Mr. Drewett, to inform them that Mr. Causton is much pleased with the quality of the linen and would ask for more, for which he is prepared to send rice and furs or, if these goods are not in good supply at a reasonable price, pay in cash.

Thursday, the 24th of November. Last night Mrs. Schweiger gave birth to a daughter, who was christened this morning. [Mrs. Rheinlaender is again showing signs of submission and has started, as she has done before on other occasions, to berate herself for her offences and rudeness toward me. I trust her all the less now, as she has previously committed much falsehood with her recognitions and confessions.] My dear colleague has been called to Purysburg, where he is to administer Holy Communion to the people there this coming Sunday, for a number of persons have expressed their desire in this respect. We have now started on the Book of Leviticus in our evening prayer hours. During my absence, my dear colleague has partly read and partly explained, with the corresponding instructions for the edification of our flock, the voluntary offerings for the building of the tabernacle, based on the relevant text in the last chapters of Exodus.

I demonstrated tonight in particular that the priests and all Israelites had to follow divine instruction meticulously in their services and carefully avoid all arbitrary means of conducting such services, however reasonable they might appear. For the Lord made a terrible example of the sons of Aaron, Nadab and Abihu, as men who were not careful in their observance but served the Lord as their phantasies directed them. In the New Testament it is also urged that we should closely follow the will of the Father in heaven in our Christian faith, our service, and our entire way of life (Matthew 7:21). It is most regrettable that only a very few recognize the will of the Lord as it is truly manifested, and instead seek their salvation according to their own convictions and impulses and by an external use of means of salvation and socially respectable behavior.[223]

It is said in Romans 7:2 that the will of the Lord must be recognized; for as long as man refuses to walk the path of repentance but continues on the easy road in his sureness and carelessness, he is truly blind and refuses to find the path of righteousness. Once he takes his Christian faith seriously, however, and reflects on his previous conduct, he will be amazed at his former blindness, wherein he quite misjudged the Christian faith; and he will thank the Lord for having finally brought him to the true recognition of His will and the truth! Oh, how necessary it is to warn the people of self-deceit and erroneous comfort. For their hearts harbor the seducer and the false prophet, and these must be made to hold their tongue by the word of truth.

Friday, the 25th of November. We have had some winter clothes prepared for a number of poor children and adults, for which the name of the Lord is gratefully praised by some, whereas others must be reminded of their duty, which they are too lazy to recognize, by us and some other Christian folk. This year there is a good crop of acorns, and our people are collecting a large stock.[224] The third transport has hopes of receiving the hogs that were promised to them in the last letters of the Honorable Trustees. Since there are numerous bears and wolves in this desolate and uncultivated area, our people have lost many hogs, a loss which causes much deprivation in these poor people's nourishment. There are many obstacles and difficulties to overcome for those who attempt to cultivate barren soil and make their livelihood on it. There are misfortunes and other unforeseen instances which are hard to imagine for those who live in a more developed country. And, since it is often the case that industrious people are not given sufficient help and support, they cannot make ends meet and must labor for others and painfully earn their living.

Saturday, the 26th of November. Our listeners are always well pleased when, during our evening prayer meetings, we and our children sing one of the less known songs which are so pleasant and well arranged both in words and melody. Some even ask the children to sing them these songs in their own houses, so that the older people may learn them the more easily. Last night we sang with much delight and edification the song: "Continue, Zion, continue in the light."[225] We have learned that this has left a strong impression on our people. The audience is silent when such quite unknown melodies are played, and the children are left to sing by themselves so that the true melody can be easily followed. The children learn such songs by heart, word by word, at home so that they can sing them without any prompting in the evening prayer hour, where there is only one candle to light the darkness.

In general, it is a great pleasure to the parents and others of good will when they hear what the children learn in school, in particular as the treasure of their learning is shared by the whole audience, both Sundays and during the evening prayer hours. I often hear remarks to the effect that our children have many advantages over others, for which they are encouraged by the Christian souls among us to say thanks and praise to the Lord. The Schweiger infant died this morning, although it had looked quite well after its birth and at the time of baptism. It was suddenly and unexpectedly seized by epilepsy on two consecutive occasions, a disease of which several of our children have died.

Sunday, the 27th of November. N. [Mrs. Pichler] has been ill for a long time, and her affliction has worsened since the time she sinned against the Lord by her grievous offences. But God seems to be reaching His goal in her, for she assured me that God has made her recognize, one by one, all the sins that she has committed since her childhood. However, in her terrible fear of heart and conscience she had loudly implored the Lord, the source of all help and salvation, for a number of days; and He had finally calmed her heart and had forgiven her for all her sins, a remission of which she was quite assured. Her husband told me that she had been quite restless and easily upset all throughout the preceding week and for some days after that, and that he could do nothing to please her. Nevertheless, she had reproached him on several occasions, for which she had subsequently asked his forgiveness from the bottom of her heart. She asked me to visit her often and said that, even if she should lose her voice and power of speech, I should read to her from the Lord's word and pray with her and for her. When I read some passages to her from John 9, concerning Lazarus and his illness, and particularly the words: "This sickness is not unto death but for the glory of God, that the Son of God might be glorified thereby,"[226] she seized her prayer book in her feeble hands and opened it at the morning prayer for a sick person, which contained the very passage that I had just read to her and which impressed itself all the more strongly on her mind since she had previously said this prayer. When Pichler came to my house to fetch something for his wife's physical comfort, I reminded him to be patient with her and her feebleness, for I have learned that he, being himself ill quite often, has on occasion become short-tempered and impatient with his wife's long illness.

Today, on the first Sunday of Advent, we have had a very cold day. However, this has not prevented us from holding both the regular service and the evening prayer meeting. These meetings are well visited by our hungry souls, so that our doctor's quite roomy kitchen, where we hold our Sunday meetings because of the cold, can barely accommodate all our listeners. We sing our strength-giving songs, encourage each other in the seriousness of our Christian faith, and pray for ourselves and for others. The Lord is among us in these meetings, He has truly revived and awakened a number among us, and He has continued to lead them and strengthen them in His mercy.

Monday, the 28th of November. I found a married couple at home on their knees; and the woman in particular complained, with many tears and much trembling, that she could not see her way for the many sins that obstructed her mind. To show me the nature of her present prayer, she quoted the words: "My prayer is full of doubting thoughts, although Thy word and comfort resound, my faith is and remains unsure, my heart appears both dead and cold and is so full of fear and hesitation and so inwardly confused that I can hardly bear myself, my mind is so led astray."[227] She added that God had persuaded her never again to sin against Him intentionally or knowingly, even if she were to die a horrible martyr's death, if only she could fight and break her way to the grace of the Gospel, etc. God be praised for placing such a serious resolve in this woman and others of her kind. May He bless this example in others, as He has done before.

Yesterday morning I received a letter from Savannah to the effect that we should retain an escaped servant if he should happen to pass through here. The Englishmen apprehended him in Old Ebenezer, and he is being taken to Savannah on our boat, which happens to travel there today. Captain Thomson has brought a whole boatload of male and female indentured servants from Scotland; and, while I was in Savannah, all adult persons among them were sold for 10 pounds sterling, for which they must serve for fourteen years.

Tuesday, the 29th of November. My dear colleague returned to us last night and told us, to the Glory of the Lord, that Christ's word was well received by the people in Purysburg and has entered their souls. Not only did they appear in great numbers both in the morning and in the afternoon, despite the severe cold; but they have actively expressed, both in word and in deed, their joy and gratitude to him who has given them God's word in the name of the Lord. He told of a mother who had come to Purysburg from her faraway plantation with her small child, had spent the night there, and had eagerly attended the sermons with her small infant, which had to be swaddled in clothes against the cold. He was much impressed by this. Since the poor people there are ill served [by their preacher] both in health and in illness (of which we do not like to give much detail), they have asked us to report, both in London and in Germany, on their great need for a proper preacher so that our dear benefactors there and the friends of the Lord might be apprised of their situation and that they might be provided for as we in Ebenezer are provided for by the Lord's providence and fatherly care. However, it is not incumbent upon us to interfere in this matter, except for an occasional mention in this diary of the spiritual want and the miserable material and spiritual conditions of these poor people in Purysburg.

A Salzburger has asked me to explain to him the saying: "I will be gracious to whom I will be gracious, and I will show mercy on whom I will show mercy",[228] because he claims that his struggle against sin is so difficult and that he can not see his way and that he is often convinced that the Lord will not take pity on him and show him His mercy. Since we had repeated these words a few weeks ago in our discussion of Exodus 34, I explained to him, solely by the following sermon, "The Lord of the Lord," in particular on the basis of the words of Moses in vv. 6:7, that our Lord Jesus, full of mercy, pity, patience, etc., clearly devoted Himself to the sinners; and, as has been shown us, he proved this while He walked visible among us and continues to prove it.

So that I might relieve this poor man of his scruples and his unnecessary fears that God might not have pity on all sinners, I quoted to him a number of sayings that make particular mention of the all-embracing love of the Lord for all poor and fallen humans. I thereupon explained to him the meaning of the words of the Apostle Paul, concerning the words in Romans 9:15, i.e., that God, in showing His mercy, will ignore all outward signs and human judgments and wishes and will act in utter freedom so as to show His mercy to all who accept His rule, be they Jews or heathen or even the most serious sinners. When He is merciful and full of pity, He is merciful with great strength and effort, so that we rightly speak of true mercy and pity.

Wednesday, the 30th of November. Our people find large numbers of acorns in this area, which they collect in places the hogs cannot reach and then bring them to their homes by boat. When we were still in Old Ebenezer, they were forced to carry the loads of acorns there on their back from this place, which caused them to spend much time and yet to little avail. When the plantations are finally allotted, a matter which is still progressing slowly, we shall in particular see to it that our people here have access to open water, be it the Savannah or the Ebenezer river, for such access is of great advantage here in view of the scarcity of horses and wagons. Also, the best earth is close to the rivers.

Mr. Vernon has sent me a copy of the letter received several months ago, and I received it through the good offices of Captain Thomson. He must be much concerned to show us his displeasure at the desire of the Salzburgers to obtain land on the other side of the Ebenezer River. We request nothing against the wishes of our benefactors and the authorities, and we have not written about this matter more than once. If Mr. Vernon and others were to understand how important it is that the first colonists here be well established, and how easy it would be for Mr. Oglethorpe to obtain such land from the Indians, who do not cultivate it themselves, he would not be so ill pleased that we should have mentioned such matters in a letter. I was present in Savannah when Mr. Causton agreed with Mrs. Musgrove to persuade the so-called king, Tomo-Chachi, to exchange his and some other Indian's present residence, which is now located between the town of Savannah and Mrs. Musgrove's plantation, for other land; and neither Mr. Causton nor Mrs. Musgrove expected to meet any difficulties in the execution of their plans. However, I am writing this only for the information of our friends, so that they might better understand our situation when it is presented in London.

DECEMBER

Thursday, 1 December. The weather is again inconstant, sometimes bringing extreme cold and then again more clement temperatures; rain, however, is quite rare. These frequent changes are probably the cause of the fever, which is still continuing. An honest member of our flock asked to speak to me privately; and, when I spoke to her, God in His mercy assisted our talk and joint prayer in such a manner that both our hearts were much strengthened in Jesus, our blessed Shepherd, Who has come to seek and save that which was lost.[229] Oh, how the sins of youth, and in particular those committed thoughtlessly and out of physical pleasure, come to haunt and frighten those souls seeking redemption. In the last few days this honest and struggling soul has recalled each sin and offence in every small detail, and it appeared to her as if the executioner were standing there so as to exact retribution on this earth for the sins once committed against all conscience and morals. Her tears streaming down her face, she said that she had even deserved physical death more than once, if God would only not reject her, for no sinner was worse than she, etc. But my remorse and my struggle is not serious enough, she added, [I should give myself up to the law, etc.]

I thereupon addressed myself in particular to the words, "we must enter through much tribulation,"[230] which people generally interpret as meaning physical suffering and want; but, once people start to disengage themselves from the ties of Satan, of the world, and of sin and do so seriously, they will better and sooner understand the saying: "the spiritual anguish and fear arising from misdeeds committed against our Lord and great benefactor surpass all feelings of physical suffering." Nonetheless, these words also contained solace for all those who repent, suffer, and are bent with grief; for Paul or another apostle did not say it is through sweet and gentle emotions that we pass into God's kingdom, but through much tribulation. Cf. Matthew 5: "Blessed are they that mourn, the poor in spirit, and those which do hunger and thirst after righteousness," etc. Our reason, unless it be enlightened, would consider this narrow path not only uncomfortable but also wrong, and least of all lawful. God did not reveal, in the case of him and others, all grave sins punishable by law; and this fact should be seen as proof of His mercy and wisdom. He fully intended to use such souls, if they would but truly convert (as such mercy is bestowed more often on whores and publicans than upon the falsely respectable) and use them to pronounce and attest to His miraculous love and to make them His tools in the conversion of other poor sinners, which goal He would be less likely to achieve if the sins committed in blindness were to be revealed to other persons in this world.

Friday, the 2nd of December. Giessendanner,[231] an engraver and seal-maker who went to Carolina with the last Swiss transport, has written me again from Oranienburg in North Carolina[232] and advised me that the German people there have chosen him their regular preacher, that he had followed their invitation, and that he had commenced in the exercise of his office by preaching the Lord's word and administering the Holy Sacraments.[233] His flock is dispersed in various parts of that country, and much of his time is taken with visits and travels for that purpose. Many of the people there also were of our religious beliefs and showed him much affection; for they knew that he had no material gains in mind. He talks much about the importance of his teaching tasks, an office with which his first sermon dealt; and at the end of his epistle he requested me to accept his brother's son as a student and to continue his instruction in oriental languages, in which he had already received a good start, as well as to provide him with instruction in other matters. He himself has exhausted whatever means he brought with him and can no longer support him. His whole letter is full of references to the love of Christ, which urges him on, and he presents many detailed thoughts on the salvation and illumination bestowed by the New Testament; but one cannot but notice that he travels a dangerous road of deviance and will surely lead his listeners onto it. [Also, as shown by the entire manner of composition apparent in his writing, he is afflicted by the natural defect of feeble reasoning and judgment; and, since he may very well have a simple, honest mind, he will probably fall into much rambling and phantasizing and confuse the minds of others with an assumed holy fervor.] He asks me to reply to him, for which may God grant me the necessary wisdom and prudence!

Last night our people received a message from the surveyor that they would receive instructions today as to their allotted land. This morning they assembled in the church, where I prayed with them before their departure and warned them, on the basis of the Lord's word, to guard against all distractions and frivolous and ill considered words.

Saturday, the 3rd of December. Yesterday and today the surveyor assigned our people their plantations in an area which he and we have found to be generally the most preferable and fertile ground. However, much of the land is nonetheless of such poor quality that little can be cultivated or harvested there. Those who have been ill served may, on their own, examine the entire area that is to be part of the town; and, if they should find good land, it will be surveyed and assigned to them upon the surveyor's return, which will be in about four weeks. The man has business with the present assembly or parliament in Charleston, with which I neither desire nor am able to interfere; but he assured me that, immediately upon his return, he is willing to bring his work with us to a full conclusion. The best land has already been surveyed and distributed. [It is hard to look without pity on those who are willing to gain their bread with the work of their hands and have suffered much hardship to this end, but who are prevented from reaching this goal because of lack of good land and for other reasons.]

Today I have again learned of the example of a man who, according to his own confession and realization, has rendered his conversion and salvation difficult by hiding his misdeeds and has not been able to struggle to the light despite all entreaty, tears, and soul searching. His shame and his realization of the horrendousness of his offence have kept him from making a full, honest confession, although he has often approached our door with a trembling heart for this very purpose, ready to let his tongue confess. May God give the requisite wisdom to my dear colleague and myself so that we may deal properly with this man's soul so as to save it through the strength of Christ, for there is a great danger here that we can only bring before the

Lord. This example, the presence of which among us I would never have suspected, will compel us in the future not only to teach the comforting lesson of the gospels but also to put great emphasis upon the law of the Lord in all its purity. This will not cause damage, but instead prepare their hearts to receive and correctly apply the gospels; for else their message and comfort will not remain and stand up in times of trial. And how necessary is it for the ministers to warn their listeners constantly not only of the deceit of sin but also of all opportunities for committing sin. May God help us!

Sunday, the 4th of December. This year my dear colleague is basing his lessons on the regular epistles as applicable to each Sunday, after having based them on the catechism throughout the last church year. A week ago, that is, on the first Sunday of Advent, he was in Purysburg; and, therefore, today he commenced with today's Sunday epistle, Romans, 15:4 ff. In the morning, again this year, we explicate the gospels and use them for joint communal edification, for which these materials offer rich ground. As an *exordium*[234] we are in the habit of quoting, and pointing out in its text, a strong and impressive verse from either the Old or the New Testament so as to prepare the mind for the texts to be discussed. Both children and adults are admonished to read and re-read it throughout the week until they know it by heart. I have made it a practice to ask for this verse in the repetition a week later and insist that they repeat it from memory without recourse to the text. Today I took as an *exordium* 2 Timothy 4:18 and Luke 21:25 ff., that is, the entire and blessed redemption of all faithful from all evil, and that 1) as a future but certain event, and 2) as full and blessed redemption. My dear colleague used 2 Timothy 3:15 as his introduction and discussed the epistle concerning the Holy Bible and its great usefulness in showing the path to eternal salvation.

Monday, the 5th of December. I have replied by today's boat to Mr. Giessendanner, who wrote me several days ago from Oranienburg in North Carolina.[235] I briefly informed him: 1) that the blessed teaching of the justification of a poor sinner ready to repent has done much good in our community and, when presented in all its purity, has laid a sound and lasting foundation of Christian belief, 2) that my work and circumstances will not let me accept his brother's son here to instruct him, as desired, in languages and other studies.

This afternoon the surveyor left for Savannah with our boat; he intends to proceed to Charleston, where he must discharge some necessary business which will not stand any delay. He has not yet completed his task; but the best land has been surveyed and assigned to the people, although some allocations and distributions of good and bad land remain to be effected if our Salzburgers are to be tolerably accommodated. Before dawn this morning I made a proposal to our people which is in full agreement with the intentions of our benefactors [but which found lukewarm reception with Ernst and his like, and thus was not eagerly accepted.]

Tuesday, the 6th of December. The weather has been as mild as spring both today and yesterday during the day as well as at night. We have also had some gentle rain. N. N.'s [Michael Rieser's] wife died this morning suddenly and against all expectations. For a long time she has had a sickness (*obstructionem mensium,* which is said to be an almost common affliction in this town) and which only an experienced doctor can treat; and, for this and other specific reasons and circumstances, we are anxious to receive such a man here among us, a prospect which has been held out to us on a number of occasions. It is true that this woman was far from prudent and careful in regard both to food and drink, as well as in her entire household; and her husband, an N. [dyer] by profession, has given her a bad example both in material and spiritual respects. A short while ago both desired to take Holy Communion; but I was forced to refuse them for good cause, asking them instead to visit me often so that I might pray with them and speak to them according to their circumstances. But neither of them has come yet, and they are poor church-goers, so that the deceased woman will have a right miserable time of it.

I took the occasion of this death to speak to N. [Pichler] and admonished him to look out for his salvation and to insist with his wife on a full and sincere conversion. I did not wish to arouse any scruples in her concerning that certain forgiveness of her sins of which she boasts. Nonetheless, it was urgently necessary to reach a true and proper conscience and to avoid with great care all pretenses which our hearts are wont to make. Pichler offended me seriously a few days ago in a fit of rage, when I was forced to speak to him on account of his careless and offensive conduct. Today, however, he recognised his fault and firmly resolved to change his ways. [I have lent him a little book for his own and his wife's use, in which there is an account of Pastor Arnensee's[236] thorough and edifying examination of the signs and obstacles to true conversion.

[Wednesday, the 7th of December. Yesterday evening the two Zublins[237] arrived here; they have been in Purisburg for several years now, and they have come to seek advice and counsel concerning their rather miserable material circumstances. Prior to the arrival of their brother, they had undergone much want and trial and had hoped that their brother's presence would afford them true and substantial help and assistance. In this, however, they have found themselves disappointed in that the latter, who is in the process of establishing a plantation near Purysburg,[238] has incurred more expense and misfortune in his enterprise than he may have anticipated when he came here. The two brothers, who are now spending a few days with us, love each other dearly; and they are honest men. It would be much to our pleasure if we could give them such advice as would enable them, after so much disquiet and illness and want, to eat their own bread and serve God in peace, without distractions. If it were but in our power to contribute substantially to their welfare, we would not hesitate, all the more as they show an honest mind directed toward the pleasure of the Lord. They barely have words to describe all the misery that is to be found among the Appenzellers, both in Purysburg and in Savannah-Town. In Purysburg, in particular, conditions relating to the conduct of church services and the material conduct of the people there are so confused that one must be shocked at the tales brought to our ears.]

Thursday, the 8th of December. Cornberger has been quite ill for several weeks but has now regained some strength so that he can get up and move around the house. I talked with him about the proper preparation for a blessed death and how necessary it is to prepare oneself in times of health for this important journey. He told me that God had blessed his sickness in that He had made him recognize his worthlessness and utter inability in matters of the spirit and that he would have to be brought to spiritual life before he should be able to perform deeds to the glory of God that would truly be worthy of merit. He is much worried that he can not yet attend the prayer meetings; for, on the occasion of discussing the institution of the Levite services, Christ in His reconciliation and dear mercy had become close and dear to his heart and he had learned what he had not realized before, how closely and pleasantly the Old and the New Testament agree with each other.

A mother told me of the manner in which she is bringing up and treating her children, trying everything so that they might be won over and led to Christ; and she told me that God had blessed her motherly endeavors in that for some weeks now she had noticed in them greater attention to the Lord's word, greater seriousness in prayer, and a more quiet manner of deporting themselves.

Friday, the 9th of December. Johann Paul Franck of Purysburg, who had been accepted among our orphan children some while ago, informed me that his mother desired him to return home so that he might assist her in working the fields and caring for their house. It is possible that he is not too content with our order here, because he has to rise early with the other children and spend his day in performing useful tasks and cannot run about on his own, although he has not shown any signs of such discontent. Also, his stay among us has not been entirely in vain, since he has not only learned the entire catechism, many important verses from the Bible, and the art of reading, but has also felt in his heart the attraction of God's spirit as alive in His word.

Saturday, the 10th of December. Seeing that only little good soil is to be found in the land that has been surveyed for the plantations and that most of the people here have been assigned poor land which, by all human judgment, will not suffice to nourish them, I have recently suggested and again urged today in our convocation that those who have been allotted good land by the surveyor for their plantations should share their good fortune with the others. This is not only demanded by common fairness and the laws of Christianity, but is also suggested by a letter in my possession in which the Honorable Trustees express their desire that each man should have at least one piece of good land that might enable him to use the less advantageous plots in the course of time. It is impossible for one person or family without fieldhands to work and plant a plantation of 48 acres; and this is another reason why several men should share in the good land, especially since one of them is as good as the other. This would have the further advantage that the fieldwork would be done not by one man working alone but by several who could assist each other in their work and it would also be advantageous in the event that one of them should injure himself or incur some danger. Good friends who stand by each other can work together and have the freedom to associate for their purposes. These propositions were well accepted by all, except for N. [the obstinate Ernst], who is said to have uttered harsh threats against all those who would want to share in his plantation, a matter on which I still wish to hear the witnesses. I fear that he might suffer the same fate as Rott.[239]

In this meeting I was also requested to permit future prayer meetings and the entire divine service to be held in the attic of the orphanage, which is well constructed and quite spacious; and I was advised that the congregation is willing to furnish proper benches for this purpose. The hut where we have been meeting is badly located and ill preserved, and also we cannot refuse its use as a night lodging for travellers passing through. Thus, it is ill-suited for a church. I could hardly refuse the people their wish, for we much desire to make life as easy and comfortable for them as possible. In any event, the new building is being constructed for the purpose of honoring the Lord, and it is our heartfelt wish that much praise be uttered to Him therein and that many souls may be led to Him through His word, which shall often be pronounced at this site.

In the trust of the Lord, Who can easily provide for more means, I am having boards prepared so that a solid flooring may be constructed on top of the first story. These will be covered with thick split shingles until the good Lord may provide us with better materials. We hope that, in time, our benefactors' providence will permit us the construction of our own church, so that this part of the orphanage may be used for other necessary activities. Also, the space there would be insufficient if, as it is hoped, more people should join us, although the present building is 45 feet long and 30 feet wide.

Sunday, the 11th of December. A raw and cold wind prevented us from holding the repetition hour, so I have repeated the morning discourse in the course of the evening prayer meeting, which is still visited by young and old after supper every Sunday with much eagerness and, as I hope, with the blessing of the Lord. The discourse thus repeated dealt with Matthew 11:2 ff., concerning the divine certainty and reassurance of the heart in the main and basic truths of the Christian faith. Several of our listeners have remarked on the manifold spiritual benefits of these repetitions, which are conducted by question and answer; and this is all the more reason for us to continue them. In these periods we reinforce points that may have been lost or unclear in the sermon by means of examples from the Bible or appropriate sayings or writings. Parents or those acting in their stead are admonished to conduct a repetition at home with the children prior to coming, so that they may be better able to furnish the correct answers and to edify the whole community.

Monday, the 12th of December. The two Zublin brothers have been forced by the miserable circumstances under which they had to live in Purysburg for a long time to leave that town and to seek their livelihood in this province. The matters that have passed between them and their brother, who is settled on a plantation near Purysburg, are not pleasant to recount; but these two men are much to be pitied for having neither land nor money but being forced to work as fieldhands with little food and at hard conditions, if they are to stay here any longer. They have asked me to place a good word with Mr. Causton on their behalf so that they might be given permission to settle here for the purpose of not only gaining their bread with the work of their hands but also of having the proper circumstances for guarding the health of their souls.

As soon as I have an occasion to travel to Purysburg, I shall ask their brother's opinion in this respect and hear how things stand. Both my dear colleague and I have earnestly advised them not to rush matters but to consider their steps carefully so that their decision might not cause them remorse later. They have gone to Savannah with my letter, and we will see what Mr. Causton proposes. Matters in Purysburg seem to go quite poorly, and it is hardly possible to take exception to those who wish to change their place of residence. If there were no province of Georgia, where poor people have an occasion to earn their bread as fieldhands, many would have to perish. Ernst has now shown himself quite small and tame; he might be afraid of danger to life and limb because of his malicious and obstinate talk. He came to me to inform me that he is now willing to let others share in the rich plantation that fell to him by lot. He complains of his wife, who renders life so difficult for him that he is prepared to run away if she should not change her ways. However, one is as bad as the other.

Tuesday, the 13th of December. When I visited Leitner on his sickbed and spoke to him about the verse, "The son of man is come to save that which was lost,"[240] a woman who was standing there recalled what I had told her about this very verse more than a year ago, during her sickness. She said she had been quite ignorant at the time, such that she did not even know this verse from the gospels; but in time our faithful Lord had taken pity on her and she had been able not only to retain in her mind several verses and words from the Bible from sermons, prayer meetings, and the readings of others (since she herself cannot read), but had moreover come to realize the wickedness of her rotten heart. She places her trust in God that He shall bring her to Him and save her completely and fully. She feels that God has rendered her a great service by having brought her here;

for else she might well have, as she added with tears welling from her eyes, remained blind and unconverted. She begged me to let her come on occasion, as others do here, so that she might pray with me and be instructed and admonished. I have had little hope for this woman, and certainly less than our loyal creator has now shown me I should have had. In this small congregation there is little that escapes our knowledge, particularly with regard to those circumstances, both material and spiritual, that prevent some of our listeners from a true and full conversion; and, if our sermons are composed accordingly, they reach these souls and they will accept the message more readily than if it were given privately and individually.

Wednesday, the 14th of December. This morning, on my way home from the prayer meeting with the orphans, a woman was waiting for me in front of her door and asked me for an opportunity to speak privately and alone. I granted her request this afternoon and learned that she is much troubled by a matter that would hardly cause much grief to others, even honest and devout people. This woman is not afraid of the law as such but rather desires to obtain her salvation with much fear and trembling; and, since she is possessed of a tender conscience, she realizes all too quickly every speck of insincerity and undue haste. After some instruction, I prayed with her and showed her the words in 1 John 2:12. She finally confided in me the many traps and wiles used by Satan to waylay her in the course of her Christian faith and prevent her from the use of the means of salvation. However, she knew how to free herself from these traps with tears and prayer.

N. [Mrs. Rheinlaender] is making a good pretense: she accuses herself, repents her coarseness such as used against me on another occasion, and attributes guilt partly to others, and partly to her own temper and lack of control. She pretends to have realized that we both mean her well, while previously she was incapable of understanding what we told her about her rotten condition. When I repeated to her, among other admonitions, my previous statement to herself and her husband, i.e., that their joint conversion would give us special joy inasmuch as we had known long since that they would have a much harder task than many others in breaking the bonds of sin, she cried bitterly and left me with the best of professed intentions. She had even been to see Mr. Causton in Savannah, who reprimanded her sharply and instructed her to observe the law and our orders. At my request he is now prepared to advance her and her family some provisions, provided that I can attest to her improvement. Such instances recall to my mind the saying in 2 Timothy 2:25–26.

Thursday, the 15th of December. Mr. Causton has replied most kindly to my letter in which I put in a good word on behalf of the two Zublin brothers; and he is prepared to allow for land and provisions for these two and for others who wish to settle among us, in accordance with my recommendation. However, he is not of the opinion that any encouragement should be given to those who might wish to leave their former place of residence and move to this colony. [He also wrote me concerning circumstances in our community, which message gave me much pleasure. At the same time I have received news that Mr. Wesley has secretly and by night travelled to Charleston via Purysburg so as to embark from there for London in great haste.[241] I do not really know what may have prompted him to such a hasty decision, which reflects badly on his office and on the name of the Lord. When I talked to him recently in Savannah, particularly about his quarrel with Mr. Causton,[242] he did not yet intend to leave his flock but rather to await Mr. Oglethorpe's return. Also, he suffers much ill repute for having taken with him two men who had made numerous debts in Savannah and have left without repaying them.

Friday, the 16th of December. We have not had such a pleasant and warm winter since we came to this country. There were several severe night freezes; but the weather always changed quickly, and for a few days now it has been as warm as is customary here in springtime. We have had the men plant a goodly number of peachtrees, which a German man in Purysburg sold to us, in the garden of our future doctor; and we intend to do a similar planting in the orphanage garden once the whole building is completed. N. N. [Stephen Riedelsperger] has again turned into himself and reflected on his sins, and he and his wife have resolved to return to the Lord. He came to me to bring me money gained improperly, which he has previously refused to relinquish. On this occasion, I reminded him in particular both of his transgressions and of the Lord's mercy, which he had worked for so strongly in his fever and of which he had given me such a full confession. He acknowledged my reprimands and is truly ashamed.

Saturday, the 17th of December. Although our Salzburgers have been assigned little good land for their plantations, they share in it in such a manner that each of them now has one good plot on which, given God's blessing, he can earn his bread until such time as even the poorer land can be prepared for use. The people are to choose their fellow workers; and thus it has come about that on each plantation good friends work in common who agree well with each other and seek each other's welfare. This is a free and profitable joint arrangement for common labor. In this manner they will soon have cleared a large tract of land so that the sun may penetrate the soil and reach the seed (for little or nothing grows in the shade); and the fencing-in, which is necessary to protect the seed from birds and game, as well as other matters, are much facilitated by this mode of work.

Sunday, the 18th of December. A tailor from Purysburg, who together with his family makes use of our services and office, has come to ask me to accept two of his children in our institutions and school so as to instruct them in the fear of the Lord and give them regular schooling. However, in this scarce year he cannot provide for their sustenance here, and instead promises to return in kind that which his children will have consumed by next fall, if God gives him some harvest by then. We shall accept the children on this condition, inasmuch as our present means do not suffice to give room and board to strange children, until such day as the good Lord shall give us richer revenues, for which we dearly hope. There are more children in Purysburg who would be accepted on these conditions. Oh, what joy it would give us to be able to take charge of such poor children, if it were only within our means. But God can cause much blessing among us so that we will have plenty of all things and be rich enough for manifold good works.

Monday, the 19th of December. I had occasion to write Mr. Zueblin[243] in Purysburg to let him know that his two brothers have come here and asked me to secure their acceptance in Ebenezer, where they intend to work for their bread with their hands and provide for their souls in the services that are offered to our Christian community here. Having found honesty, sincerity, and a good manner of living in them since I met them, I have always held them close in my affection and thus am now prepared, from the bottom of my heart, to recommend them to Mr. Causton and the Honorable Trustees. This I would do all the more readily if I could obtain his views on this matter. I added that I believed a further sojourn there [in the deserts of Purysburg] would be to their grave material and spiritual detriment, a conviction that he would come to understand in the course of time. I also let him know that I found his youngest brother[244] to be skillful and loyal; and, God willing, we might be able eventually to use him as an instructor in our orphanage and school.

N. [Mrs. Pichler] has again fallen ill and must keep to her bed, nor is the condition of her soul according to my hopes. A few weeks ago, in the course of illness, she pretended cleverly that God had made her recognize her entire circumstances, how much she had sinned since her youth and how much she had loved the world; but He had taken pity on her and forgiven her for all her sins, etc. All this had come to pass so quickly that her comfort and pretended state of grace appeared quite suspicious to my mind; and I therefore carefully admonished her as well as her husband, when the latter came to me privately, to step most carefully and circumspectly and to make sure of the state of her soul, for self-deception was a common error, etc. I also gave him the careful tract [by the Reverend Arnensee, dealing with the symptoms of and obstacles to conversion, i.e.], *Instructions on the Commencement of a Christian Life,* etc.,[245] so that he and his wife might read it for their edification.

When I passed by their house one evening, she confided in me her doubts and scruples; but these were not serious sins but all trifling and material worries, which are not even worth repeating. Her husband added comments on her previous acts and words which much shocked me. I earnestly admonished her to guard her soul, for Satan was surely to be found close by and would try to ensnare her into perdition with the very bonds of which she had just made mention. I also repeated some appropriate sayings to her, such as: "The Lord is at hand, Be careful for nothing," etc.; Philippians 4; likewise, "I grieve for my sin, etc."[246] How hard it is to tear the heart away from sin and world if it has grown attached to them by long habit and neglect.

Tuesday, the 20th of December. Yesterday and today I have had many requests from those who wish to go to the Lord's Table on the second day of Christmas, and those among them who are serious about their Christian faith have given me much spiritual joy. On this occasion several have complained of a young man[247] who is said to have spoken in a most careless and offensive manner so that we should remonstrate with him for his annoying conduct if he should desire to be admitted to Holy Communion. Our poor people are much aggrieved by the fact that this matter has caused a certain sort of people who are residing in Savannah [the Herrnhuters], who have heard the young man and his words, to speak badly about our community; I should add that the latter seem to be well versed in the art of making general conclusions from one instance and of spreading the fame of one to the entire congregation. Had they wished to act in a Christian manner, they should rather have confided their impression of the offensive words uttered by this reckless young man to one of us, instead of to others, in particular as my dear colleague has only recently spoken to some members of their society. The young man in question was at my house yesterday and his complaints and humble and dejected manner had already shown me that something was troubling him, although I learned of his misconduct only today.

It grieves me much that many think it sufficient to lead half a Christian life, consisting in abstention from and detestation of gross sins and in the exercise of outward virtue, whereas we have always publicly and urgently insisted on their horrible fall into sin, the consequent deep rottenness of the human heart, and the terrible anger of the Lord lying upon it. There is no doubt that it is this which most urgently requires a thorough change of heart and justification in the blood of Christ.[248] I often hear that the people feel the strength of God's word as leading them to a recognition of their selves, but they must admit that they are negligent in the faithful use of the means of salvation, in particular that of urgent and constant prayer, despite their best resolutions. May God grant us that His word may effect lasting good in many people during this week of preparation.

Wednesday, the 21st of December. Now that it is time to go to the Lord's Table, N. [Gschwaendel] pretends to many good intentions, well recognizing that, despite his industrious reading, listening, singing, and praying there is still much amiss with him. The worries of this world cause him many obstacles, and until now he has not been ready to forswear all, even his own piety and justice.[249] I have read him and others who have come to me in these days a certain passage from the blessed Luther, which I find of much edification for myself also. He describes it thus: "The Christian life is such that he who has embarked upon it believes he has gained nothing but must continue and strive to obtain a blessing. Nothing is of greater danger to a faithful believer than the idea that he has already reached his goal and need not seek further; for this causes many to fall back and they perish in the security of their assumptions and their neglect. Therefore, he who has commenced being a Christian must realize that he is not yet a Christian but must have the desire to attain this state. He who is a Christian is not yet a Christian; that is, he who believes he has become a Christian, whereas he has not yet become one, is nothing. Our old self must be renewed from day to day, and woe upon those who believe that they have been quite renewed, for in those there is not even the beginning of a new faith, and they have never tasted what it means to be a Christian. For he who has truly started does not hold himself to be a Christian but seeks with great seriousness to become a believer; and the more he progresses on this path, the more he seeks to continue to it, and the less he claims to have reached his goal.''

The German cobbler from Purysburg[250] has returned and is making shoes for our people. He remains a careless fellow, although he has repeatedly made many promises. We have had quite enough of him; but, in view of the lack of a better cobbler, we have no other recourse but to use his services. He has caused much offense in Purysburg, and the people there are not as well served by him as might have been the case formerly. I am quite prepared to buy such shoes for our people as come from London or New England to Savannah until such time as we shall be supplied by a more conscientious man of this trade. The wooden shoes and Indian footwear which some of our people wear do not suffice during the winter and the rainy season. A cobbler who not only knows how to make shoes but is also versed in preparing the leather would find great demand for his services in this country. Cow and ox hides are quite cheap, but the people who might prepare them for use are lacking.

Thursday, the 22nd of December. N. [Mrs. Rheinlaender] is most insistent on being admitted to Holy Communion, for she cannot bear the thought that the people here should consider her as excluded from the congregation. This shows much false pride and arrogance. With many tears she asserts that she regrets her sins, particularly those committed against me and my office, and that they have caused her much fear and pain; but I do not trust her, particularly as I have learned that she does not reveal this sorrow in the presence of others but rather shows herself in her old ways. She has been heard to pray in her hut, which she does not fail to mention; but she refuses to forswear all and recognize that she is as deeply rotten and wicked as natural man is depicted in God's word.[251] I explained to her the two passages in John 9:40–41 and Revelations 3:17–18 and showed her that these people had run into perdition because they had refused to recognize their pitiful blindness but had trusted more in their own thoughts than in the Lord's words and had been resentful of Christ and his stern admonitions.

The cold has been as severe for a few days now as last winter, but by all appearances this does not prevent any of our listeners from coming to the evening prayer meetings, which are now concentrating on the preparation for Christmas and Holy Communion.

Friday, the 23rd of December. Since the second story in the orphanage has not yet been floored and the benches are not yet ready, each of the Salzburgers has contributed 10 roof shingles, which have been used to cover and restore the old hut wherein we have until now conducted the services. This has been done to prevent inconvenience at Christmas in the event of heavy rains. Even when the services are no longer held in this location, the hut and its fireplace will serve in the winter for the instruction of our pupils; and travellers and passing strangers may use it as a shelter at night. In tonight's prayer meeting I interrupted the lesson on Biblical history which now deal with Chapters 13 and 14 of Leviticus; and, instead, I treated a subject which would prepare us for Christmas, just as most of the prayer meetings during this week have been largely used for this purpose. The gracious Lord let me know, through a few couples who visited my hut with tears and sighs as well as through some others of whom these spoke to me, that today's readings and instructions have not been without benefit. In my discourse I have recalled the spiritual blessings I enjoyed in Halle before and during the holidays among the children, who eagerly came for prayer and contemplation of the divine word both during the day and at night, and among the adult people. I encourage our people to share in these blessings in joyous imitation. In the preparation tomorrow, if God will, I shall treat Romans 8:31-32 and the exceedingly great mercy of the New Testament; i.e., 1) that our Father has given us His son, 2) that in Him He desired to give us Himself and all things.

Saturday, the 24th of December. N. [Mrs. Pichler] keeps urging her husband to move to Pennsylvania, because N. [Rheinlaender] and his wife have persuaded her how comfortably one can live there for little money and how easy it is to earn money there. Physically she is quite miserably off and much more to be pitied, therefore, for her material desires and preoccupations. The husband was much taken by her entreaties, but in last night's prayer meeting God touched his heart and made him realize the danger for his soul should he move away from here.

Today he spoke seriously to his wife and told her that she should drop all thought of leaving; for he would not follow her, since that would be against the will and the glory of the Lord, as he confided in me today. N. [Rheinlaender] and his wife constitute a bad influence among our people because of their hidden wickedness and their ready tongues; they will not improve despite the many benefits we have bestowed on them to this end.

After the severe freeze, God has sent us mild weather, which is much welcome for the holidays. Today, with God's blessing, we have attempted to prepare for the days of Christmas by the message of the divine word and much prayer. To this end we assembled in the church around 4 o'clock and in the doctor's hut between 6 and 7. The two Zueblin brothers show great joy at these occasions for edification, and others also show their pleasure. The former came to me after the preparation and attested that they would be well content with poor food and lodging, seeing that the Lord so richly provided for their souls.

Sunday, the 25th of December was Christmas. Last night we had a heavy storm which brought back the cold weather. This did not keep any of us from attending the Christmas services. The repetition was shortened somewhat because of the cold, and that which was partly omitted was repeated at night in the kitchen of the doctor's house. The subject was Christ's meritorious poverty. Many of the children attend these evening meetings so that we may speak to them for the edification of the adults present. Tomorrow, on the second day of Christmas, 51 persons will go to the Lord's Table. N. [Ernst] and his wife again demanded to be admitted, whereas neither of them shows any desire to cease their annoying behavior, much less to convert to the Lord. Only last week two little girls came to me, one complaining that, in passing in front of their parents' hut, N. [Ernst] had mocked their joint singing. The other accused him of having attempted to seduce her into lying and, when she refused to speak according to his wishes and lie to another so as to please him, he had threatened to beat her, etc. When I reproached him for this in his wife's presence, he denied everything, as is his custom; but he did not get very far with that. The woman is quite ignorant[252] and should have come to me previously for instruction; but she offered many excuses, such as her own and her child's ill health, and she now promised me to come right after the holidays.

Monday, the 26th of December. N. [Pichler] wanted to go to

the Lord's table, but he refrained on my advice. His wife also desired to take Communion on her sickbed; but, since she is full of ill faith and love of the world and is unwilling to forgive those who have sinned against her, although she refuses to admit this, I could not give in to her wishes. She is quite angry at her husband and made many serious charges against him yesterday when I visited them; but their nature was such that they revealed all her material desires and rigid heart. The husband would do well to postpone Communion, for he is full of grief and worry because of his wife and must suffer much contradiction from her in both material and spiritual matters.

Together with us, he must work on her in a tender and forgiving spirit; and, if God lends mercy and makes her well, he must enjoy Communion jointly with his wife. He was present at last night's prayer meeting and attested today that God had let him hear a message that stands him in good stead in his present miserable condition. He believes that God means well with him in so chastising him and is giving him the strength to bear his fate well; if he had learned this in his former state, when he had less insight in and instruction of God's ways and guidance, he would have refused to accept this lesson as unbearable. While his wife looks back upon the fleshpots of Egypt and desires the bygone days, he will thank the Lord in her presence for saving him from the service of man and the days of material well-being, for at that time his Christian faith and his salvation were remote.

Last night Mrs. Crause was struck mortally ill and we expected her demise; but the good Lord soon blessed our medications so that she could rise today and take Holy Communion in her house, a blessing which she much desired. A married couple entreated me to treat them harshly and reprimand them severely if they should reveal ill ways, for they much needed such strictness. The woman recounted, for the glory of the Lord and with much humility and joy, that before the holidays she had been full of sorrow that she might not find the true spirit of Christmas because of her slovenliness and lack of faith. But the Lord had ordained things so well that she had gained a little in the recognition of herself, of Christ, and of His love for her. In yesterday's repetition, I spoke, as an introduction, the words: "Ye know the grace of our Lord Jesus Christ" etc.[253] as a test for each of them whether or not he had celebrated Christmas in the proper spirit; for those who had not become richer when God so richly offered His mercy in Christ His son could not have celebrated Christmas well. And here I mentioned material wishes and imagined riches (Revelations 3:17 and Luke 12:21) as a serious obstacle and as a warning.

Tuesday, the 27th of December. Cornberger, who was ill some time ago but has recovered, resumed his work today and was felling a tree to make shingles of the wood. Before the tree was about to come down, he put a piece of wood on the ground so that the tree would come to rest on it and provide space for sawing. However, as he was bending down in this task, the tree came down and threw him to the ground; and he was seriously hurt on on his left side. He himself told me that, if he had been but one inch further in, he would have been crushed by the trunk. Is this not a sign of the grace, patience, and forbearance of the Lord that has thus protected him as he himself acknowledges? May this instance confirm what he was shown, by yesterday's passages and admonitions, as requiring his repentance; and may God give him the strength to use it such.

Wednesday, the 28th of December. Mrs. Crause was taken ill again yesterday, and as badly as the other night; but she soon improved when God blessed our medications and hot compresses. I visited her today, and she spoke in a most edifying manner. She well realizes that God is seeking her soul with great seriousness, and she only regrets her inability to pray well. We showed her, however, that she should but present her needs quite simply, as a child to its father, as was done by dear Jacob upon learning that his brother Esau was coming upon him with 400 men.[254] She took this occasion to tell me that in her prayers she had the habit of presenting this or that passage to the Lord, and in so doing often experienced much shame; for she realized that things were not yet as described in her prayer. Such simple people are easy to deal with, for they gladly accept all our teachings so that the Holy Spirit and its merciful blessings can work in them.

In yesterday's and today's evening prayer meetings we have discussed the gospel for the third day of Christmas, John 1:1–14, which our dear and generous Lord will not fail to bless in us. Oh, may the incarnate God Jesus Christ grow in us with His merited grace so that all that is in this world may mean nothing to us and He mean everything. For has He not given to all those who have accepted Him the glory, power, and honor of becoming the children of the Lord, the magnificent and blessed one? For it is written, "is Ephraim my dear son? Is he a pleasant child?"[255] May He give grace so that everyone may go forth so that the King may render him as beautiful and enjoy his beauty.

Thursday, the 29th of December. Late tonight I returned with our little boat from Savannah, where I had gone Tuesday because of Cornberger's injury and other matters that had to be discussed with Mr. Causton. The loving Lord, who has given us all His son, this highest and dearest gift, has richly blessed our travels, for which His name shall be praised and honored. Mr. Causton has now presented to me as a gift, and on his own decision, several items that we had received from the storehouse on behalf of the community and that had been charged against my credit, nor did he fail to offer his further services in a most generous manner. The bill for the provisions has finally been written; but I received it to take home for examination and approval, and whatever is still outstanding in the way of provisions for the Salzburgers is to be sent here.

Since he is well aware of the discomfort which we suffer in our huts, he has given me permission to have a proper house constructed at the expense of the Honorable Trustees. While there is not enough money available for this purpose at this time, he hopes that he will easily persuade the Honorable Trustees to provide more funds for this purpose. However, inasmuch as our people must now seriously begin their work in the fields, I shall postpone this construction until the fall, as was done this year for the orphanage; and we shall therefore gladly bide our time in our present huts. Perhaps we shall meanwhile receive permission and funds for such a house from London, as well as for the erection of a church and a school.

A few days ago a boat full of Germans from the Palatinate[256] came to Savannah, the passage for whom was provided by the Honorable Trustees, in return for which these people and their children are bound to work as servants for a number of years. These people had heard of us and our teaching in Ebenezer and therefore requested Mr. Causton to arrange for us to preach God's word to them and give them Holy Communion. They all, large and small, congregated in the newly built, commodious church; and, after the singing of hymns, I spoke to them and gave them some instructions, admonitions, and comfort from the word of the Lord. This service passed not without blessing, thanks to God's mercy. I began with the last words of the 33rd Chapter of Acts 10, so as to prepare their minds for the sermon, which was Psalms 50:14–15, from which I reminded them simply and with heartfelt words of their duties both in regard to past and future gifts received from the Lord and of the mercy shown by the Lord both in regard to their past, present, and future needs. After the sermon, in the presence of the congregation and also of some Englishmen and Jews who had come out of curiosity, two of the couples from the Palatinate were given in marriage.

In the coming week, Mr. Causton desires to speak to these people through my offices, so as to offer some proposals as to how their children, of whom there are many among them, should attend school while pursuing their work. At the same time some of these people who, in my opinion, will be well prepared therefor, shall be given Holy Communion. Some of them are quite coarse and rude people who will cause much anger and offence in Savannah, against which I have warned them loyally from God's word. It remains to be seen whether this group can be kept together, for there are many Reformed among them.[257] I am intending, instead of the preparation for Holy Communion, to instruct them in several lessons about the main cause and additional circumstances for this act, for which purpose I shall have to spend several days in Savannah. May God accept and smile on these plans for the sake of Christ.

Near Charleston a large English ship was thrown on a sand-bank during the last strong wind and badly damaged by 18 blows.[258] If the wind had not abated and if the tide had not returned to set it adrift, the whole boat and all the merchandise aboard might well have been lost. They fired the canons on board often, and a sloop came to take off the passengers. The boat had already taken in 7 feet of water.

Friday, the 30th of December. While in Savannah I took the occasion to inquire among certain people [the Herrnhuters] in regard to the shameful statements alledgedly uttered by N. [Bruckner],[259] and I interrogated all those assembled in the kitchen. However, none of them will acknowledge knowing anything about this matter, except that they had noticed, on Mr. Causton's plantation, the disorderly and frivolous behavior of this man, for which they reprimanded him. Nor did they wish to acknowledge that they had spoken ill of our community; instead, they claim to have seen God's blessing in some of our people who had lodged with them. I cannot reconcile what our people have told me with what I have now learned directly; but am much delighted that the Herrnhuters at least deny this incident ever took place. At the same time, I received a letter from Mr. N. [Spangenberg] from N. [Pennsylvania], in which he informed me of the proper delivery of the letters we had entrusted to him and enclosed a receipt by a merchant to whom he had in turn delivered them.

Franck, the boy from Purysburg who so recently had desired to return to his mother and had been dismissed from our school, now wishes to return and longs for us, having learned the difference between Ebenezer and Purysburg. Both mother and son came to see me in Purysburg yesterday and asked me to accept the boy once more. However, I could not grant their request; for this benefit has already been promised to another, and we are not in a position to treat the children of strangers such as we would wish. The new structure, which is now being completed, has, contrary to our expectations, cost so much that our funds are exhausted and we have even incurred debts. But God's fountain has plentiful water and is inexhaustible.[260] Hallelujah!

Saturday, the 31st of December. Upon my return from Savannah I was told by several people that God (may He be praised!) has blessed our reading of the gospels this Christmas, so much that some even say they have never celebrated such a Christmas before. May God be praised! The cobbler, Reck, from Purysburg now wishes to follow the two Zublin brothers and live with his family among us. He has seen and heard that his salvation, if it is to come, will have to be gained not by the common ways of the world but in a quite different manner. He realizes that he is often touched by God's word; but, since he is entangled in the love of the world rampant in Purysburg, he quickly loses the good gained, which he hopes to preserve and use in a better way were he to live here and permanently close to the Lord's word. I have shown him the statutes of this country and admonished him to take his time, so that he might not later wish to leave again, for the Honorable Trustees were not interested in such people. He is a clever cobbler and we could use him and would love him well if were to move here in accordance with God's will and convert to the true faith.

After the regular prayer meeting, which was arranged according to the new time change,[261] some of our people came to the doctor's hut to assemble there; and we ended this year in the praise of the Lord and in prayer and begged for new blessings for us and others to be granted in the coming year from the riches of Jesus. May our faithful Father in heaven be humbly praised for all the physical and spiritual strength He has mercifully bestowed on us for the exercise of our office. We recommend all our work, in public and in private, with both children and adults, to His blessing; and we ask for forgiveness, on behalf of Christ His son and His blood of reconciliation, for all sins and weaknesses committed in the exercise of our office and otherwise. And may He reinforce us in our resolution, made with his mercy, to show true seriousness and faith in this year and for as long as the Lord may give us life, so that we and those who listen to us may gain the goal of faith that is the bliss of our souls. Amen for Jesus' sake, Amen!

 *Notes*

1. George F. Jones, ed., *Henry Newman's Salzburger Letterbooks* (Wormsloe Foundation Publications, No. 10. Athens, Georgia, 1966.)

2. Samuel Urlsperger, ed., *Ausführliche Nachricht von den Saltzburgischen Emigranten . . .* (Halle, 1735 ff.)

3. *Franckesche Stiftung—Missionsarchiv Abtheilung 5A.* All missionaries sent out by the Francke Foundation were required to submit regular reports, which were then entered into letterbooks still found in the archives of that charitable institution.

4. *The Journal of the Rev. John Wesley, A.M.* (London, 1907), I, 52.

5. See notes 241 and 242.

6. Walter L. Robbins, ed. and trans., "John Tobler's Description of South Carolina (1753)" in *South Carolina Historical Magazine* 71 (1970), 148.

7. Typical Pietist tenets are expressed in the entries for 8 Jan., 30 July, 6, 22, Aug., 4, 25, 30 Oct., 5, 24 Nov., 20, 21, 22 Dec.

8. *O Jesu Christ, dein Kripplein ist.* Hymn by Paul Gerhard.

9. Isaiah 41:17.

10. Johann Paul Francke. See entries for 27 Feb. and 8 March. His mother was probably the same as Ann Barbara Frank, who received 100 acres in Purysburg on 17 March, 1735. Henry A. M. Smith, "Purrysburgh," in *The South Carolina Historical and Genealogical Magazine* 10 (1909), 212.

11. Boltzius meant to say the Bartholomäus Riesers. Balthasar was the second son, then aged thirteen. Jones, ed., *Newman Letterbook,* 371. See note 1 above, also entry for 19 May.

12. In his journal under May 5, Wesley wrote: "I was asked to baptize a child of Mr. Parker's, second Bailiff of Savannah; but Mrs. Parker told me, 'Neither Mr. P. nor I will consent to its being dipped.' I answered, 'If you certify that your child is weak, it will suffice (the rubric says) to pour water upon it.' She replied, 'Nay, the child is not weak, but I am resolved it shall not be dipped.' This argument I could not confute. So I went home; and the child was baptized by another person." (p. 29). This refusal was the fifth of ten bills presented to the grand jury that tried Wesley. (p. 56). *The Journal of the Rev. John Wesley, A. M.* (New York, 1907) 29, 56.

13. Benjamin Ingham. See entry for 12 March.

14. The Halle copy of this entry ends at this point. The remainder was added by Urlsperger in his *Ausführliche Nachricht.* (See note 2.)

15. Burning off the woods, which was standard procedure until a generation ago, is still permitted under certain conditions.

16. *Hallelujah, Lob, Preis, und Ehre.* Anonymous hymn. The child's retarded speech probably resulted from brain damage caused by the high fever suffered by all the children.

17. This was Christian H. Müller, whom the Earl of Egmont lists separately (not as one of Friedrich Wilhelm Müller's dependents) as servant to Ernst Ludwig von Reck, the commissioner's younger brother. E. Merton Coulter and Albert B. Saye, *A List of the Early Settlers of Georgia* (Athens, 1967), 37.

18. Johanna Margareta and Johanna Agnese. There was one other daughter, Frederica, and two sons, Johann Simon and Johann Paul (in addition to the son in the note above). Their mother was Anna Christiana.

19. Boltzius writes this name as Schmannsgruber, Schomansgruber, and Schoemansgruber. George F. Jones and Marie Hahn, eds., *Detailed Reports on the Salzburger Emigrants . . .* (Athens, Ga., 1972), 116, 124, 189. On 16 Sept. 1738 fifty acres of land

in Purrysburg were granted to George Schonman Grober. Smith, 214. See note 10.

20. Those preparing for Holy Communion.

21. The first pastor there, Joseph Bugnion, left Purysburg for St. James in Santee in the fall of 1734. His successor, Henri François Chiffele arrived with Purry at that time (See entry for 22 Nov., 1974). Frederick Dalcho (*An Historical Account of the Episcopal Church in South Carolina* [Charleston, 1820], 386) is in error in stating that Chiffelle did not arrive in Purysburg until 1744. Chifelle lived until 1765 (the same as Boltzius), during which time he received many land grants under the name of Chivillet, Chevelis, Chefeille, and Shiffle. Smith, 212, 213, 217, 218. See note 10.

22. When Boltzius writes "potatoes," he means sweet potatoes. He used the word *Erd-Apfel* (earth apples, *pommes de terre*) for white potatoes, which are now generally called "Irish" potatoes in that part of Georgia.

23. Boltzius never furnishes evidence for his paranoic fear of the Herrnhuters' calumny. In this case he should have suspected Rheinlaender's ingratiating gossip.

24. This is the commandment against adultery, which is number seven in the King James Bible. Like the Vulgate, Luther's Bible combines the first two commandments and divides the tenth, thus changing the number of all the intervening ones.

25. See note 24.

26. Against adultery and stealing. See note 24.

27. He got only as far as Pennsylvania, where he settled.

28. *contra septum*, against stealing. See note 24.

29. Here Boltzius is following a tradition of medieval theology in which all persons and events of the Old Testament are proved to be prefigurations of those of the New Testament.

30. Chiffelle. See note 21.

31. Johann Paul Francke. See note 10.

32. Sweet potatoes, See note 22.

33. Zwifler seems to have come from an area now in Slovakia.

34. Johann Paul Francke. See note 10.

35. This was a certain Jacob (?) Matthews, whom Mary married after Musgrove and before the Rev. Thomas Bosomworth.

36. Mary Musgrove was valuable as interpreter and liaison agent with the Indians, she herself being a mixed blood.

37. Urlsperger changed *casus necessitatis (case of necessity)* into *Notfall* (emergency).

38. Ross. See entry for 3 June.

39. Tertian malaria.

40. Boltzius' spelling for Uchee, which he must have only heard.

41. Asotion, dissoluteness, sensuality. Related to Lat. *asôtiâ.*

42. *Dominica Judiaca,* the 'Judgment of God,' apparently the title of his sermon.

43. Pastor Bonaventura Riesch had ministered to those Salzburgers who had sojourned in Lindau. See Jones, ed., *Newman Letterbooks,* 482, 553 (note 1, above).

44. Boltzius contrasts his present *ungeschmaltzen Brot* (bread without butter) with *Mehlspeise,* or desserts made of fine flour.

45. This passage begins with verse 13 in the King James version, which numbers some Psalm verses differently from the Luther version.

46. E.g., the favorable reports that appeared in *An Extract from the Journals of Mr. Commissary Von Reck, . . . and of the Reverend Mr. Boltzius . . .* (London, 1734).

47. E. g., *Short Description of the Present Status of South Carolina* (Neuchâtel, 1733). Jean Purry's claims were typical of the promotional literature then flooding South Germany and Switzerland. Since Purysburg lay at 32 latitude, the same as Jerusalem, it had to be a paradise. See entry for 8 May.

48. The medieval church had taught that any sexual activity was sinful unless solely for the procreation of children in wedlock. The term *peccatum onaniticum* (see Genesis 38:9) was incorrectly used to designate masturbation.

49. I John 2:1; I John 1:7.

50. Bach was later scalped by the Spanish Indians.

51. This was the group of Appenzellers brought by Johann Tobler. See entry for 8

May. See Charles G. Cordle, "The John Tobler Manuscripts," in *Journal of Southern History* V (1939), 83-93.

52. *Du bist ja, Jesu, meine Freude*. Hymn by C. T. Koitsch.

53. Pirogue, a large dugout. Boltzius used the Spanish term *periagua,* a folk-etymological corruption of a Carib word.

54. Christ, the convert, suffered from consumption.

55. Like many others in Purysburg and elsewhere, Kieffer had cleared his land only to find that the title was faulty.

56. David Zubli(n), father of Johann Joachim Zubly, who was a leader of Dissenters in Georgia and member of the Continental Congress. Six hundred acres of land were granted to David Zubli in Purysburg on 14 Dec. 1739. Smith, 216. See note 10.

57. Sebastian Zuberbuehler, son of Bartholomäus Zuberbuhler, Anglican leader in Georgia. One hundred acres in Purysburg were granted on 9 April 1743 to Savastian Zuberbukber. Smith, 217. See note 10.

58. *Girrendes Täublein, die Gebundene Seufzerlein eines mit Gott verbundenen Hertzens, . . .* (Leipzig 1731.)

59. *Geh auf, meines Hertzens Morgenstern.* Hymn by Johann Scheffler.

60. This allusion seems to confuse Psalm 124:7 with Proverbs 6:5.

61. *Jesu, deine heiligen Wunden.* Hymn by O. C. Damius.

62. *Ein' feste Burg.* Hymn by Luther, anthem of the Lutheran church.

63. The term "late Professor" always refers to the father, August Hermann Francke, the founder of the Francke Foundation.

64. Believing his readers familiar with this passage, Boltzius wrote only the first verse; but Urlsperger added: "few there be that find it."

65. Boltzius uses the word "teacher" *(Lehrer)* to mean minister of the gospel. A school teacher is a *Schulmeister*.

66. At Savannah-Town, in New Windsor Township.

67. It is amazing how much editing Urlsperger performed in order to conceal the fact that there were marital squabbles in Ebenezer.

68. A medication manufactured by Johann Caspar Schauer, a benefactor of the Salzburgers in Augsburg.

69. This refers to the son, Sebastian. See entry for 29 April.

70. Johann Tobler, mathematician and former governor *(Landeshauptmann)* of Appenzell. See note 51.

71. Revelations 21:7.

72. *Solt ich meinem Gott nicht singen.* Hymn by Paul Gerhard.

73. See note 70.

74. "So-called" because it was built by the Salzburgers in the Indian manner. Boltzius wishes to make it clear that he is not trying to encroach on Indian property.

75. Allusion to Lazerus Spengler's hymn, *Durch Adams Fall ist gantz verderbt.*

76. Fort Moore.

77. For some reason Urlsperger changed the last sentence to read: "To be sure, we need a shoemaker, but perhaps a Christian man will be sent from Germany with the fourth transport." This Reck (sometimes written Röck) was probably the Jacob Reck who received fifty acres in Purysburg on 16 Sept., 1738. Smith, 214. See note 10.

78. Boltzius uses the word *justitiarius.* He repeats this threat on 1 June.

79. John 3:19.

80. "As in parody."

81. Friedrich Wilhelm Müller.

82. Sometimes called Ernstdorf. Baron von Reck picked up this indentured family in Savannah.

83. To stimulate production, the Trustees had paid a shilling subsidy for each bushel of corn harvested. See entry for 15 Dec., 1736.

84. A typical Pietist tenet.

85. Ortmann had been a lieutenant. See entry for 2 March, 1736.

86. The Society for Promoting Christian Knowledge, which paid Boltzius' and Gronau's stipends.

87. See note 46.

88. Luke 18:7–8 is more appropriate in the Luther version than in the King James version, because it speaks of "saving" rather than of "avenging."

89. Noble Jones, who surveyed Old Ebenezer. Jonas is the German name of the man swallowed by the whale.

90. In his entry for 28 April, Boltzius reported that Riedelsperger and Rieser had gone to Mary Musgrove's cowpen. In his entry for 21 May he reported that Rauner and Leitner intended to go to Savannah-Town.

91. *Was Gott thut, das ist wohl gethan.* Hymn by Samuel Rodigast.

92. By "Altamaha" Boltzius means St. Simons Island.

93. Boltzius dated this and the following entries as 15 and 16 June, but Urlsperger changed them to the 16th and 17th.

94. Boltzius wrote *Glaubens-Bekenntnis,* or "confession of faith."

95. *Man lobt dich in der Stille.* Hymn by Johann Rist.

96. In the Luther version this is Psalm 22:7. See note 45.

97. Here Boltzius is following a literary convention popular throughout the Middle Ages, that of clothing allegory.

98. Boltzius used "he" to refer to Prof. Francke, but the typesetter in Halle thought it referred to God and therefore capitalized it.

99. Boltzius does not make it clear that Christian Ernst Thilo had accepted the call to Georgia.

100. The war of the Polish Succession, 1733-35.

101. Scene of missionary activity in India maintained by the Francke Foundation.

102. *Lobe den Herrn, den mächtigen König der Ehren.* Hymn by Joachim Neander.

103. "He who is absent must do without."

104. See 2 Timothy 1:16.

105. *Kans Doch nicht ewig währen, oft hat Er unsere Zähren, eh mans meint, abgewischt. Wanns bey uns heisst: Wie lange wird mir so angst und bange? so hat Er Leib und Seel erfrischt.* Apparently from a hymn.

106.*Nun gute Nacht, du stilles Welt-Getümmel, . . . Solt ich denn wol mein Glücke selbst verschertzen? Das könt ich ja wol nimmermehr verschmertzen.* Unidentified hymn.

107. *Gott lässt uns zwar ein wenig sincken, aber nicht ertrincken.*

108. *Er wird zwar eine Weile mit seinem Trost verziehen,* etc. . . . *Wirds aber sich befinden, dass du ihm treu verbleibst, so wird er dich entbinden,* etc. From an unidentified hymn.

109. Matthew 11:28.

110. *Zu dir Herr Jesu komme ich.* Hymn by J. A. Freylinghausen.

111. See note 90.

112. Another typical pietist sentiment.

113. Urlsperger lengthened Boltzius' shortened quotation to: *Meine gute Werck die galten nichts, es war mit ihnen verdorben, der freye Wille hasste Gottes Gericht,* etc. Apparently from a hymn.

114. *Kommt, denn alles ist bereit* (Matthew 22:4) The King James version gives "Come unto the marriage."

115. Psalm 103:10. In this case, Urlsperger shortened Boltzius' quotation.

116. Baron Christoph von Ploto, the Prussian envoy to Salzburg, had attempted to collect debts and other sums due the Salzburgers who had emigrated to East Prussia.

117. Boltzius failed to fill in the blank, so Urlsperger re-worded the sentence.

118. John 7:37.

119. This was the son, Charles Purry, merchant in Purysburg.

120. *Zu dir, Herr Jesu, komme ich* (see note 110). *Wer ist wol wie du, Jesu?*

121. The "dear man" is not Spangenberg, but Freylinghausen!

122. By authority of the king.

123. "All others being excluded."

124. Frederick William I of Prussia.

125. Samuel Quincy, the Anglican pastor in Savannah prior to Wesley.

126. In his edition of these reports, Urlsperger began a new volume at this point, which continued through 31 March, 1738. See note 2.

127. Boltzius failed to fill in these two ages.

128. See note 99.

129. The book of Sirach is found in the Apocrypha.

130. *Wo der Herr Jesus ist, da ist Segen.* This is not a quote from Luke 5, but perhaps the title of Boltzius' sermon. See entry for 10 July.

131. Psalm 73:25. Luther renders this quite differently: *Wenn ich nur dich habe, so frage ich nichts nach Himmel und Erde.*

132. According to the entry for 4 July, Arnsdorf had been in Danish military service.

133. See note 75.

134. John 8:47.

135. It should be noted that this cruelty was practiced by Gronau, not Boltzius. Compare his treatment of the widow on 17 July.

136. While Georgia was fearing an attack from St. Augustine, merchants in Charleston and the northern colonies continued to supply that city.

137. Boltzius is quoting Luther's rendition of Jeremiah 18:12 *Daraus wird nichts; wir wollen nach unsern Gedancken wandeln.* The King James version says, "There is no hope; but we will walk after our own devices."

138. Boltzius says a *Quadrat von sechzehn Englischen Meilen,* but he means a four-mile square. See note 192.

139. *Ein Lämmlein geht und trägt die Schuld.* Hymn by Paul Gerhard.

140. *Ich weiss, du kanst mich nicht verstossen, wie köntest du ungnädig seyn dem, den dein Blut von Schuld und Pein erlöst, da es so reich geflossen,* etc.

141. *Nur frisch hinein, es wird so tief nicht seyn.* This appears to be from a hymn.

142. These are from Luke 6:35 and Isaiah 43:24.

143. Urlsperger saw fit to add the following warning footnote:

> The dispute about quinine (Urlsperger calls it fever-bark) or *china de china* is so general and so complicated that entire treatises have already been written about it. Therefore we will not be able to treat it in sufficient detail in this note. Nevertheless, a necessary warning can be expressed in a few words: Quinine requires a great caution, which cannot be expected of many people. Over a thousand people have lost their lives through the misuse of this bark, as cannot be denied by its proponents. All cold fevers can be thoroughly cured without this bark, and therefore one does not need to select this slippery and questionable method. The precaution that is taken with the previously given emetic is a clear proof that its inventor does not understand the nature of a cold fever. For in the most extensive medical practice we have scarcely six kinds of circumstances in which the emetic can be used without harm. Therefore it is certain that this recommended emetic will cause harm more often than the quinine itself. For, through useful additives and good preparation, quinine can be so restricted that it will not produce its usual dangerous astringent effect. *In forma enim Decocti et additione remouentium partes Terrestres adstringentes crassiores excluduntur, teneriores autem disjunguntur.* Nevertheless, if one considers what has been reported about this cure on 17 August of this year, one might well hesitate to use this quinine.

144. Galatians 6:7.

145. This seems to be a conglomerate of various Biblical passages.

146. The name Uselt, which appears as Unselt in the entry for 7 Nov., was borne by various members of the Ebenezer congregation during the Revolution. See index of A. G. Voigt, trans., *Ebenezer Record Book* (Savannah, 1929). See entry in present work for 7 Nov.

147. Married to Jörg Schweiger.

148. It is ironic that Boltzius' very next report should be lost, or at least delayed, in the mail. See note 149.

149. Boltzius' journal for the period 1 Aug. through 14 Nov. was lost or delayed, with the result that it was not entered into the current Halle letterbook. It did, however, reach Germany in time to be included, well expurgated, in Urlsperger's next volume. Consequently, his deletions cannot be restored. See notes 2 and 3.

150. "M" is Muggitzer and "C" is Causton. See entry for 21 May.

151. The Virgin Islands then belonged to Denmark.

152. This must have been Herrnberger, who left Hungary to visit Protestant countries in the Holy Roman Empire. See entry for 20 March.

153. For Boltzius, a true Christian was a true Pietist.

154. Christian H. Müller. See note 10. The Earl of Egmont writes his middle name as Hervack, which must be an error for Heinrich.

155. Apparently Zwiffler. See entry for 25 Feb. But why the deletion?

156. Surely this is Mrs. Holtzer. But why is name suppressed here and mentioned in the next entry?

157. *Amt der Schlüssel.* Fifth section of Luther's *Small Catechisim.*

158. A good example of Pietistic faith in rebirth in Jesus.

159. Hans Schmidt was the only Salzburger with those initials.

160. See Introduction, p. xii.

161. Boltzius often uses the word *Anfechtung* in the sense of "doubt," that is, the temptation to lose faith in Jesus.

162. *Sein Wort lass dir gewisser seyn, und ob dein Hertz sprach lauter Nein, so lass dir doch nicht grauen.* Apparently from a hymn.

163. Boltzius is referring to the orphanage, in which she is to reside.

164. *Mehr in einem gesetzlichen als evangelischem Geist.* More in the spirit of the Old Testament than in that of the New, more according to the outward observance of the law than to rebirth in Jesus.

165. *Die Stillen im Lande* (the Quiet ones in the Country). A term of derision for the Pietists, later accepted by them as an honor.

166. The Gichtelianers were followers of the religious zealot Johann Georg Gichtel (1638–1710).

167. These were Indian beans, a kind of field pea that is still a major source of protein in the area.

168. From St. Gall in Switzerland. See entry for 15 Oct.

169. See entry for 12 Aug. and note 155.

170. Boltzius uses the word "honest" *(redlich)* of those who share his Pietistic principles.

171. Another expression of Pietistic viewpoint.

172. Bruckner. See entry for 30 Dec.

173. This is from Luther's translation of Psalm 65:10 *(Gottes Brünnlein hat Wassers die Fülle).* The King James Bible has "the river of God, which is full of water."

174. Boltzius was in error here. The "Trustee lots" were not reserved for wealthy men but for the common good.

175. Apparently Zettler. See entry for 11 May.

176. Probably the Ortmanns. See entry for 29 Sept. Their feud seems to have been with the Rheinlaenders.

177. Mrs. Arnsdorf.

178. Naturally, as indentured servants for a specific period of time to pay for their passage.

179. Reports from missionaries sent from Halle to the East Indies, like those sent from the "West Indies" by Boltzius and Gronau. Boltzius was probably reading from *Der Königlichen Dänischen Missionarien aus Ost-Indien eingesandte Ausführliche Berichten.* Halle 1735.

180. At this point Urlsperger added the reassuring footnote: "As already known, not only has good land been given since then to all the inhabitants of Ebenezer, but also many additional benefactions have been sent from Germany and England."

181. Clearly the schoolmaster, Ortmann.

182. He did go to Germany, but he returned bringing his sister and other female immigrants.

183. Boltzius' time was not short. He served for twenty-eight more years, until his death in 1765.

184. These were ricebirds, pests in the rice fields but considered song birds in the

North, where they wear bright plumage and are called bobolinks *(dolinchonyx oryzivorus)*.

185. Our good pastor is better at describing the means to salvation than the means to grinding meal. His words are: "Der oberste Stein, welcher an eine eiserne Spille und daran befindlich Quer-Eisen vest gemacht ist, wird mit einem geraden in die Höhe gehenden Stock, der oberwärts in einem ausgebohrten Brett-Loch, auf dem Steine aber mit dem Stachel in einem Löchlein steckt, herumgetrieben. Unter dem Unter-Steine liegt grade durch das ausgehohlte Holtz, darin die Steine liegen, ein Quer-Holtz, darauf die Spille in einem etwas ausgehohleten Eisen liegt, welches Quer-Holtz durch zwey untergesteckte Keile, die von dem dicken Ende spitz zu gehen, auf beyden Seiten bald erhöhet bald erniedriget werden kan, wenn man grob oder klar mahlen will."

186. Another expression of Pietistic point of view.

187. These were Rauner, Michel Rieser, Stephen Riedelsperger, and Leitner. See entries for 28 April, 21 May, and 13 June.

188. See Introduction p. xii.

189. The Society for Promoting Christian Knowledge, which paid Boltzius' and Gronau's stipends.

190. *nach der sie allein anckert.* An unusual expression.

191. He went the whole way to Herrnhut.

192. A *Viereck von 16 Englischen Meilen.* He must mean a four mile square. See note 138.

193. Boltzius consistently calls the slaves *Mohren.*

194. Boltzius, or Urlsperger, is probably suppressing the fact that these were Kieffer's slaves.

195. This is so obviously Purysburg that nothing was accomplished by suppressing the name.

196. *Guldenes Schatz-Kästlein der Kinder Gottes* (Halle, 17??), devotional tract by Carl Heinrich Bogatzky.

197. Another expression of Pietistic thought.

198. See note 225.

199. John 3:16, I Timothy 1:15 or 2 Timothy 2:11, Matthew 11:28.

200. This is probably Mrs. Schweiger, née Unselt. See entry for 7 Nov.

201. More Pietism.

202. John 4:46 ff.

203. No doubt at Mary Musgrove's cowpen. The Pietists did not approve of dancing.

204. Probably the Holzer girl.

205. Windhausen, in Hanover, was von Reck's home.

206. See note 173.

207. "I have no pleasure in the death of the wicked." Ezekiel 33:11.

208. More Pietist propaganda.

209. *Sey fröhlich im Herren, du heilige Seele.* Hymn by J. E. Schmidt.

210. *Ich will dich lieben, meine Stärcke.* Hymn by Johannes Scheffler.

211. Friedrich Eberhard Collin, *Das Gewaltige Eindringen ins Reich gottes* (Frankfurt/Main, 1722).

212. Savannah-Town.

213. To Jörg Schweiger. See entry for 30 Oct., also George Fenwick Jones, ed., *Detailed Reports on the Salzburger Emigrants* . . . (Athens, Ga., 1969), 143.

214. No doubt as given in his *Ordnung des Heils, Nebst einem Verzeichnis der wichtigsten Kern-Sprüche,* etc. Halle 1724.

215. Prof. Francke. See entry for 3 Nov.

216. At this point the letterbooks include the marginal note: "The portion of the diary from 1 Aug. to 14 Nov, 1737, is still missing and probably was lost at sea." See note 149.

217. Chivelle. See note 21.

218. The German people at Purysburg were either German Swiss, and therefore mostly Zwinglianer, or else Palatines, who were largely reformed. Language was, however, a stronger bond than confession, at least within the Protestant persuasion.

219. Romans 4:25.

220. Matthew 25:1–12.

221. *Anfang Christlichen Lebens.*

222. By "French" Boltzius meant French-speaking Swiss. Quite a few of these Swiss, mostly from Neuchâtel, left descendants who believe themselves to be of Huguenot ancestry.

223. Another illustration of Boltzius' fear of "natural honesty."

224. Acorns for the hogs. The Salzburgers discovered the Red Bluff while gathering acorns. See Jones, ed., *Detailed Reports,* II, 191 in note 212, and entry for 30 Nov., below.

225. *Fahre fort Zion, fahre fort im Licht.* Hymn by J. E. Schmidt.

226. John 11:4.

227. "Mein Beten ist voll zweiflender Gedancken, wenn gleich Dein Wort und Trost erschallt, so ist und bleibt mein Glaube doch voll Wancken, mein Hertze scheinet todt und kalt, und ist so voll Angst und Zagen, und ganz in sich selbst verwirrt, ich kan kaum mich selbst vertragen, so gar ist mein Sinn verirrt." Unidentified hymn.

228. Exodus 33:19.

229. Matthew 18:11.

230. Acts 14:22.

231. Johann Ulrich Giessendanner, who opposed the policies of Dobler and Zuber-bühler, broke away from the main party, which went to Savannah-Town, and founded a settlement at Orangeburg. See Cordle, 86, in note 51.

232. Boltzius means Orangeburg in South Carolina.

233. After being ordained in London, Bartholmäus Zouberbuhler tried to arrogate Giessendanner's position, but the latter's congregation stood by him. Here we see an early example of the frontier tendency to prefer a plain man of the people, even if uneducated and unorthodox, over the polished and theologically qualified ministers of the coastal regions.

234. The first of the seven parts of a sermon, which serves to catch the hearer's attention.

235. See notes 231–233 above.

236. This name had to be corrected both here and in the entry for 19 Dec.

237. These are the two unnamed brothers of David Züblin.

238. See note 56.

239. Georg Bartholomäus Rott (Roth), a Bavarian distiller, had been banished from Ebenezer for bad behavior and died soon afterwards.

240. Both Matthew 18:11 and Luke 19:10.

241. Wesley did not depart secretly. He had announced his intention to depart and denied Causton's authority to detain him. Causton gave orders for his arrest but took no steps to enforce the order. Thus it appears that Causton hoped that he would leave under a cloud of suspicion. See Martin Schmidt (Norman P. Goldhawk, trans.), *John Wesley,* (New York, 1962), I, 205–207.

242. Causton and Williamson, Sophie's husband, claimed that Wesley had repelled her out of pique because she had jilted him. Actually, at the advice of the Herrnhuters Wesley had decided to remain celibate.

243. This is the oldest and propertied brother.

244. It is strange that Boltzius never identifies these brothers, whose names were Ambrosius and Johann Jacob.

245. See note 221.

246. The first of these verses is in Philippians 4:5–6. The second is not.

247. Bruckner. See entry for 30 Dec.

248. These are more illustrations of the Pietist fear of "natural honesty."

249. See note 248, above.

250. Reck. See note 77.

251. See note 248, above.

252. Mrs. Ernst was a convert from Catholicism.

253. 2 Corinthians 8:9.

254. Genesis 32:6.

255. Jeremiah 31:20.

256. The Rhenish Palatinate, the region extending from Heidelberg to the French border, often devastated by Louis XIV. So many immigrants came from there that the term "Palatine" was applied to all German indentured servants, regardless of from what area they actually came.

257. Since the Reformation, the established church of the Palatinate had fluctuated between Lutheranism and Calvinism.

258. Boltzius uses the word *Stösse*, which could mean either gusts of wind or impacts against the bar.

259. See entry for 20 Dec.

260. See note 173.

261. Boltzius does not explain what he means by "time change." *(Zeitwechsel)*.

Index

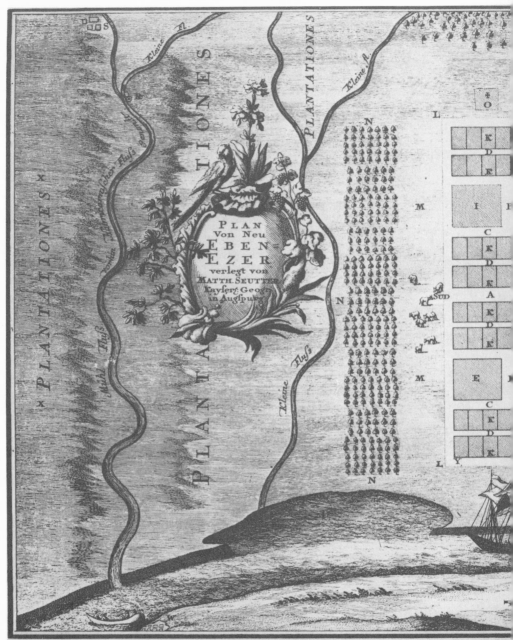

A. Haupt Straßen. B. Marckt Plätz. C. Mittle Gaßen. D. kleine Gäßlin. E. Store Hauß. F. Pfarr Wohnungen. G. die Kirchen
rer ein jeglicher Zehen Wohnungen faßt; So in einem Hauß Hof u. Garten bestehet. L. ein Schindel Zaun Sechs Fuß hoch
welcher ebenfals eingezaünt. P. Holtz. Q. Eigenthumlichs Land einer kleinen Nation Indianer. R. die Mühl. S. Fabricorn
Land wo die Saltzburger ihre Vieh Ställe haben. Y. Sind 20 Hauß Plätze zwischen drey Straßen. so Hr: General Ogleth.

This Plan of Ebenezer first appeared in Urlsperger's *Ausführliche Nachrichten, 13te Con-*
tinuation, Erster Theil (Halle and Augsburg, 1747.) A tinted copy is in the De Renne Collection, University of Georgia Library.